IN GENERAL AND PARTICULAR

Also by C. M. Bowra

IN GENERAL AND PARTICULAR

C. M. Bowra

THE WORLD PUBLISHING COMPANY

CLEVELAND AND NEW YORK

The quotation from Isaac Rosenberg is reprinted by permission of Schocken Books Inc., from *The Collected Poems* of Isaac Rosenberg, edited by Gordon Bottomley & Denys Harding, Copyright 1949 by Schocken Books Inc.

The lines from Dame Edith Sitwell's "Song of the Cold" are reprinted by permission of the publishers, The Vanguard Press, from *The Collected Poems of Edith Sitwell*. Copyright, 1948, 1954, by Edith Sitwell.

The quotations from Thomas Hardy's *The Dynasts* are reprinted by permission of Macmillan & Co. Ltd., London, and St. Martin's Press, and the Trustees of the Thomas Hardy Estate.

The poetry of Robert Frost is quoted from *Complete Poems of Robert Frost*. Copyright 1947 by Holt, Rinehart and Winston, Inc. Reprinted by permission of Holt, Rinehart and Winston, Inc.

Published by The World Publishing Company

2231 West 110th Street, Cleveland 2, Ohio

Library of Congress Catalog Card Number: 64-12062

FIRST EDITION

CONTENTS

ACKNOWLEDGMENTS

I AM much obliged to the publishing houses who have kindly given permission to quote from their publications : to the Trustees of the Hardy Estate, the Macmillan Company of Canada Ltd and Macmillan and Company Ltd for permission to quote from Thomas Hardy's *The Dynast;* to Macmillan and Company Ltd for permission to quote from Edith Sitwell's *Song of Cold;* to Chatto and Windus Ltd for permission to quote from *The Collected Poems of Isaac Rosenberg;* and to Jonathan Cape Ltd for permission to quote from Robert Frost's *Why Wait for Science.* I am also grateful to the following for permission to include various chapters : to the Manchester Literary and Philosophical Society for permission to include 'Some Aspects of Speech'; to the Birmingham and Midland Institute for permission to include 'Poets and Scholars'; to the Classical Association for permission to include 'A Classical Education'; to King's College, Newcastle-upon-Tyne, for permission to include 'The Meaning of a Heroic Age'; to the University of London for permission to include 'Medieval Love-song'; to Faber and Faber Ltd for permission to include 'Songs of Dance and Carnival' from their publication *Italian Rennaissance Studies,* in which it first appeared; to the Taylorian Institute, Oxford, for permission to include 'The Simplicity of Racine' and 'Poetry and the First World War'; to the Journal of the British Institute of Persian Studies, Vol. 1. 1963, for permission to include 'Edward FitzGerald'; and to the English Association for permission to include 'The Prophetic Element'.

I

SOME ASPECTS OF SPEECH

[Clayton Memorial Lecture delivered before the Manchester Literary and Philosophical Society, 1959]

IN THE animal world man is unique in possessing the gift of speech. Other animals are indeed capable of some sort of communication with one another through their own kinds of noises, which sometimes have a differentiated character and are directed towards a special end. When a chimpanzee is in danger, it utters a peculiar cry, which brings its fellows to its succour. Lions roar at one another, and in so doing challenge their rivals to a test of strength. A cock utters one kind of cry when he sees a hawk in the air, a second when he hears rats or mice, and a third when he calls a hen to enjoy a worm or other tit-bit. But these sounds are not speech. Their range is extremely narrow, and they are connected with only a very few, recurrent, familiar occasions. Unlike speech, they do not vary from place to place but are constant over the whole world. Above all they cannot be broken up into units such as words, and for this reason they forbid both variety and advance. They record fixed responses to certain situations in an extremely limited way, and from this restriction there is no escape. Man alone produces the vast range of different and separate sounds which constitute speech. Bees get over this handicap to some degree by various kinds of dance which indicate the presence of pollen or nectar, but this is a silent code, and though it may serve as an alternative to speech, it too is very narrow in its range and confined to purely immediate and practical ends. Though all animals react to stimuli very much as man does when he is afraid or angry or excited or pleased, and make their own appropriate noises for them, they never approach anything that can be called speech. Even a parrot which can imitate human sounds does not use them as a means of communication but enjoys them for their own sake and for the opportunity which they provide for showing off. Man remains the sole master of speech, and to this he owes not only his difference

9

from other animals but much that is most distinctive in his own development.

We do not know when man began to speak or how he spoke when he began. Physically he seems to have been capable of it when he emerged from his simian and hominid ancestors. But the capacity for speech does not necessarily mean that it was put into practice at once, and the formation of intelligible sounds must have been slow and reluctant. On the other hand even so remote a figure as Peking man, who some half a million years ago used simple stone tools to make holes in the skulls of his fellows that he might eat their brains, may conceivably have been able to celebrate his glory and his gluttony with suitable noises. No doubt such noises were inchoate and restricted, but once they began, they could extend their range and their significance as man extended his needs and his experience. At first such sounds must have been akin to the cries of beasts, but gradually they widened their scope and formed the beginnings of real language. Language starts when the inarticulate cry becomes a call with some definite content beyond the mere expression of a mood, and from the call come the three primary parts of speech, the command, the question, and the statement, or, to use the jargon of the grammarians, the imperative, the interrogative, and the indicative. The first might, for instance, be a call for help, the second a question about what is the matter, and the third a factual account of it. There is no reason to think that human speech emerged at a single place at a single time. All attempts to find by comparative philology an evolutionary counterpart to the language of Adam sought by such men as Jakob Boehme in the seventeenth century, an *Ursprache* or original language, from which all other languages are descended, have failed. It may be possible to reduce the varieties of human speech to some dozen families, but beyond that we cannot go. Even the most elementary words are not constant, and it is noteworthy, for instance, that in Georgian the word for father is *mama* and for mother *deda*. Just as man himself seems to have emerged separately in widely divided parts of the earth, so speech must have done the same. Nor need it, once it began, have developed quickly. The slowness of material advance in the Early Palaeolithic Age may well have been due in part to the inefficiency of primitive speech and the inability of men to form and communicate ideas. Once it started on its course it must have been closely connected with the making of artefacts since the exercise of the hands is related to the brain, and the manufacture of tools and weapons is a social activity which calls for communication and instruction in their use. When in the stupendous Neolithic revolution man turned from hunting and gathering to agriculture and the domestication of animals, his increased rate of material progress must have been accompanied and aided by an increasingly richer and more serviceable command of words. Without this he could never have made so vast a change in his habits or developed such magical and religious notions as are implicit in the pictures which he painted on the walls of caves at Lascaux and Altamira. We may be reasonably certain that by the Late Palaeolithic Age, that is *c.* 30,000 B.C., man had evolved methods of speech which went far beyond his immediate physical needs and expressed what can only be called ideas.

This is the heart of the matter. Whatever rudimentary intelligence we may attribute to animals, we cannot really think that they have ideas, whereas the whole conception of *homo sapiens* means that he has. Now it is true that not everyone thinks always with or in words, that some people think largely in pictures, others in patterns or figures, a few in what may best be described as pure thoughts. But the mass of mankind thinks in words, or, to put it more precisely, thought calls for words to make itself clear, and words provoke thought through their own exercise. We all know how at times an idea may seem clear enough in our minds and yet we fumble for words to express it, and conversely we know how words, once shaped, may stir thoughts to start in a new direction. Words and thoughts work together in an indissoluble alliance, and each assists and stimulates the other. This is not to say that thinking is identical with speaking. It is possible to utter words mechanically without thought, and it is equally possible at times to think without words. But words are indispensable to thought as a means both of formulating it and of communicating it to others. The difference between articulate speech and cries like those of animals or babies is that these convey no more than an undifferentiated, emotional state; they do not communicate anything except at an incoherent level, and they are never truly informative. Speech begins its proper task when more or less specific information is passed from one human being to another in words, and once this begins there are in theory no limits to the possibilities before it, since in the end ideas always find words for their expression, and words help ideas to become common property. It is through this means of communication with his fellows that man has become what he is. When Aristotle laid down his famous and influential doctrine that it is the possession of reason which differentiates man from the animals, he might equally have said that it is the possession of speech; for in the only world of which we have any knowledge reason and speech act in close collaboration and perform what is in the result a single task.

Once such an instrument as language has come into existence, it can move in many different directions, and not all are equally adventurous or equally conducive to enlargement of experience. Though language is often a potent instrument of change, it can in certain conditions restrict the exercise of thought and therefore of social development. There still survive in the world languages spoken by peoples who are indeed primitive and even savage, since their economy is based entirely on hunting and gathering, and they are living fossils of the Stone Age. Western civilization, in the form of disease, enslavement, and murder, has slaughtered them at a hideous pace, and just as the nineteenth century saw the extermination of whole peoples like the aboriginal Tasmanians and the Kalang of Java, so the twentieth is on the way to seeing the inhabitants of Tierra del Fuego, the Andamanese, and the Bushmen follow the same brutal path to oblivion. We know enough of these peoples and of a few others, more fortunate because more isolated, like the Pygmies of equatorial Africa or the Eskimos of Arctic America, to know what life is in a truly savage society. But none of these peoples, not even the Tasmanians, who lived in Palaeolithic conditions, speak a primitive language. Their languages differ enormously from one another and from the great linguistic families of the rest of the world, but they have certain common characteristics, which are due not to descent or any external relation but to similarity of circumstances, and they are in their own way extremely complicated and imply a long history of change and adaptation behind them. Though in thousands of years these peoples may have added to the mechanism of living very little that was not known to Palaeolithic man, it is unlikely that their speech is in the least like his. Indeed the most striking feature of these primitive languages is their extreme elaboration. For instance, Yamana, which is, or was, spoken in the extreme south of Tierra del Fuego, is said to have a vocabulary of some 30,000 words, which is far more than a well-educated Englishman uses, and though this may include some variations due to differences of dialect, there is no doubt that a primitive vocabulary is always and necessarily enormous. This is because it deals not with ideas but with impressions, not with embracing concepts but with visible particulars, not with simplifying generalities but with individual objects. We are so accustomed to abstractions that we take their existence for granted and do not stop to think how enormously they simplify language and reduce its vocabulary. Languages which lack them work very differently from our own.

These languages have certain advantages. They are remarkably subtle and expressive when they deal with anything in the visible world. They record the impressions of the senses, in such matters as colour, shape, and smell, with far more accuracy and sensibility than a highly developed language can; they are able to deal competently, if pedantically, with the endless ramifications and grades of relationship in a totem-system or a kinship-group; they concentrate an unusual amount of power into a few words, and this makes them impressive instruments for religious and magical ceremonies and for the songs which accompany them. By our standards their grammar may look a little flimsy, and we may be surprised by their inconstant use of sounds, as if it were quite in order for a word not to have a fully fixed shape. None the less, for their own purposes they are perfectly well fitted. Indeed this is their trouble. They are so well fitted that those who speak them are so tied to them that they cannot advance beyond their inhibiting limitations. Just because they are so well shaped for the description of particular objects, they are almost incapable of treating general ideas. The social disadvantages of such a system are revealed when their speakers come into contact with Europeans. Among the less consciously lethal of their visitors were missionaries, who had at least benevolent intentions, but what were they to do with the Andamanese, who seemed to have no word for God, or with the Fuegians, who failed to understand what is meant by life after death? These were failures alike of vocabulary and of thought. The words did not exist because no ideas existed that called for them, and in the last resort the nature of speech almost forbade the formation of such ideas which extend beyond the visible scene. These peoples had names for the many and various spirits who encompassed and harassed them at every turn and to whom they paid a lively, apprehensive attention, but they had no notion of a separate world of spiritual beings as such. For them spirits were quite as real and individual as the members of their own human clan or family, and they felt no call to ascribe them to a special category of being. The same kind of difficulty arises in more mundane matters. The Tasmanians and some aboriginal Australians do not count beyond two, and there is seldom any need for them to do so. They have words for 'few' and 'many', but, if they have to be precise on a question of number, as for instance in saying how many people were present on a given occasion, they have no difficulty in enumerating them all by name.

The languages of these peoples suit them nicely until they are forced to adapt themselves to new and unprecedented conditions. Isolated for thousands of years from other cultures, they have worked out their own system of life which meets their elementary needs so long as they are left alone, and it is remarkable how in their odious climates the Fuegians and the Eskimos have succeeded in surviving at all. But this kind of primitive life is based on a very careful adjustment to natural surroundings, and especially to the search for food. The equilibrium between survival and starvation is perilously poised, and if anything goes wrong, a whole tribe may perish. For this reason it is dangerous to alter any established habit, and custom is lord of everything. Every little detail in hunting or gathering, every point in beliefs in the supernatural or in the strange philosophy of totemism, is worked out with precision to suit circumstances which are thought to be immutable. Language is intimately adjusted to the conventions and assumptions of existence. It is indeed so well adjusted that it allows no opportunity of looking beyond them or conceiving any alternatives to them. This means that these peoples have been frozen in their natural conservatism by the nature of their language, and though this reflects their social and economic circumstances, it holds them in a frame which they assume to be eternal and forbids change even in such matters as we might think to be perfectly acceptable to them. Even hunting, on which life depends and which occupies a large part of every day, has stimulated the invention of almost no weapons which were not known in the Ice Age. A complex language tyrannises over those who speak it and obstructs the free movement of the mind into new regions of experience. In so far as these languages change, and they certainly do, it is towards an ever greater elaboration in their own special methods of dealing with individual impressions and with the finer shades of difference in social relations. It is not surprising that men who spoke them were quite unable to understand what was happening when white men shot them for breaking rules which were to them totally unintelligible.

The languages of these savages hinder development in other ways than this. Such peoples are usually organized in small groups of a few families, probably closely related, which work together as a social unit and seldom number more than three or four hundred members and often much less. Such a group tends to live a more or less isolated existence, confines even its hunting to a recognized area, and seldom has anything to do with other groups, unless they invade its hunting grounds. In such conditions each group is likely to develop its own dialect, which may with the passage of years become a distinct and independent language, not fully intelligible to neighbouring groups. This must account for the bewildering variety of indigenous languages in South America, where there are so many that the philologists have not been able to arrange them in families. Even in so small an area as Tasmania there were two distinct languages, each of which had its own marked dialects. This tendency to splinter into groups and then to develop independently may be contrasted with the wide spread of a single language when conditions encourage it. Northern Chinese is spoken by some three hundred million people, and its diffusion owes nothing to the use of writing, which is organized separately from the spoken word; the Turkic languages have indeed local variations but are more or less mutually intelligible from Adrianople to north-eastern Siberia. Such languages have so vast a spread because their speakers are based on a social system different from that of primitive hunters. The Chinese are largely agricultural, the Turks largely nomadic, but in both of them social units are forced into contact with their neighbours, learn much from them, and are under no pressure or temptation to keep their habits or their speech to themselves. The marked tendency of modern Stone-agers to live in small, self-contained groups means that they develop their languages in isolation, and in due course find themselves separated by linguistic obstacles from units with which they were once closely related. Since the development of culture depends largely on the interchange of ideas and techniques, it is not surprising that these groups are deeply embedded in their habits and change them only from the inside without any thought of what might be done to extend their scope and possibilities.

This inhibiting rôle of language among savage peoples may of course be exceptional. It cannot have been the case with the hunters of the Magdalenian epoch, who not only perfected their remarkable visual arts but seem to have formed new ideas about what happens to the dead. No doubt they were helped by a greater freedom of movement than has been possible for modern Stone-agers and were able to profit by contacts with other peoples on a far wider scale than is permitted by the storm-swept mountains of Tierra del Fuego or the rain-forests of equatorial Africa or the deserts of central Australia. Indeed the ability of language to develop and assist the growth of ideas suggests that its inhibiting activities in these peoples are a social phenomenon created by restricting and exacting conditions of life. The twofold process by which thought calls for words and words stimulate thought can work with ample freedom and ease only when the struggle for existence does not demand all a man's efforts and most of his time, and when we turn from these savage people to others who are more advanced we see at once how influential language is in their development, and how differently it works with them.

The development of language, with the incalculable impulse which it brings to thought and action, is largely a matter of organizing words to meet social needs. For this it must have grammar, which is nothing more than a system of rules by which a language is controlled and made to do its work properly. Though English is less rigorously organized than none too distant relations like Latin or Russian or German, it has enough vestiges of grammar to express without trouble differences of number or time or case or probability. Its original Indo-European ancestor, whose main characteristics may

be deduced from its large progeny, was a highly inflected language
with eight cases for the noun and a rich range of moods and tenses
for verbs, and though we might think some of these unduly fussy,
their aim was to secure clarity at all costs. It is perfectly reasonable
to have both an optative and a subjunctive to show the difference
between remote and near possibilities, and even to have, as still
exist in Russian, two aspects of the verb, the perfective and the imperfective, which indicate whether an action is complete or still in process. The absence of such aspects from English accounts for certain
difficulties which foreigners find in speaking it and leads them into
such strange but entirely reasonable sentences as 'I fix it', which is a
perfective present with a future sense, or 'My aunt is having a house
at the sea-side', which is an impeccable imperfective present. Neither
of these happens to be right in English, but from an Indo-European
point of view they are natural and even necessary. Indeed though
English has abandoned most of its inflections, it has been forced to
find substitutes for them, notably in auxiliary words, and to this
degree it remains more or less faithful to its heritage. But the Indo-
European method is only one way among many of imposing order on
language. At the opposite pole to it is Chinese, which seems once
to have had some kind of syntax but abandoned it long ago for a
different system. Chinese has no tenses or moods or cases or genders,
but it remains a highly subtle and exact language which is able to
rise to any occasion and settles everything by placing words in the
right order and relation to one another. How it works may be seen
from Pidgin English, which is a word-for-word translation from it,
aided by some ingenious adaptations of European words, not necessarily or always English. I hope that you will allow me to illustrate
this with an episode from my own early life of which I have no personal remembrance. In my first year I once howled for my food half-
an-hour before the right time. My Chinese amah wanted to give
it to me, but my mother pointed to the clock and said it was too early,
at which the amah said : 'Maskee mississy clock. He no savvy. Baby
clock, he inside tummy, he savvy.' This delicate and scholarly statement shows how admirably the Chinese system of ordering words
surmounts deficiencies which might seem insuperable to us. But what
matters for the moment is not how a language is organized but the
fact that it is, and indeed some measure of organization is essential
if language is to make itself felt in the whole range of thought. Once
its foundations are assured, it is able to build on them and to increase
with confidence its means of communication between man and man.
The desire for organization is clear enough even in savage languages,
and can be found to some degree in Tasmanian and other primitive
vernaculars. But in them the degree of grammatical order is still

small, and this is a sign of incomplete mastery. The more capacious and adaptable the order, the more likely is a language to act as a civilizing force.

A second important element in the development of language is its ability to suit itself to new calls and new conditions. This means a great deal more than absorbing new words, though of course it also does this. Even the most primitive peoples have no difficulty in taking over strange words like 'steamer' and 'gun', and every language does the same kind of thing. When the Greeks first reached the Aegean Sea, they had no words for sea, bath, bean, pumpkin, and hyacinth, and took them over from the earlier inhabitants. The English language has always borrowed lavishly from abroad, and there has been a steady sequence of assimilations from Norse, Latin, and French. Nor are less obvious sources lacking. *Orang-outang,* which means 'man of the woods', comes from Malaya, *tea* from Amoy in Southern China, *bungalow* from India, *taboo* from Polynesia. Not all imported words are used correctly, and at times we wonder why they are used at all. Why, for instance, do the French insist upon referring to aftertoon-tea as *le five-o'clock,* or a walk as *un footing,* or a dance as *un dancing?* Hardly less whimsical is the Russian habit of calling a railway-terminus *voksal* after our own Vauxhall. Yet even when such queer words as these are adopted they must be properly acclimatized and brought to discipline. Modern Greek can hardly be blamed when it calls the cinema not *kīnēma,* as in theory it should, but *tsĭnĕma,* or when its menus offer ham and eggs as *amenex,* or its nightclubs advertise opportunities for *ailaif.* More severe is Arabic, which insists that, no matter how foreign a word is, it must conform to Arabic usage. Thus both *football* and *jolly-boat* are in current use, but are made to form plurals in *fatūbīl* and *jalābit.* The relevance of these acclimatizations is that they show how languages borrow from one another and in so doing increase the experience of their new employers. This is by no means the only or the most productive way of expanding a language, but it shows how such an expansion marches with the introduction of new ideas and new techniques.

A language can also develop its own inherent resources from inside, and this may be extremely productive and profitable. At no point does a civilized language show its capacities more impressively than in the construction of abstract words. Just as the lack of these is a dangerous hindrance to savage societies, so an ability to form them is one of the most civilizing functions which language can perform. A notable example may be seen in classical Greek. When from the beginning of the sixth century B.C. the Greeks began to speculate about the nature of things and to ask what really makes them what they are, they laid the foundation of philosophy, science and mathematics. All these have to deal with abstractions, and the Greek language, which had hitherto been polished largely for poetry and was exceedingly well equipped to deal with the senses and the emotions, had few abstracts ready to hand. But they were rapidly and skilfully formed, partly from adjectival roots, partly by very simple metaphors, as the notion of *dikê,* or right, is an extension of the word for 'boundary' and comes to stand for the right limits to anything in thought or conduct, however unsubstantial. With this happy adaptability we may contrast the slowness of the Romans to develop their own more practical language in the same direction. They may have been hampered by their taste for the minutiae of legal regulations, which tend to confine themselves to particular details, and even when Cicero, with an extraordinary dexterity, translated Greek philosophy into his own tongue, he had to invent words on Greek models, but when he had done so, they did not pass easily into currency, and it was not until the end of the fourth century A.D. that Latin found in the work of St Augustine a philosophical vocabulary at all comparable in range and ease with that of Greek. A similar and no less striking contrast can be observed between Chinese and Japanese. From an early date Chinese formed abstracts for its own philosophy, which is indeed not at all like Greek but in its own way hardly less fine and exact. This was done by using familiar words with a new extended significance but without in any way disturbing the security of the language. In this the pictographic script helped, as in the character for 'benevolence', which is that of 'man plus two', and suggests that a man thinks of another, and in 'happiness', which is 'one mouth supported by a field'. Japanese on the contrary is curiously poor in abstracts, and often, when an educated Japanese wishes to use one, he will draw a Chinese character on his hand and show it to you. There is a whole world of difference between the Greek or Chinese ability to form abstracts and the inability of savages to speak of anything which is not present to the senses. The development of abstract words has not only provided man with a means to generalize about experience and so to be prepared for many contingencies which the savage cannot imagine, but it has also opened the way to philosophy, mathematics and science, all of which deal with general laws deduced from particulars. The famous definitions of Euclid may not be so final as we once thought, but they are triumphs of linguistic ability and show how things which are in their very nature invisible can be described with apparent ease and clarity.

Language promotes ideas, and ideas promote language. The process seems so natural and so inevitable that we may not always appreciate how remarkable it is and how easily in the end men are able to express their most intractable and unfamiliar thoughts or to approach unexplored or undefined subjects. From one point of view the advance of language is towards an ever embracing clarity, a readier ability to frame thoughts cogently and definitely, to say exactly what we mean so that our hearers are left in no doubt. It is in this respect that civilized language differs most from that of savages. Just because it is so well organized and receptive and adaptable, it is able to cover an increasing field of meaning with precision and firmness. This a savage cannot do. Thus when an aboriginal Australian of the Arunta was shown a photograph of himself, he said 'That one is just the same as me; so is a kangaroo'. This was his way of saying that the figure in the photograph was very like himself and that he himself was in some sense a kangaroo, since this was his totem. In strict logic he confused two kinds of relation—that between a photograph and its original and that between a member of a totem-group and the totem itself—and he did this because for him there was no real distinction between similarity and identity. In his mind these relations were the same because his language had no means to differentiate between them. For most purposes of life clarity is essential. It need not be, and seldom is, of the highest order, but in speaking our first aim is usually to make ourselves understood. This may take peculiar, specialized forms, as in the rebarbative and almost secret languages of law, business, and bureaucracy. Yet hermetic and wilful though these are in comparison with common speech, their aim is presumably to produce fool-proof statements in the hope that they will have only one meaning and resist any attempt to interpret them otherwise.

Language communicates by giving information, but it does much more than this. The man who gives it may be affected by what he has to say, and his mood will enter into his words and do something to them which makes them more than a mere intelligible statement and produce an effect on his hearers which is more than mere understanding. Words have nearly always a meaning, but they can also appeal to something else than the pure understanding and evoke emotions or fancies or associations which are not easily explained but stir a man's whole being and not his intellectual faculties alone. This emotive function is inherent in language from the very start, since it is derived directly from the original, undifferentiated cry. From this it passes easily into the call, the statement, and the question, all of which may in appropriate circumstances involve anxiety, curiosity, urgency, or other emotions. There are of course many occasions when words are purely informative, notably in technical treatises, manuals of military law, Bradshaw, and the weather forecast, but in ordinary intercourse this austerity is less common. Few of our statements in conversation have the detached impartiality of Whitaker's Almanack or an Act of Parliament, and in our common dealings with one another emotions enter almost without our noticing them. Just as the desire for clarity has led to the creation of special vocabularies, so the urge to convey something more than a merely intelligible meaning has created the arts of poetry and rhetoric. In the languages of savages the emotive element is stronger than the intellectual, because they are intimately concerned with action and its chances and choices. But they too use words in both these ways, and often combine them. The balance between the two functions of language may be different in civilized societies, but both exist in them, and both are often interwoven. Indeed when we think of the art of words, we usually mean not so much their obvious power to convey a simple meaning as their emotional and imaginative effect upon us. Such an art must be extremely ancient, and it is noteworthy that savages, who have almost no handicrafts, have usually quite an advanced art of words, especially in song, which provides them not only with instruction and entertainment but with an outlet for their emotions on occasions which might otherwise be too much for them. Civilized man is their brother in this respect. He too needs this art, and through it feels more at home with his world and with himself.

The double function of language accounts for a paradoxical element in its history, its combination of persistent attempts to master new territories and its innate conservatism. New thoughts require new methods of speech, but appeals to the emotions rely on psychological association which are largely unconscious and must be treated with respect and delicacy. That is why we cling instinctively to certain habits of speech; they are habitual to us and touch us in tender spots. But they may well have an inhibiting effect. The French word *gloire* may indeed be translated by *glory*, but *glory* has nothing like the strength of appeal for the English that *gloire* has for the French. *Glory* is a less refulgent, less commanding, even shabbier word, with certain dubious pretensions, but *gloire* calls up the tramp of triumphant armies and summons to reckless and even ruthless endeavour, allowing no excuses and defying all protests. A characteristically English word of high social influence is *cad*. It is not so powerful as it was forty years ago, but then it stood for almost everyone who, from some uncontrolled and insensitive ebullience, rebelled against the established routine of an entrenched class, and it condemned utterly any attempt to escape from it by display or self-assertion. Its application was deadly, and it is illuminating that no other European language has an equivalent to it, but perhaps an orthodox Edwardian would have argued that this is because all foreigners are *ex hypothesi* cads and therefore do not need a special word for it. Single mastering words may even exert pressure on serious thinking. When Confucius and his followers paid much attention to *li,* which means 'principles of social usage', they spoke of something at the centre of their social and political system, of the whole way of life which dominated China for over two thousand years and has only recently been dethroned. Such a word embodies a gospel and shapes generation after generation in obedience to it. To somewhat the same order belongs the German word *Pflicht,* which we translate 'duty', but which has associations both stricter and more embracing. When Kant made it the basis of his metaphysic of morals, he derived it from the current speech of Prussia and made it keep its character as an imperative call to obedience, which advances no reasons for itself and expects none to be advanced against it. This may indeed promote both efficiency and sacrifice, but it also leads to irresponsible servility and to that unquestioning respect for men in superior station which has crippled the moral and political growth of the German people. These are only a handful of instances in a vast multitude, but they illustrate how words may not only shape the outlook of societies but keep it at work long after it has outlived its usefulness.

Language is also a political force in an obvious sense. The consciousness of possessing a single language is the most powerful element in the cult of nationality which has dominated politics for some two hundred years and shows no signs of abating its vigour. The Arabs and the Cypriots are merely repeating what the Italians and the Germans did in the nineteenth century, and it is as useless now, as it was then, to raise arguments of expediency or legality or racial origin against the compelling claims of a common language. What drives a linguistic group to clamour for unification is the deep and natural feeling that all who speak the same language are in some sense brothers and have far more in common with one another than with anyone else. Yet even this comparatively modern phenomenon has its roots in a distant past and is probably much more ancient than we allow. The conviction that language creates a special bond goes back beyond national and international politics and may be seen at work in truly savage societies. A remarkable case may be seen in the Pygmies of the Gabon, the Congo and Ruanda. To strangers, white or black, they speak the language of whatever negro people lives around or near them, and though they are fluent enough in it, they speak it with a special intonation and a tendency to insert the clicks which seem to be a primordial heritage of the Pygmoid peoples of Africa and are used by the Bushmen and the Hottentots, who have imposed them upon the Zulus. It may be the case that the Pygmies are in fact bilingual and have also a language of their own, which they speak to each other and never consciously before strangers. They are afraid that, if it becomes known outside their own circle, they will betray one of their most sacred secrets to alien and hostile powers and suffer greatly in consequence. A language is so intimate a part of society that even at this savage level it is treasured as a holy possession, because it binds a group together as nothing else can and gives to its members a peculiar sense of being united to one another. In such conditions it is not surprising that when Caribs from South America invaded the Antilles and ate the Arawak men and married the women, the women continued to talk Arawak to each other, although, or perhaps because, their new husbands neither understood nor liked it. The view that a language is a peculiarly special tie between those who speak it is far from being a modern eccentricity and goes back to the most primitive kinds of society.

Despite this powerful impulse to keep them intact, languages, like other living things, struggle with each other for survival and are condemned to the doom that they must either devour others or be devoured themselves. The world still contains pockets in which unusual, often ancient and primitive languages are still spoken by a few people. Yet they have survived simply because of their geographical isolation. Burushaski has been preserved by the mountainous masses of the Karakoram, Yukagir, Chukcha, and Koryak by the unwelcoming tundra of north-eastern Siberia, the Khoisan languages of south-western Africa by the Kalahari desert, Eskimo by the frozen Arctic. The many languages of South America have survived because white settlers have not been able or willing to penetrate the tropical jungles where primitive tribes still live· But once a more or less primitive language is faced by another more highly organized it is doomed to defeat. It is ill fitted to deal with the impact of new ideas and new outlooks, and just as its speakers must in other ways either come to terms with the intruders from outside or perish, so must the language itself. Even a very slight difference of power or culture may extinguish one language before another, as the Dama of the Kalahari now speak the language of the Hottentots, from whom they are physically and historically quite distinct, and the Veddas of Ceylon, who still practise the habits of the Stone Age, speak Sinhalese. The greater the cultural gap between the speakers of one language and the speakers of another, the greater is the danger to the language of the less cultivated group. Languages survive only if their speakers are strong enough to maintain some of their original, independent pattern of existence and even then something may have to be done to keep it intact. In the face of such perils there is more than one solution. A desperate remedy is to adopt the language of the intruders, and that this is not so difficult as we might think is clear from a Samoyede tribe which twice changed its language in two generations, first to a Turkish dialect, then to Russian. A second remedy is to develop a compromise, as many Africans under British rule speak their own versions of English. Indeed gossip reports that when the governor of one of our smaller African colonies addressed his subjects in English, his speech was translated not into any local vernacular, but into Pidgin, beginning with the introductory words : 'Number one white man he say'. Yet even this is possible only if the people which employs it is sufficiently numerous and self-contained to be able to maintain its own habits and with them its own language at least for its own purposes.

The independence of a language may be threatened by forces more powerful even than this. No society can exist in complete isolation, and the need for communication with foreigners is always to some degree present and grows rapidly with the increase of communications and the spread of mechanical devices. The quest for an international language is by no means new. In the middle ages Latin served as a *lingua franca* in clerical circles throughout Europe, and today English or American seems likely to win an ever increasing vogue in many parts of the world. The need for an international language has prompted the creation of Volapuk, Esperanto, and Basic English. It is true that none of these has had a very wide success, and perhaps this is because they are all based on the linguistic structure of Indo-European languages and seem unnecessarily alien to those whose speech is governed by different principles. The process of internationalizing existing languages provides a useful substitute, and it is noteworthy how many scientific and technical words remain more or less unchanged in all the languages into which they are introduced. It is possible that in a foreseeable future technical speech will indeed be international, based on standard words accepted everywhere with some help from symbols which transcend the limits of speech.

Language is both conservative and progressive. On the one hand it likes to maintain established usages long after they have lost their first purpose or meaning. Even in English such a phrase as 'It rains' implies some undefined, supernatural power at work, which is much older than any religious or scientific belief about its identity. The French *quatre-vingt* is a survival from an archaic system of numerals, still in vogue among some Papuans of New Guinea and the Chukcha of Bering Strait, in which twenty was a fundamental unit derived from the sum of a man's fingers and toes. The dual in classical Greek,

Lithuanian and some Uralian languages must be a relic from a time when men, like some primitives today, did not count beyond two. The remarkable fact that most vocatives are the roots of words which are otherwise declined, and are morphologically related to the imperative, suggests that they go back to the primaeval cries and calls of earliest man. The insistence of many European languages that nouns must be divided into masculine, feminine, and neuter has nothing to do with modern ways of thinking and dates from very ancient classifications of objects according to their religious or magical significance, and it is worth noting that Hittite, which is closely related to Indo-European, does not agree with it in this respect but sensibly divides nouns into animate and inanimate, as if it felt able more than three thousand years ago to dispense with what was already an outmoded arrangement. Such archaisms do not interfere with the main task of a language which is to establish communication between one man and another, and they have a certain usefulness, since they keep contact with the past and help to maintain that continuity which is indispensable if a language is to be learned and understood.

On the other hand language continually faces new challenges and has to meet them, and this presents special problems in an age of vast intellectual changes like our own. In general it looks as if the informative and emotive functions of language were growing further and further apart and each were developing more specialized techniques in its own sphere. In the strict world of science, with its increasing desire for precision and its search for general laws, symbols have long begun to replace words, and the tendency, which began with mathematics and physics, has spread to economics, biology, and even logic. Statistics are almost part of the ordinary apparatus of thinking, and diagrams are common for many subjects which resist lucid or concise exposition in words. There is little doubt that this process will continue and expand, as the different sciences discover new principles and evolve more abstract formulae. It is not possible to forecast how far such symbols will replace words, but it looks as if the common man would find science more and more difficult to understand, while even the scientist will not understand any branch of science outside his own speciality. To this degree language will lose its immemorial function as a general means of communication between men on all topics. Parallel with this grows an increasing concentration on the emotive function of words in the finer branches of literature. The scientific and imaginative approaches to experience, which were even in the nineteenth century closely related, are growing more and more separate. This is due partly to a recognition that their functions are obviously different, but it has been aided and accelerated by the conviction that each must go its own way without paying attention to the other. It looks as if in the future the scientist who wishes to understand poetry, and the man of letters who wishes to know something about science, will have to be almost bilingual, and speak alike in abstract formulae and in emotive words. Of course common speech will continue, and both classes will use it, but it will not suffice for all their needs, and language, which has for centuries been simplified and made more useful, will become more difficult and call for greater efforts if it is to fulfil its indispensable duties.

Whatever future waits in store for human speech, its known achievement is enough to excite our wonder and awe. At every turn we see how it accentuates and promotes the difference of man from the beasts. In the natural world all creatures, except man, are helplessly and irredeemably conservative. The elephant of today is identical in form and habits with his ancestor of Tertiary times; the crocodile has not changed its odious character since the remote age when reptiles were the lords of creation; the ungainly coelacanth is just what it was at least two hundred million years ago when it was fossilized into the Devonian sandstone. Animals do not change their habits of their own volition, and such changes as befall them are due to external forces, such as alteration of environment and climate, or capture, domestication, and breeding imposed and conducted by man. Man alone initiates and carries out changes by his own premeditated choice. We may well claim that he is able to do this because he thinks, but thinking would not have got him very far if he had not been able to formulate his thoughts in words and communicate them to his fellows and thereby to cooperate with them in mastering the resources of the world in which he lives.

II

POETS AND SCHOLARS

[Presidential Address delivered to the Birmingham and Midland Institute on 15 October 1956]

THE CONNECTION between poetry and scholarship is so familiar that we do not often stop to think about it. Because it reflects the part which poetry has for centuries played in education and culture, and the need for it to be presented with respect and care, we do not probe the motives or the usefulness of scholars, but take their work for granted as something which presumably has to be done, even if for most people it is of little interest. That students of literature should on the whole prefer poetry to prose is natural enough. It has more to yield to their enquiries because it is more concentrated, more carefully fashioned, more obviously derived from the whole being of those who write it. If humanly it promises finer entertainment and richer rewards, technically it offers many puzzles and problems to tempt ingenuity and invention. The application of scholarship to poetry has happened in most countries where poetry is studied as part of an educational system. In Europe it was born when Greek scholars of Alexandria collected, edited, and annotated the texts of classical masterpieces, and it was reborn with the revival of letters in the fifteenth century. In Asia, notably in China, Persia, and India, it has for centuries held an honourable place in civilized society. That is perhaps why we do not pay much attention to it or notice that it raises some searching questions which concern both poets and scholars and cannot for long be ignored by anyone who is concerned with the intellectual idiosyncrasies and innovations of our time.

At the start let it be said that scholars are not the same as critics. A good scholar, like W. P. Ker, may, in his sanity and his perspicacity, also be a good critic; a good critic, like Sainte Beuve, may, in the range and the solidity of his learning, rightly be regarded as a scholar. But the two classes pursue different ends and employ

27

different means. The scholar's first task is not to judge but to make judgment possible by the preparation and elucidation of texts; to this he must give his full attention, and it may well occupy all his time and all his powers. He may, if he wishes also be a critic, but nothing in the nature of his duties compels him to be one, and there are many scholars, who, whether from modesty or from arrogance, shrink from it. On the other hand the critic's task is to judge a work on its merits, to decide what in it is good and what is bad, to relate it to the society in which he lives, and to other works with which it is in some sense comparable. What he needs is insight and judgment. Knowledge indeed he cannot do without, but as an instrument to help him, and not as the goal of his endeavours. He may sometimes require a wider range of knowledge than most scholars, but in any given field it need not be, and can hardly hope to be, so detailed or so deep. He needs sensibility more than austerity, an open mind more than exclusive concentration, judicious intelligence more than organizing intellect. Both scholars and critics live on the creative work of poets, and both can, if they do their work well enough, provide something that is worth having.

Critics have for centuries been a target for the gibes and strictures of poets, and there is nothing in this to surprise or shock us, since after all the critic can make or mar a poet's reputation, and the poet may not find it easy to accept verdicts passed on his work by men whom he often regards as having taken to criticism because they have failed in poetry. But on the whole the scholars have fared better. For some centuries they have been accepted as a tolerable, and not wholly useless, adjunct of poets. They owe this to the unity of culture which prevailed in Europe from the fifteenth century to the close of the nineteenth. In this period polite education was based mainly on the study of literature, and especially on that of Greece and Rome. Poets might not know this with the precision of scholars, but they were brought up on it and applied to it their own informed, professional insight. The scholars made it easier for them to study, and were usually wise enough not to complain if poets departed from ancient precedents and forged new means of expression. Poets and scholars moved in the same circles of cultivated society, and, though they might differ enormously in tastes and temperament, they had sufficient regard for one another and enough interests in common to take their place together in the traditional structure of intellectual life.

In this period respect for scholarship was maintained because many poets were not merely well educated but had substantial claims to be thought scholars. From Dante to Hopkins the learned poet has been the rule rather than the exception, and though the exceptions might be said to include Shakespeare, he is after all always a law to himself, and the rule covers men so different in their gifts as Chaucer, Ronsard, Camoens, Tasso, Racine, Goethe, Swinburne, and Carducci. Even Rimbaud, who was in many ways the prophet and the pioneer of the modern revolution in poetry, not only won prizes for Latin verse at school but made a generous exception for the Greeks when he derided the career of European poetry as 'avachissement et gloire d'innombrables générations idiotes'.[1] Poets might have their own ideas about obeying classical precepts or following classical examples, but their independence was at least tempered by a quiet agreement that the classics could not be ignored.

What such a tradition could mean to a poet can be seen most remarkably in Milton, who dedicated the best years of his life to the great work which was to be the justification and the fulfilment of his calling, and for which he set out systematically to master the whole of ancient and much of modern literature as a necessary preliminary to a truly complete and comprehensive poem. In this he put into practice the accepted theories of his time as Italian teachers like Vida had formulated them. Nor did this prodigious effort hamper his creative energies. On the contrary Milton's scholarship gave strength to his poetry, and the years of his silence were consumed not by his love of learning but by his sacrifice of personal ambitions to public needs. This spirit lasted into the nineteenth century, when it found a characteristic exponent in Leopardi, who combined an omnivorous scholarship with rare poetical powers. He was indeed more consciously a scholar than Milton in that he pursued scholarship for its own sake and made noteworthy contributions to it. We might perhaps think that he would have written more than the handful of poems which were his life's work if he had not been impeded by his attention to learning, but his poetry arose largely from it and owes its flawless economy in an age of romantic ebullience to his respect for classical art.

This alliance between poetry and scholarship has had its lurid patches. Sometimes scholars have forgotten their proper business and interpreted poetry by irrelevant consideration for alien ends. There are few works of the spirit which cannot be darkened by misinterpretation, and poetry has suffered like the rest. Homer would certainly have been surprised, if from the fields of asphodel he could have seen how his poems, composed to give a noble enjoyment to festal audiences, were turned into manuals of instruction for Greek youth or subjected to bizarre allegorical interpretation. The Chinese *Shih*

[1] Letter of 15 May 1871, to Paul Demeny, *Oeuvres complétes*, ed. La Pléiade, p. 253.

Ching, or *Book of Songs,* which is a collection of delightfully fresh and vivid songs composed for a variety of human occasions, was for centuries used as a hand-book for politicians and bureaucrats. Confucius surely helped the process, since he is reported to have said :

> Little ones, why is it that none of you study the *Songs*? For the *Songs* will help you to express your grievances. They may be used at home in the service of one's father; abroad, in the service of one's prince. Moreover, they will widen your acquaintance with the names of birds, beasts, plants, and trees.[1]

If the Master treated the *Songs* in this business-like spirit, it is not surprising that even pieces concerned with love and courtship were interpreted as allegories of political life, and the lover sighing for his beloved became the image of a man groaning under oppression from the government.[2] Nor is this fate less odd than that which befell the *Song of Songs,* ascribed to Solomon. By some happy caprice this sensuous, candid love-poem found its way into the Hebrew scriptures. With the triumph of Christianity it had to be accommodated to different and more exacting ideas, and everything in it was treated as a prophetic symbol. So 'I raised thee up under the apple-tree' was thought to foretell the tree from which the Cross was made, and the love of the poet for his beloved that of Christ for His Church.

Such cases belong to the eccentricities of history, but there are others in which poetry and scholarship are not so much at cross purposes as openly at war. We have only to recall Pope's treatment of Lewis Theobald in the first version of the *Dunciad* to see how a poet can savage a scholar. Theobald was in fact a highly gifted pioneer of textual criticism, whose emendations in the text of Shakespeare were not perhaps always what the poet actually wrote but were often what he might have written and showed an intuitive and well founded understanding of him. But Pope dismissed 'Tibbald' with deadly contempt :

> Studious he sate, with all his books around,
> Sinking from thought to thought, a vast profound !
> Plung'd for his sense, but found no bottom there;
> Then writ, and flounder'd on, in mere despair.

Yet even this is not really the hatred of poetry for scholarship, but the hatred of a poet, who has pretensions to being a scholar, for a better scholar than himself. What roused Pope's fury was Theo-

---

[1] *Analects* XVII 9. Translated by Arthur Waley.
[2] *The Book of Songs.* Translated by Arthur Waley, pp. 335 ff.

bald's destructive treatment of his own work on Shakespeare, and his motive was more injured vanity than artistic disdain. A poem like the *Dunciad* could be written only in a society where poets were themselves scholars, even if they made mistakes in scholarship, and it could be appreciated only by men who shared both their taste for poetry and their respect for scholarship.

More formidable perils than this lurked in the old tradition. Scholars were indeed so emboldened by general esteem and so confident in themselves and their methods that at times they made hideous blunders by insisting that poetry should conform to standards which were not relevant to it. This was perhaps hard to avoid when such standards were inculcated at schools and universities, and scholars, who are often out of touch with their time, obeyed them too conscientiously and assumed that what was right for one kind of poem was necessarily right for another. A fantastic, terrifying case of this is Bentley's edition of *Paradise Lost*. With what looks very like wilful perversity he eliminates or alters vastly for the worse almost everything in the poem that we regard as Milton's best and most characteristic work. He expurgates both the savage, mocking account of Limbo, and the magical comparison of Eden with the renowned gardens of legend and song. If we turn to almost any lines that we love or admire, we find that they have been transformed into gawky, ponderous, lifeless dummies. So the vast vision of Satan as he surveys the universe :

> So high above the circling Canopie
> Of Nights extended shade; from Eastern Point
> Of *Libra* to the fleecie Starr that bears
> *Andromeda* farr off *Atlantick* Seas
> Beyond th' Horizon,

(P.L. III 556-560)

becomes
> So high above the most extended Cones
> The limiters of Night.

So the last two lines of the poem :
> They hand in hand, with wandring steps and slow,
> Through *Eden* took their solitarie way.

(XII 648-9)

becomes
> Then hand in hand, with social steps their way
> Through *Eden* took, with Heaven'ly Comfort cheer'd.

We can only gasp with amazement and horror, and it is no comfort to remember that Bentley was the greatest classical scholar of his age, whose special strength lay in the establishment of poetical texts. However we choose to explain his extraordinary aberration, whether we say that he deceived himself into believing that Milton's printer really rewrote the text, or that behind the pretence of emendation he exercised his own notion of what the poem ought to have been, he should in either case have known better, and his lack of self-criticism is a damaging comment on the integrity of his scholarship. Yet even this would not have happened if there had not been an accepted notion of what poetry ought to be and if scholarship had not believed that it understood this and must keep it alive before the world.

If Bentley's handling of *Paradise Lost* is a grotesque farce, the treatment of Torquato Tasso by the learned Italian academies of his time is a heartrending tragedy. In 1575, when he was only thirty-one years old, he completed his *Gerusalemme Liberata*. It was an astonishing work of genius, his incomparable masterpiece and unique contribution to the spiritual experience of mankind. In it he enlivened the heroic epic, as his age understood it, with many magical elements drawn from romance, and the Italian academies condemned it, without reservation and without pity, for its failure to conform to correct classical models. Unfortunately Tasso listened to them and continued almost until his death in 1595 rewriting it to suit their demands. He made it more traditional, more classical, more respectable. He pruned, almost out of existence, its chivalrous and romantic elements. He brought his heroes, in despite of themselves, closer to those of Homer and Virgil. He expunged the passages which might shock the most austere morality. There was no academic stricture, however pedantic or trivial, to which he did not pay respectful and obedient attention. The result was the *Gerusalemme Conquistata,* which, though it is longer than the earlier poem, adds nothing at all to it. As we might expect, it failed completely to please the academicians, who proceeded to point out new and equally reprehensible faults. That does not matter. What matters is the work itself. It lacks one thing, and lacks it absolutely—poetry. The poetry, which was so brilliant and various and daring, has gone. Everything that we love in the *Liberata* has been eliminated or wrecked. Tasso wrote the first poem from the abundance of his genius, the second from a depressed and servile desire to please the professors. No doubt in these later years his powers were failing; for a man cannot put all that he has into a long poem and continue to write with the same ardour and abandon. No doubt too his mental disturbances hindered his creative powers and prevented him from reaching his proper level. None the less the *Conquistata* is a horrifying warning both to academicians and against them. In this campaign they won a resounding victory, and it was one of the sorriest disgraces in the history of literature.

Yet, despite Bentley and the Italian academies, poetry and scholarship maintained some kind of equilibrium and even some degree of mutual understanding and respect. Even when new forces began to change the situation, the nineteenth century still held scholarship in high regard, and poets were often good scholars. If there was a general point of view, it was that which Browning dramatized in *A Grammarian's Funeral,* where he justifiably transposes to the Revival of Learning an attitude still characteristic of his own time. The scholar is indeed revealed as a different being from the poet. He pursues his own august and mysterious ends, and deserves honour for his self-sacrificing devotion to them. What he does may be incomprehensible to most men, but it is none the less worth doing; for it is inspired by a lofty vision of man's powers and worth :

> Did not he magnify the mind, show clear
> Just what it all meant?
> He would not discount life, as fools do here,
> Paid by instalment.

The Victorians were still conscious and proud of their continuity with the past, still ready to assume that in some far-off event scholarship and poetry might meet and be married in a final harmony.

Yet beneath this decorous exterior fiercer forces were already at work. The romantic spirit was not prepared to acquiesce in the old assumptions. The poet now asserted himself in his fullest possible individuality and claimed everything that he could as a natural right. He no longer thought it his duty to conform to established rules, but assumed that the only relevant rules were of his own making, and that what mattered above everything was the self and its personal claims. This spirit passed from the Romantics to the Symbolists and their successors, and is still vigorous today. In its refusal to yield to conventions, no matter how hallowed by time or theory or success, it rejects anything that savours of the 'academic', and by this it means almost anything that tries to drill the poet by precedents.

So when Rubén Darío wishes to speak for the unfettered and uncommitted activity of the creative genius and sees it embodied in the figure of Don Quixote, he says :

> de las epidemias, de horribles blasfemias,
> de las Academias,
> libranos, Señor.

·   ·   ·

> from epidemics, from horrible blasphemies,
> from Academies,
> Lord, deliver us.

For him the sin against art, the hideous malady which is its deadliest enemy, is precisely subservience to academic rules, and from this it is but a short step to disowning scholarship and any association of poetry with it. A similar spirit can be seen in W. B. Yeats, who was deeply touched by the ideas of the Symbolists and was not in vain a poet of the nineties. In his poem *The Scholars* he shows what a great poet, who was himself by no means without an interest in learning if not exactly in scholarship, thought about its professional exponents :

> Bald heads, forgetful of their sins,
> Old, learned, respectable bald heads
> Edit and annotate the lines
> That young men, tossing on their beds,
> Rhymed out in love's despair
> To flatter beauty's ignorant ear.

> All shuffle there; all cough in ink;
> All wear the carpet with their shoes;
> All think what other people think;
> All know the man their neighbour knows.
> Lord, what would they say
> Did their Catullus walk their way?

Now we might feel inclined to dismiss this as a momentary fit of spleen in a man of genius, and argue that it does not reflect anything very fundamental or representative. But the signs are otherwise. No one who examines the poetry of the last fifty years can fail to notice that it has rejected many of the old ties with the past and the familiar respect for them. So far from being exceptional, Yeats seems rather to have given voice to what lies in the minds of many poets and rises from their demand to be unmistakably and unrestrainedly themselves.

The romantic creed contained another article, which was no less damaging to the old acceptance of scholarship. Blake and Coleridge, Wordsworth and Keats, alike insisted on the primary importance of the imagination, and by this they meant the sense of some transcendental order revealed in their moments of inspired vision. This was quite a different ideal from the traditional notion of poetry as something built on the accumulated wisdom and art of the past. Coleridge was indeed in his own extraordinary way a scholar, and Keats would have liked to be one, but neither created his best work from anything to do with scholarship. For Blake, who carried the conviction to its limits, the only real world is that of the imagination, and he is perfectly consistent when he associates it with an uncompromising individualism :

I must Create a system or be enslav'd by another Man's.
I will not reason and compare; my business is to create.

Such a belief meant that poets felt no obligation to the past and might well not be interested in it. What mattered was that they should soar on their own wings into the uncharted empyrean in the hope of finding something entirely new.

These two tendencies, which were the products of the Romantic outlook, have been greatly enhanced and fortified by the vast educational changes of the last fifty years. With the spread of education to whole classes which before did not have it has come the breaking up of the old unified curriculum into many branches. Even highly educated circles have no longer the common basis of culture which still existed in the nineteenth century. It is not merely that Latin and Greek have ceased to be the staple of teaching at schools and universities, but that almost everyone becomes sooner or later a specialist who pursues his own speciality in unconcerned separation from others. The new situation has indeed created an impressive variety of educated people, and it is useless, if not wrong, to wish it to be otherwise, but it means that the strength which poetry once drew from a single, accepted, and familiar tradition has been lost. The poet must now work on his own, fashion new images and symbols to replace those canonized by the past, gather his learning wherever chance or whim may lead him, and strain every nerve to express an individual vision through individual means. The educational changes of our time, have, so far as poetry is concerned, completed the work begun by the Romantic revolution. Poets, who are no longer trained in a knowledge of the literary past, may not be unaware of scholarship but may also regard it with estranged and even suspicious eyes.

This widening rift between poetry and scholarship has led some to the conclusion that after all the two have nothing to do with one another. A marked instance of this flourished in France after the First World War as the cult of 'la poésie pure'. Eloquently advocated by the Abbé Bremond, and not without echoes in Proust, this doctrine maintained that poetry, deprived of accidental trappings and reduced to its essence, does not need, and in fact does not have, a

meaning which appeals to the intelligence, since its appeal is to
something else. Through its sounds and rhythms and the vague
associations which these awake, it creates a state which is not understanding but akin to the enraptured awe and wonder in which an
ignorant peasant-girl listens to the Latin of the Mass. This was but
one example of a general notion, which took different forms, but
always insisted that the intelligible content of poetry was not indispensable and that it did not really matter whether it was there or
not. This conviction underlay the attempt of the Surrealists to
breathe a new force into poetry by exploiting the unconscious self,
the notion of Paul Valéry that the meaning of a poem varies from
reader to reader and that no poem has 'un sens véritable, unique,
et conforme ou identique à quelque pensée de l'auteur',[1] the
attempt of certain English poets to give ambiguity an essential part
in their work because of the multiplicity of associations which it
evokes. That something was gained from these experiments cannot
be denied. At least they introduced a new element of excitement and
even of mystery and got rid of the caution and the flatness which
seemed likely to reduce poetry to the cosy domesticity of a fireside
chat. But the denial of any need for it to be understood was a reckless expedient, which was neither sound in logic nor profitable in
practice.

It was this movement which made much modern poetry almost a
private affair of the poet. His readers might well derive a certain
thrill from it, but they could never feel quite at home with it or be
sure that it meant the same to them as it did to him, or indeed that,
in any strict sense, it meant anything. An image or a symbol which
a poet derives from his private life may indeed convey much to him,
but it is quite likely to convey nothing to others who have not
shared his experience. This is particularly true of any too trustful
reliance on the unconscious self as the source of images, since it is
notoriously cryptic and capricious. It was unwise to forget that
almost all poetry begins by appealing to the understanding. Once it
has done this, it can and must do much more; but this at least it has
to do. The absence of any really intelligible content is an unsur-
mountable obstacle. Poetry reaches its unique end and achieves its
unique effect by appealing, at first at least, to the understanding,
and in so far as it is intelligible, it may always need scholars to interpret it.

There has in recent years been a reaction against the view that
poetry is a purely emotive activity to which sense is ultimately
irrelevant. In England the latest generation of poets recognizes the

[1] *Variété* III p. 80.

claims of intelligibility and is eager to see that it gets its due. Nor
are they declared enemies of scholarship. Some of them indeed are
professional scholars, and others have profited from what scholars
have done to bring such literatures as Chinese, Japanese, Provençal,
and modern Greek within the range of English readers. But though
they may mark out in scholarship their own spheres of influence,
which enlarge their horizons and enrich their resources, they have no
close or stable relations with the special world of scholars. Nor is
this surprising. The culture which they have inherited has been so
divided into specialized departments that it seems to them an im-
pertinence to look beyond their own boundaries into the domain of
strangers who have other aims and methods and outlooks. Since
there is no hope that the old unity of culture will be restored, and it
is for many reasons not desirable that it should, the poets are right to
accept things as they are and to make their own corner in whatever
kind of scholarship may appeal to them. This has the incidental
advantage that between them they cover a wider range of reference
than in the past, but it also means that this is to some degree private
and subjective and not always fitted for common consumption. It
is dangerous for poetry to fall in the hands of cliques and coteries,
whose members write mainly for one another; for if it does, it loses
the strength and the confidence which come from having a lively
general interest behind it. The old culture provided links with a
large part of the educated public, and poets were conscious of it
and throve on it. Now that they build their own private systems of
symbols and allusions, there is a risk that they will be understood
only by one another or by their intimate friends, and if this happens,
they may squander their powers on technical trivialities and esoteric
by-play.

There is another side to this, of which poets are not sufficiently
aware. Some of them may in their heart of hearts wish to write
only for one another in the hope that they will then be properly
appreciated without having to make concessions to readers who are
not poets and therefore in the last resort incapable of seeing all that
they are trying to do. Such a hope lurks in many writers and artists,
who accept the public as a necessary evil but cherish a dream that
they would be happier without it. It is an egregious illusion, and
it defies reality in its assumption that poets are even normally com-
petent to appreciate each other's work. The facts point in the opposite direction. The better a poet is, the less he seems able to understand what his fellows do. He is so occupied with solving his own problems that he often fails to grasp that others have different problems
and look for different solutions. History, both ancient and modern,
provides many salutary examples. Pindar compared Bacchylides

with an ape; Sophocles said of Aeschylus : 'Even if he does the right thing, he does it without knowing it'; Greene called Shakespeare 'an upstart Crow, beautified with our feathers'; Goethe failed to see anything in Hölderlin; Milton must have had poets like Herrick and Suckling in mind when he spoke of 'libidinous and ignorant poet-asters'; if Byron made fun of Keats as 'spoilt by Cockneyfying and Suburbing', Keats called *Don Juan* 'Lord Byron's last flash poem'. I have myself heard Bridges say of Yeats at the height of his powers 'Poor Yeats, he's finished', and Yeats say of Housman 'I like only his humorous poetry'. Poets are by no means the best equipped to appreciate the poetry of others, and the notion that such scholarship as poetry needs is best provided by them bears no relation to actual experience.

If in this century poetry has moved in one direction, scholarship has moved in another, and both might be thought to be pursuing more closely their own special aims and obeying their true natures. While poetry has been more concerned with the fundamental tasks of the creative spirit, scholarship has become more scientific, not merely in its development of new techniques for the study of the past but in a more vigorous and more self-denying concentration on its age-old duties. The personal element, which is never absent from Scaliger or Bentley, is viewed with growing suspicion. It is not enough that a scholar should show knowledge and insight; he must show them through an apparatus of scientific proof. It is significant that authors like Aeschylus, who used to be edited with a copious array of emendations, which were not certain but often plausible and at least provided a readable text, are now edited so conscientiously and with so nervous a fear for human fallibility that any passage which is at all disputable is left obelized and uncorrected,[1] and the reader has either to improvise his own text or acquiesce in frustration and defeat. The same is becoming true of Shakespeare. The more we learn about the way in which the First Folio was printed, the further we seem to move from an accepted or acceptable text. Scholarship has become so severe and so highminded in its pursuit of certainty that it prefers to admit ignorance rather than say anything about which there is a possible doubt. This outlook has its own intellectual dignity, but does not make it easier to study the great works of the past as living things, and it means that, just as poets tend to cut themselves off from a large public in order to bask

---

[1] Gilbert Murray told me that A. W. Verrall used to quote with reference to some scholars the Homeric line:

μίστυλλόν τ' ἄρα τἄλλα καὶ ἀμφ' ὀβελοῖσιν ἔπειραν

and translate it: 'they set *obeli* about it and made a hash of the rest.'

in each other's approval, so scholars produce work which only other scholars can endure.

The present situation impels us to reconsider the relation of scholarship to poetry and to ask what, if anything, can or should be done. Their relations have undeniably changed, but though the difficulties are great, it is clear that the old obligations of scholarship should still be seriously treated in the new conditions. Of these the first is to see that the works of poets is preserved and presented to the world. This is in one respect less difficult than when the librarians of Alexandria collected the works of Greek poetry from many sources, or Poggio ransacked the monasteries for Latin manuscripts. The prevalence of printing makes it likely that once a poet's words have been published, they will remain known. There is of course always a hope that some undiscovered genius, who failed or refused to get his works printed, may be revealed, and scholarship will be needed to see that he is treated properly. This has happened in different degrees with Clare, Blake, Hölderlin, Hopkins, and Rimbaud; it may conceivably happen with someone else. More urgent, and more immediate, is the need to see that works which have long been familiar are published correctly. It is indeed surprising to learn, for instance, how inadequately even Shelley, who left a large mass of unpublished texts, has been presented by his first editors and how much he yields to perceptive and precise study.

In recent years the careful examination of poets' manuscripts has led to the appearance of editions on an unprecedented scale of exactness and detail, in which almost every word that they wrote is carefully printed, whether they themselves kept it or abandoned it. What the Soviet Academy of Sciences has done for Pushkin, the Stuttgart editors are doing for Hölderlin, and each edition is a majestic piece of scholarship which shows how these poets worked, by what stages they moved from a first, originating impulse to a finished poem, how they rewrote poems that might seem to us already complete. If a poet is good enough, every word that he wrote adds something to our knowledge of him, and a few scattered or unfinished lines may tell us something that we should never have guessed for ourselves. Mere scraps which he cast aside may contain the seed of what was to bear fruit later; a scribble in the margin may reveal a second thought which alters the whole intention of a poem. Behind the finished achievement that we already know appears the effort which went to its making, the selections and the rejections which show the poet in his workshop and make him more real and more vivid than any account of the external events of his life could ever do. This is the right material for his biography, because it shows him at work in what mattered most to him and absorbed his finest energies.

This is, of course, by no means the only thing that scholars can or should do. Though 'pure' scholars usually suspect and shirk anything that savours of interpretation except in the narrowest and safest sense of knowing what the words mean, there is no doubt that this too is a scholar's duty. Its ideal was formulated by Pope :

> A perfect Judge will read each work of wit
> With the same spirit that its author writ.

This is never easy and becomes more difficult as the past recedes into an ever dimmer distance and the present bursts into new complexities which confuse those who were brought up to something different. It may in the last resort be impossible to know a poet as his intimate friends know him or as he knows himself, but this is not quite what the scholar has to do. His business is to know him in his work, which is after all the central and most serious part of his existence. Though we cannot catch the tone of his conversation or the casual movements of his mind, we can at least remove some of the obstacles set by time and place between his books and ourselves; we can discover what he was trying to do and how he set about it; we can study his language with its nuances and idiosyncrasies, its individual tone and its relation to that of his contemporaries. Our task is to see his work as it really is, in the efforts which went to its making, in the assumptions upon which he acted, whether political or social or doctrinal, in the artistic ideas and ideals which he learned from others or shaped for himself, in the literary forms which he found to his taste or fashioned for his special ends. We must get to know him as well as we can, with all the means at our disposal, and even then we must recognize that there is much which eludes our chase and which we shall never discover. It is not surprising that many scholars shrink from so exacting a task or think that it can never be accomplished. None the less it can be attempted, and it is not always doomed to failure.

A good example of what scholars can do in this way may be seen in a case not very distant in time from ourselves. Shortly before Mallarmé died in 1898, Arthur Symons, who was among the first to introduce him to English readers, wrote of him :

> In the course of a few centuries, I am convinced, every line of Mallarmé will have become perfectly clear, as a corrupt Greek text becomes clear with time.[1]

In 1897 this may well have sounded foolish; for Mallarmé was then

[1] *Figures of Several Centuries* p. 307.

regarded as ultimately unintelligible, and the comparison of his work with Greek texts was hardly convincing, because with him there is no question of corruption by the transmission of manuscripts through time. His work is as he left it, as he meant it to be, and if it defeated his contemporaries, it was even more likely to defeat posterity. Yet Symons was, in his main contention, right. The elucidation of Mallarmé has come far more rapidly that Symons foresaw, and has been the work of scholars, who, by studying everything that he wrote or that can be found out about him, have unravelled the main secrets of his art and proved that, so far from courting ambiguity, he maintained a hard core of intelligible structure behind the mystery which he loved and expressed through evocative symbols. What scholars had already perceived was confirmed by the publication in 1948 of a letter from him to Sarah Helen Whitman about his sonnet *Le Tombeau d'Edgar Poe*. In this he gives a literal translation of the poem into English and makes it quite clear that he worked on a firm sequence of unambiguous ideas.[1] The discovery proved that the scholars were right in denying that he was guilty of wilful obfuscation, and now many of his poems, which seemed to resist coherent interpretation, are seen to have a solid intellectual intention, while even the most refractory are slowly yielding to treatment. The process reveals Mallarmé's genius in its true splendour, and we are now beginning to enjoy his poetry as it really deserves. He trusted in posterity to interpret him rightly, and his trust was not misplaced.

Something of a similar kind has happened with Hopkins. Bridges has been freely and unfairly blamed for keeping his friend's poetry unpublished for nearly thirty years and for presenting at first only small bits of it in his anthology *The Spirit of Man* in 1916. But Bridges judged the situation correctly. If he had published the poems immediately after Hopkins' death in 1889, they would have made little impression on a generation soaked in a very different poetry. Their appearance in 1918 was well timed, since a new spirit was abroad, and men were on the look out for ways to break away from poetical conventions which had outlived their usefulness and become a hindrance to new effort. Though the poems were slow to make an impression, in the end they succeeded, and it was enormous. But much of the growth of Hopkins's reputation and popularity is due to the scholars who have worked on him, published his letters and note-books, unravelled his theories of metre and rhythm, showed how he coined new words and gave new associations to old, defined the sphere of sentiment with which he deals, placed him in his Victorian setting, fitted the poems into the events of his life, and

[1] Gardner Davies, *Les 'Tombeaux' de Mallarmé* p. 90.

illustrated them by what he sought and suffered in his religious calling. By this process a poet, who was on his first appearance so original as to be indeed forbidding and formidable, has been assimilated, and the rare experience which he has to offer has been made available to all who love English poetry and are not afraid of finding surprises in it.

This process of elucidation and analysis becomes the more necessary as poetry moves further from its traditional moorings and seeks unknown horizons. The poetry of our time often calls for interpretation, not merely among those who are not trained in its evocative and allusive methods, but among academic students who are expected to understand the whole of English literature in the spirit in which it was written. Now that poetry is not only a private pasttime but an educational discipline, it makes new demands on scholarship to present it fairly and fully. Boys and girls who no longer have to construe Aeschylus can display their talent for conundrums on more modern works which call for no less agility and erudition. What Pindar said of his own poetry is true of more than one poet today:

πολλά μοι ὑπ' ἀγκῶνος ὠκέα βέλη
ἔνδον ἐντὶ φαρέτρας
φωνάεντα συνετοῖσιν· ἐς δὲ τὸ πᾶν ἑρμανέων
χατίζει.

> In the quiver
> Under my elbow are many swift arrows
> That speak to the wise, but for the crowd
> They need interpreters.

The task of scholarship is to meet this need, to bridge the gap between the strangely personal experience of the poet and the understanding of other men. If the scholar of modern poetry does not need quite so systematic an apparatus of learning as his classical counterpart, he needs a like insight and a like concentration, and he must be no less aware of the conditions in which a poet lives and works. Though his task falls in new fields, it remains essentially the same as before. His first duty is to grasp with the full capacity of his sympathetic intelligence the works of art with which he deals.

The scholar, then, is a 'middle man', whose business is to see that certain goods are purveyed to the public which wants them, and that they are not soiled or spoiled in the process. Whether he deals with ancient or with modern writers, with his own or with foreign languages, he needs the same gifts and faces the same issues. It is not necessary that he should himself be a poet, and it may even harm his scholarship if he is. But he must know what poetry is, what poets try to do, what their unique contribution is. He may, and indeed must, do much for this by study, but study is useless unless it is based on a penetrating and sympathetic insight. If he lacks an immediate response to poetry, an inborn taste for it, and an eye for 'the real, right thing', he would be well advised to confine his activities to those more purely scientific branches of learning where it is not required. His business is not to create but to understand, and what matter for this are the delicacy of his sensibility, the degree with which he is able to submit his own personality to that of the authors whom he studies and at the same time to stand apart from them, the precision with which he records his observations and his conclusions. If he has these qualities, he may legitimately indulge in speculations and theories and judgments, but these will have little value unless he maintains before his task the modesty and the self-criticism which alone enable him to work as he should. It is not for him to teach poets their business or to compile manuals on the practical problems of poetry. If there are authors whom he finds unsympathetic or unintelligible, he is wiser to say nothing rather than to voice his distaste in condemnation. He may be a pundit but he must not pontificate, and he must always remember that his first responsibility is to enable others to share his own hard-won understanding of the great works of men.

Yet, though the scholar's task is derivative and secondary, it has a considerable significance for any society which claims to be civilized. In the end it is he, and he alone, who maintains continuity with the poetical past, who is responsible for seeing that the masterpieces of creative genius are not lost through neglect or falsified by prejudice or mutilated by ignorance. This past is indeed alive, but only because scholars keep it so. Because they exist for its service, it is not a curiosity preserved for the benefit of a few antiquarians but is free to thrive among us and to become part of our lives. We have already lost too much to be able to dispense with any means that keeps this tradition safe against the many pests, whether physical or doctrinal or moral, which lie in wait to devour it. It not only survives but grows and expands as each generation adds something to it, and it is the business of scholarship to see that new developments also are assured of their right opportunities and their hopes of survival. The process must go on, and it can do so only if scholars are vigilant and devoted in their care for it.

Scholarship has its own creed, its own code, and its own pride. If it seeks to teach or to persuade or to convert, it can do so only by making truth its first and indispensable goal. Though the pursuit of truth may be aided by inspired insight or personal experience or happy accident, it must always dominate the scholar's mind and keep his reverence. He cannot hope that even his finest work will survive the centuries, that it will not be superseded by the work of others who take up the enquiry where he left it, or that his methods, however impartial and impeccable, will not in due course be outmoded. The artist who really creates something creates it for ever, but the scholar is at the mercy of expanding knowledge and changing habits of thought. Yet he has abundant recompenses. A long and intimate association with masterpieces is an invigorating and enjoyable profession, which brings unexpected rewards from many quarters, not least to the solution of the scholar's own troubles and to the enrichment of his experience and the enlargement of his vision. Unforeseen moments of illuminating discovery and the sense of satisfaction in seeing recalcitrant material mastered and brought to order are his consolation for efforts which may sometimes seem to be humiliating and soul-destroying, for failures to realize his hopes or to prove his theories, for much drudgery and doubt and defeat. In the beginning of mankind was the Word, and though nearly all words fade on the air for ever, some few endure and give light and life to men. It is with these that the scholar of poetry is concerned, and they provide him with a calling for which he need not apologize.

III

A CLASSICAL EDUCATION

*[Presidential Address to the Classical Association, delivered on
4 April 1945]*

THE WAR has not been any kinder to the classics than to other
branches of humane education. At the universities male students of
the classics have shrunk to negligible numbers. At schools natural
science has enjoyed a great tactical advantage in that it offers to its
best adherents not only exemption from military service but a free
education at the university. It is inevitable that the number of boys
taking classics in the Higher Certificate should shrink, and it has in
fact shrunk to nearly half of what it was in 1939. No doubt this
figure is partly to be explained by the early age at which boys are
called up, but that is not all that there is to it. Some schools, which
ten years ago boasted of famous and flourishing classical sides, now
report a great diminution in the number of classical students. One
school, which has in its day produced scholars of eminence, has
ceased to teach Greek because it finds no demand for it. This sudden
diminution is a new thing. From 1919 to 1939 the number of
classical students at the universities remained at an almost constant
figure, despite the attractions of new courses and the ingenious lure
of such titles as 'Modern Greats'. It looks as if there were a real
slump in the classics through the country. We may well speculate
about the causes. Perhaps the war has turned the thoughts of parents
to science and 'modern subjects'; perhaps there is a shortage of
classical teachers; perhaps, as of old the Carthaginians sacrificed
their first-born to Moloch in time of war, so the English sacrifice
their elegances and luxuries, including the classics, to the God of
Battles. Whatever the causes may be, the situation exists.[1] If the
classics are to revive, it would be foolish to assume that the revival
will come in the ordinary course of nature and that we need take

---

[1] This was certainly my impression in 1945, but the situation has greatly
improved since.

no steps to promote it. We must look to our business and see not only why it slumps but what permanent benefits it has to offer to the young, what advantages it possesses that belong to no other course of study in the same quality or the same degree.

When the foundations of classical training were laid in the fifteenth and sixteenth centuries, it was assumed that the classics were an indispensable part of any complete education. In those golden days the writers of Greece and Rome were honoured for more than one reason. For an age passionately interested in theology the ancient languages preserved not only the holy books and evidences of faith but all the important commentaries and works of exegesis upon them. This supremacy in matters spiritual was equalled by a supremacy in matters temporal. The Greeks and Romans were the accepted authorities on astronomy, geography, zoology and medicine. Experience might sometimes indicate that Pliny or Ptolemy or Galen was not always right, but they remained the chief founts of knowledge, and new discoveries were treated as *addenda* and *corrigenda* to them. Finally, the classical supremacy was acknowledged in all matters relating to the art of words, in rhetoric, in philosophy, in history, in poetry. When Machiavelli or Montaigne or Bacon wishes to point a moral about human nature, he turns almost inevitably to ancient history and garnishes his lessons for the present with examples drawn from Livy or Cornelius Nepos. The ideal models for generations who really believed in the importance and power of oratory were found in Demosthenes and Cicero. Even in poetry the emergence of new forms and styles did not destroy the belief that the best sort of poetry, whether epic or dramatic or lyric, was what the ancients had written in these kinds. What the moderns had to do was to rival these as well as they could in their own language and conditions.

This state of affairs could not last, and it collapsed with the advent of the scientific spirit. By claiming to explain at least the physical nature of the universe natural science ousted theology from its old place as the queen of the sciences. Pliny, Ptolemy and Galen soon yielded their supremacy to the new spirit of experimental investigation. Even history, which still has uneasy suspicions that it may have as much to do with art as with science, took on new tasks which lay far away from the belief that the only models were Livy and Tacitus. What remained was fine literature, and on this classical education concentrated. From the seventeenth century till yesterday the Greek and Roman classics were studied as works of art which were pre-eminent not only in their technique but in their intellectual insight and imaginative range. It was assumed that however wrong they might be on matters of mere fact, they still possessed qualities which are not commonly found in modern works and that the writers of Greece and Rome held the keys to a world of exalted beauty which was in its way unique and a knowledge of which was indispensable to any man or woman who claimed to know about literature. On this basis the study of the classics was established. They were read and emulated both because of their form and because of their content. They were honoured because they provided a training both in taste and in human nature. The classical education grew from the Humanism of the Renaissance and kept its pride of place so long as the humanistic outlook prevailed. And if today there are signs of a depreciation in the classics, it is because this humanistic outlook has itself been assailed and shaken.

The classical education was created by men who believed in an aristocratic ideal and was intended primarily for those who were free from pecuniary anxieties and could develop their interests and personalities freely. It helped them to polish their taste, to enlarge their understanding, to practise that magnificence which was the peculiar glory of the Renaissance, to feel that they belonged to a splendid European tradition and that they must be worthy of their origins. Such an education was an elegance, a luxury and a pride. Of course it might have practical uses. Milton would not have become Latin Secretary to Cromwell if he had not been one of the foremost scholars of his age; many young men of obscure origin rose to power and place because they were good scholars and could put their knowledge at the service of others. Even in the nineteenth century Dean Gaisford could end a Christmas sermon with the inspiring words : 'Nor can I do better, in conclusion, than impress upon you the study of Greek literature, which not only elevates above the vulgar herd, but leads not infrequently to positions of considerable emolument.' But though the classical education provided a way to such prizes, it was not intended to be vocational or, in any vulgar sense, useful. Its aim was to create a full man, not to find him a job. This outlook has changed. It would be idle to deny that in a democratic age most education is expected to be in some degree useful and vocational. It must prepare a man not merely for life in general but for a special task or profession. In a world like our own where specialization is on the increase and technical training is a primary necessity for many, the uses of a classical education are not immediately obvious to everyone. It may be delightful, but is it practical? Does it prepare a man for the life that he has to live and for the work that he has to do? Can parents afford to give their children a training which offers no certain prospects of income or promotion? From the sixteenth to the nineteenth centuries such questions were hardly asked. Education was mainly a privilege of

the few who had enough money for their needs and could afford
to learn something which did not give them a living. The rise of
universal education has altered the whole situation. Whether we like
it or not, we have to consider what use education is to the educated
and what place the study of the classics has in any educational scheme.

It is clear at the outset that if the classics are to survive they cannot make such claims for themselves as they once did. Few of us
would demand that every boy and every girl should have a classical
education, and even if we were to demand it, we should not find a
popular response. We must indeed admit that to many the old monopoly of the classics did more harm than good. To assume that they
are the only education for everyone is to fly in the face of facts. We
all know gifted and clever persons who were taught the classics at
school and have kept nothing but a hatred for them. It is sad, but it
is true, and it is not enough to argue like Mr King, when he heard
Stalky refer to Regulus : 'It sticks. A little of it sticks among the barbarians.' The barbarians need something else and are determined to
get it. There are many boys and girls who care neither for language
nor for literature and for whom the classical discipline is a meaningless and hateful drudgery. We have no right to assume that such
people are unfit for education. Experience shows that some who cannot learn Greek and Latin can become good scientists or historians.
There are many for whom the civilization of the ancient world is so
shadowy and remote that it has no reality and no significance. But
they should not for this reason be sacrificed. They must have whatever education is suited to their tastes and capacities, and it should
not be classical. I would not indeed say that they would not be better
for some preliminary training in the rudiments of Latin Grammar, if
only because it makes them ask what words mean and what a sentence is. Nor would I assume that those who are unable to derive
benefit from the classics are the vast majority of mankind, still less
that many forms of education now in vogue are worth having. Nor
does it follow that a boy will be a good historian because he is a bad
linguist or a good scientist because he is congenitally inaccurate. But
I do think that the old classical system erred in claiming a monopoly
for itself and that in doing this it not only deprived many intelligent
people of some other education better suited to them but also in-
curred considerable odium and contempt for itself.

A second defect of the old system was that it was mainly linguistic
and grammatical. Of course we cannot appreciate or understand any
literature, even our own, unless we know what the words mean.
Language is a perfectly legitimate end in itself for those who like it,
and the austere scholar of the old school who shrinks from a mistake
as from an unclean thing is a noble and admirable figure. But the

special claim of the classics is that linguistic knowledge is also a means to an end, to the study and appreciation of two great literatures. If the classics were valuable merely as a training in language, the same might be argued for Finnish or Turkish, whose syntax and vocabularies are quite as ingenious and as complicated as those of Greek and Latin. The special claim of Greek and Latin is that a knowledge of the languages opens the door to the literatures. And this, I cannot help thinking, has too often been neglected. The strict old spirit is immortalized in the story of the headmaster who said to his sixth form : 'Boys, this term you are to have the privilege of reading the *Oedipus Coloneus* of Sophocles, a veritable treasure-house of grammatical peculiarities.' I have some sympathy for that great man. The *Oedipus Coloneus* is indeed such a treasure-house. But it is not only nor mainly that, and the headmaster was wrong to insist so strongly on it. Nor is this spirit entirely dead, at least in our older universities. There are still those who look askance at any interest in the classics as literature and feel that it is indecent to speak about them as if they touched our own thoughts and lives. Even those who spend their time in the study of ancient poetry have been known to describe any criticism other than textual as 'gush'. Now such a position is indefensible if only because it throws an implicit contempt upon those who happen to be fascinated by classical literature and because it discourages and depresses the young who feel this magic and should not be damped in their enthusiasm for it. This point of view determined a habit that used to prevail at schools of reading only half a Greek tragedy or half a speech of Cicero. This may have led to greater accuracy and to a greater attention to detail, but it destroyed the main reasons for reading such works at all. To even a clever schoolboy half a play or half a speech is meaningless. He might as well confine himself to a book of unseen passages and be none the worse off so far as any knowledge of ancient literature is concerned. We can hardly be surprised if clever pupils, who really love good literature and are not uninterested in language, are seduced by modern languages or English, in which they can at least see some reward for their efforts.

I have dwelt on these two points because they indicate the spirit in which the traditional classical education was often conducted and account for some of the criticism which it has received. They are easily remedied and have been remedied in many places. Let us assume that the classics provide a suitable training at least for those who care for language or for literature or for both. We may then ask what special advantages a classical education has to offer in an age when it has to compete not only with natural science and modern languages but with history and that amorphous mass of subjects which our leaders in education demand for an understanding of the modern world. It is not enough to say that the classics teach accuracy; the same can be said of mathematics. Nor that they inculcate taste; the same can be said of French. Nor that they open avenues to important fields of speculation; the same can be said of history. Nor that they are indispensable to the correct use of English; the same can surely be said of English itself, and I have not found that classical scholars are inevitably masters of their own tongue. It is of course true that such grammar as English can boast and such order as can be found in English composition owe a great deal to Latin, but that is because our language has in the past been shaped by spoken and written Latin, not because our present writers are classical scholars. The real and special claim of a classical education is something different.

The study of the ancient languages is a training not only in words but in thought. The Greeks and the Romans presented their ideas in a way quite unlike ours. They are not necessarily more direct or more natural than we are. It would, for instance, be hard to find anything in English so terse and concentrated as some passages of Thucydides or so rich and rhetorical as much of Cicero. The Greeks and Romans expressed themselves in ways unlike ours because their minds moved differently. To understand them we have to make an effort which we do not have to make in our own or in any other contemporary European language, and in making this effort we widen our understanding and make our intellects more supple. We find that ideas habitual to us did not exist for the Greeks and Romans and that for some of their fundamental ideas we have no exact equivalents. It is this intellectual exercise, this adaptation of our minds to something alien and unfamiliar, that the classics have to give us. The differences between our use of words and theirs are enormous. There are few sentences in either Greek or Latin which can be translated literally into English without losing something essential; there are few sentences in English which can be translated literally into Greek or Latin without being absurd. To understand the classical languages we must get past the words to the ideas which they express, past the grammatical structure and the vocabulary to the precise colour and tone of their matter. Herein lies the special claim of the classical education.

It is sometimes maintained that the training afforded by the classics in this way, though undeniably true, could just as well be got by studying some language nearer to our own lives and more useful than Greek or Latin. The advocates of this view wish to kill two birds with one stone and to secure an education which both trains the mind and has practical uses. Why not, they ask, study

French or German or Russian? They are languages with rich vocabularies and difficult grammars; they are hard to read or to speak fluently; they should give an intellectual training as good as any given by Greek and Latin and yet useful in the modern world. There is much to be said for this claim. The languages of modern Europe are well worth learning. They open doors to great literatures, and they demand a high degree of accuracy and even of scholarship. To this claim there are two answers. In the first place there is no reason why classical students should not also learn modern languages. They normally learn French, and there is no unanswerable reason why they should not learn another language as well. Indeed their training in the essentials of grammar well equips· them to do so, and the war has shown how easily those who have studied the classics at school can take up languages so distant as Chinese and Japanese. Secondly, and this is more important, the dead languages have an advantage over the living just because they are dead. The structure of thought in any modern language is very much the same as in English. Abstract and technical words are often common to several languages. The ways of thinking and of expressing ideas are similar. When all is said, modern languages are concerned with much the same ideas as English, and on the whole present them in much the same way. However strange we may find the matter of Nietzsche or Dostoevsky, we must admit that the actual way in which they present their thoughts is very like our own. They can be translated literally into English, while Plato or Cicero cannot. The modern languages are too near to us to provide that training in understanding ideas which is provided by Latin and Greek. To read even the most difficult modern works we do not need so great an effort of the understanding, so sharp a penetration past the words to the sense, as we need for the classics. And just for this reason modern languages are an inferior instrument of education. We can understand their words and translate them correctly without being compelled to understand their full implications. With Greek and Latin this is all but impossible.

It is because the classics provide this special kind of training that, at least in England, such attention is paid to translation and composition. It is through these that we learn not only what words mean but how ideas are expressed. The difficulties of translation are endless, and in making it a central part of an educational system we set the young a hard task. Not only have they to know the grammar and the mere meanings of the words; they have to translate words for which there is no single or obvious English equivalent. How are they to translate λόγος ἀρετή or *pietas* or *religio*? How are they to find English equivalents to Homer's epithets or Aristotle's concentrated sentences or the seductive ambiguities of Virgil or the fierce epigrams of Tacitus? How are they to convey the ingenious fluency of Euripides, the marmoreal brevity of Horace, the mellifluous expansiveness of Cicero? Beyond the mere words they have to find equivalents for the ideas which are expressed and for the manner in which they are expressed, for the aroma and the atmosphere which hang round them. Translation, as we all know, is in the last resort, impossible. But the effort to do the utmost possible, to transfer to English not only the meaning of words but their associations and character, has to be made. It is the essential discipline of the classical system and makes it what it is. Only by this effort and this attempt to get close to the full original meaning can we interpret the spirit of the ancient writers and get the utmost possible out of them.

The practice of composition in Greek and Latin raises rather different questions and demands different gifts, but it is ultimately directed to the same end. False assumptions are made about it. The good composer is not necessarily the only kind of good scholar; there are good translators and good editors who are indifferent composers. It is not really true that a good composer of Greek and Latin verse must himself be a kind of poet. Good verses can be written from a retentive memory and verbal dexterity; they do not always imply inspiration. Composition, even, has its dangers. The assumption that Latin elegiacs must be modelled on Ovid has at times led to an undue neglect of Tibullus and Propertius, and it is comforting to see that the noble verses which Housman set at the beginning of his Manilius are written, without regard to precedent, as only he could have written them. But when we have made allowance for all these points, the fact remains that composition does in one way what translation does in another. It makes us ask what the English words really mean and find the Greek or Latin way of expressing the essential ideas behind them. When we write prose or verse in an ancient tongue, we have to find out the thought in what is said and to transpose this into a different medium. When I was an undergraduate, I had the wonderful fortune to go to a small class in Greek composition conducted by Professor Gilbert Murray. It was an enthralling experience, because by some peculiar magic he was able to make us see how elaborate English expressions could be transmuted into a limpid, elegant Attic. I do not know how he did it, but I remember the electrical effect which his own compositions had on us. There was in particular a piece by William James on *The Moral Equivalent of War*. It was a somewhat turgid piece of English, full of abstract words and imperfectly defined ideas, and there was one sentence which challenged our powers : 'The horror makes the thrill, and when the question is of getting the extremest and supremest out of human nature, talk of expense sounds ignominous.' I shudder to think what pompous pseudo-Plutarchean Greek I tried to write for this, but I still remember the vivid, surprised delight with which I heard Professor Murray's own version :

δι᾽ αὐτὸ γὰρ τὸ δεινὸν καὶ τὸ λαμπρὸν γίγνεταί᾽, αἰσχρὸν δέ πως ἐν οἷς τὰ μέγιστα καὶ κάλλιστα ἐνεργεῖ ἐν τοιούτοις περὶ δαπάνης ἀργυρίου λέγειν.

The fluff has all vanished, and what remains is the essential meaning, clear and vigorous and delightfully Greek. If we can ever do anything at all like this, we have found what composition has to offer. We have pierced past the mere form of the English words, extracted their meaning and transposed it into quite a different medium. The exercise requires knowledge, insight, concentration and effort, but of its value there can be no doubt.

So far I have considered the classical education simply as an instrument for training the mind, and I have laid emphasis on what seems to me the most important element in it from this point of view. But it is much more than this, much more than a means to teach us how to think. The technique which we acquire so laboriously and so imperfectly and with which even professional scholars busy themselves all through their lives is primarily a means to gaining an experience. We learn Greek and Latin that through them we may recapture, so far as the nature of the material and our own abilities allow, the experience of the ancient world. What this means only a study of the intellectual and spiritual history of Europe can show, and I shall not attempt to recapitulate what has been said with more eloquence and knowledge than are at my command. But there is one thing that I must say. When we study the classics, we should study them without any preconceived idea of what we shall find in them and without any desire to make them justify our own wishes and beliefs. However much the Greeks and Romans may have anticipated some of our deepest convictions, we should not study them merely for that reason. For instance, Plato's doctrines may well appeal to our educational reformers, but that is not the only or the right reason for reading Plato. It is equally important to know where he differs from modern ideas. So too Virgil may well be interesting because he anticipates some of the ethical outlook of Christianity, but he does much more than that, and he must be studied in his entirety, without any desire to isolate in him only what is familiar to our own ways of thinking. This way of reading the classics falsifies our understanding of them. To know Plato we must know everything that he wrote, and we may then find that not all his views are to our taste. It is for instance hard to give an unqualified welcome to the society which he sketched with such meticulous detail in the *Laws*.

Again, whatever forecasts Virgil may have made of Christianity, it is wise to remember that Fathers of the Church like Lactantius and Augustine were dubious of his influence and particularly critical of his good Aeneas. If we look to the classical authors simply for elements which we already have in modern life, we shall not only miss much of value that they have to offer but we shall fail to widen our experience or to gain that independence of outlook which comes from the study of a world which is not our own.

The distance and the difference of the classics from ourselves are a matter of fundamental importance. In reading them we do not find our own habits of thought or our own way of looking at things. We are indeed liable to misinterpret them because they are so different. The long history of the Homeric question is an important lesson on how wrong honest and intelligent men can be when they examine a kind of art which lies outside their own experience. It is only in recent years that the study of oral epics in various countries has shown in what kind of conditions the Greek epic must have arisen and how unlike its methods were from those of Virgil or Milton. Mistakes equally grave can be made in questions which involve the thought and outlook of the ancients. The attempts made before the war to treat Augustus as a forerunner of Mussolini were not confined to Italian scholars, and some of our dialectical materialists still insist that the Pythagoreans must have been reactionaries in politics just because they studied pure mathematics. Much of course is to be gained from applying the lessons of modern experience to the study of the ancient world. It forces us to ask new questions and to look at old problems in a new light. But the danger is that we shall treat antiquity not on its own merits but as a pale reflection of ourselves. If we do this, we run the risk of being seriously wrong and of missing the special virtue of the classics which lies in forcing us to examine unfamiliar chapters of experience and to see how differently even common events can be seen and judged.

The English tradition of classical learning is based on the humanistic faith that man is worth studying for his own sake. The first Humanists turned to the study of Greece and Rome because they found in them an example of this outlook, which was not to be found in the theological doctrines of their time, and because the candour and clarity of the classics, no less than the perfection of their form, made this interest in man all the more powerful. Thus from the start the classical discipline was based on a twofold appeal, to the intelligence and to the imagination. It was not merely a subject for intellectual inquiry nor merely a way to an enchanted and enchanting world. It claimed to justify man's belief in himself and to reveal to him how rich experience can be. The devoted and noble labours which English scholars have given to their work have often been inspired by the conviction that the classics contain spiritual riches which have no equal and which it is their task to discover and display. This outlook gave them an inestimable advantage in their chosen fields of work. They kept their eye on the texts and regarded it as their first duty to interpret them. No one for instance can read any of Bentley's work without realizing that he carried a large part of classical literature in his head, and it was said of Badham, whom academic indifference exiled to Australia, that he knew the whole of Greek poetry by heart. The special quality of English scholarship lies in this close acquaintance with the originals. That is no doubt why it is rich in textual criticism and commentaries. Textual criticism is a means by which a man who loves the classics can express his love for them. He wishes to present them without flaw or blemish and trusts that his own knowledge and insight will help to do this. Of course this love, like other forms of love, may sometimes be blind to the real qualities of the beloved or see qualities which are not actually there. The textual critic may come to a point where he ceases to emend and begins to improve. What Bentley did on a small scale in his Horace and on a fabulous and fantastic scale in his *Paradise Lost* is an interesting comment on the allurements of textual criticism. But the peculiarities are at least related to a literary ideal. Bentley wished Horace and Milton to conform to his notion of what a work of literature ought to be. His ideas were those of his time, and we can afford to laugh at them. But they were based on a great tradition and on a belief that literature is a serious pursuit. The same can hardly be said of Nauck or Wecklein whose labours on the Greek tragedians, despite a remarkable erudition, are guided by no literary standards whatsoever. This closeness to literature is the special claim of the English textual critics. At their best they seem to be inspired, so near are they to the temper and style of the authors whom they emend. Though we may sometimes feel compelled to disagree with Porson or Munro, and we shall do so at our peril, we must admit that even if they are wrong, they write what their authors might well have written and perhaps would have written if they had only thought of it.

The same attention to the text and similar literary standards inspire the best English commentaries on classical works. If England can boast of few great exegetical commentaries before the nineteenth century, that is because English scholars still felt that their first duty was to produce texts. But the nineteenth century passed beyond purely textual criticism to explanation and commentary. There are many kinds of commentary, and the editor who wishes to dilate upon his author has many choices before him. Wilamowitz, for instance, used Euripides' *Heracles* as a starting-point for a discussion of many interesting and important matters, such as the nature and origins of Greek tragedy. The English editors observe on the whole their national tradition of keeping to what the author says and explaining it. What Munro does with such masterly brevity for Lucretius, Jebb does with full apparatus of learning for Sophocles. It is, I am told, fashionable in another place to depreciate Jebb. The English of his translation is no longer admired in an age which has outlived the vocabulary of Victorian archaism; his explanations of lyric metres blind the eye and confuse the mind; even his knowledge of Greek grammar is said to be sometimes at fault. Yet even with these defects his seven majestic volumes of Sophocles are a remarkable achievement. There were few difficulties that he did not face, few problems that he did not try to solve. When all is said, his text is surely better than any text of Sophocles which has tried to improve upon it, and his commentary makes most modern work look shoddy. What really counts with Jebb is his feeling for the poetry, for the words which Sophocles wrote. It is this which keeps him right when other editors go wrong. He was a man of letters and a lover of letters, and he worked not as a mechanic but as a sensitive and intelligent devotee of Greek poetry. The same in a smaller degree might be said of other English editors. The special qualities of Burnet's *Phaedo* or Neil's *Knights,* are this concentration on what the author means and this intimate acquaintance with his habits of speech and thought. Through these the editor is able both to ask the right questions and to find convincing answers to them.

The literary ideals and standards which have in the past inspired English scholarship have in recent years been threatened from more than one quarter. The greatest danger comes from the purely scientific spirit which seeks to treat the classics without reference to their importance as literature. Of course there are branches of classical learning where this does not matter. In the study of manuscripts, of papyri, of inscriptions, of grammar and metric, literary values hardly count. But when we come to the great authors they are intensely and unavoidably relevant. And it is in this respect that German scholarship, with all its energy and its industry, has been most deficient. The ideal of *Wissenschaft,* with its insistence on methodology and its desire to escape from the snare of subjective criticism, has too often fallen into other snares. The commentator is so eager to say all that can be said about his author and to miss nothing that any of his predecessors has said, that he is liable to run into two dangers. First, he deals with so vast a mass of material in editions and learned journals that he cannot but lose his independence of judgement and his freshness of approach. He is so sunk in what has been said that instead of asking new questions and trying to consider the material anew he tends to concentrate on the familiar, traditional questions. In this method the study of the great authors loses half its vitality since it is reduced to the examination of certain stereotyped problems. What matter are the freedom and freshness of approach, the liveliness with which we read the classics, and the new ideas which they force upon us. These inevitably suffer if we concentrate less on the authors themselves than on what modern scholars have said about them. It may ideally be the editor's duty to read every word that has ever been written about his author, but let him beware of allowing this to fog his own judgement and of thinking that what the critics have said is in any way comparable to what the author himself says. It is far more important for an editor to be soaked in classical literature than in learned articles, and if he must choose between the two, he must choose the first.

Wissenschaft has a second danger, hardly less great. The ideal of a scientific approach to the classics excludes anything that resembles subjective criticism. But when we deal with great literature we cannot avoid being to some degree subjective. If we try to interpret an author, we cannot but say what we think and feel about him, and we are right to do so. We form our own conception of him and are guided by it in our work on him. It is of course possible to avoid this if we say nothing about his work as literature and concentrate purely on its technical or historical aspects. But this is to shirk half our duties. If the classics have any value, it is as literature, and as literature they must be treated. The Germans know this well enough, and are not afraid of making literary judgements. But these judgements are not always made with the seriousness and the hard thought that their subject deserves. Even Wilamowitz, who was a man of vast learning and eager curiosity, sometimes treats Sophocles with a superficiality which strikes us as almost frivolous, and Pindar with an ultimate lack of sympathy, if not of understanding. He does not bring to his literary judgements the same devotion and concentration which he brings to purely philological matters. This fault is by no means confined to German scholars. It may be seen wherever classical scholars assume that anything outside the range of strict knowledge is not a serious subject. There can be no greater mistake. Such matters are extremely serious, and we shall do well to pay proper attention to them. Otherwise the English tradition of scholarship, which has grown up in close touch with English letters, will lose its most striking quality.

How close the connection is between the classics and creative literature, the whole history of English poetry shows. Though Chaucer drew much of his manner and his material from the

vernacular literatures of France and Italy, it was not to them that he
turned for his ideal but to Virgil :

> Glory and honour, Virgil Mantuan,
> Be to thy name ! and I shal as I can
> Folow thy lantern as thou gost biforn.

Where Chaucer led the way, the later poets followed in companies.
In the sixteenth century the classics were not only the direct
inspiration of Marlowe and Jonson but indirectly, through the translations of North and others, of Shakespeare. In the seventeenth
century they set the standard equally for Milton and for Dryden.
In the eighteenth century the periwigged circles of Pope and Samuel
Johnson tempered their natural dignity and common sense with
what they believed to be the authentic fire of the ancient world. In
the nineteenth century Shelley, Keats, Tennyson, Browning, Arnold,
Swinburne and Hopkins turned in their several ways to the Greek
and Roman worlds for examples and inspiration. Even in our own
time Mr Eliot has been President of the Classical Association and
of the Virgil Society. Not all these poets were scholars in a strict
sense. Shakespeare, as we all know, was reproached by Ben Jonson
for his 'want of learning and ignorance of the ancients', and Keats
knew Homer only in Chapman's translation. But Milton, Browning
and Swinburne were good scholars who read the ancient literatures
with accuracy and devotion. Whatever else Shelley did or failed to
do at Eton and Oxford, he managed to learn Greek, and Hopkins
was for a time a professor in Dublin. But these differences between
the poets are of little importance. What matters is that they were all
deeply affected by the current classical education of their times and
found in it an enlivening and inspiring power. They might well have
been poets without it, but, since it existed, it gave a special direction
to their development and was a notable force in shaping their art.
  On such a matter it is difficult to generalize, but we cannot but
ask in what main ways the classics touched these poets and their
work. On a rough estimate this influence seems to work in two ways.
The classics both curb and inspire English poets, both regulate their
art and reveal inspiring vistas to them. This combination of apparently contradictory effects is perhaps due to the paradoxical nature
of the English character which combines a sensuous exuberance with
a Puritan austerity. On each the classical masterpieces exerted their
power and effected remarkable transformation. In the first place
they curbed the natural ebullience of English poetry and gave it a
shapeliness which it might otherwise have lacked. The English arts
have not the sense of order which has existed in France for centuries

and tend to rely more on *ingenium* than on *ars*. But when English poets come into touch with the Greeks and Romans, even through translations, they seem at once to curb their exuberance of thought and of language and to write in a more shapely and more considered way. In his Roman plays Shakespeare catches much of the restrained dignity of Plutarch, and we feel that he fuses it into his own spirit, as when he takes North's account of the death of Cleopatra : 'One of the souldiers seeing her angrily sayd unto her : Is this well done Charmian? Verie well sayd she againe, and meete for a Princes discended from the race of so many noble kings.' Shakespeare takes this over, and his result is both classical and English, both Plutarch's and Shakespeare's :

> It is well done, and fitting for a princess
> Descended from so many royal kings.

The classical spirit has entered into Shakespeare's language and given it a peculiar power and directness. Something of the same purifying discipline can be seen in Keats and Swinburne. Before he read Chapman's Homer Keats allowed his fancies to take him where they would, and his early verse is uncertain in its touch and in its taste. But once he heard the call of ancient poetry, he mastered his waywardness and loaded 'every rift with ore'. A line like

> Aeaea's isle was listening to the moon

is the very voice of Keats, but is it not also Virgilian? Swinburne never achieved this mastery, but in his inspired youth, when his head was full of Aeschylus, he found a fullness and a richness which he never regained and at times broke away from his 'rum Old Testament ring' to something austerely and nobly classical like that line of his *Atalanta* which seems to contain all that is best in Swinburne and is yet indisputably Greek :

> O sweet new heaven and air without a star.

Again and again in English poetry we find this happy harmony of ancient and modern effects. The ancient poets have shown the modern how to purify their art and achieve magnificent results through concentration and order.

Parallel with this influence and no less powerful is the warmth and colour which the classics have given to the otherwise Puritan temperament of the English. The supreme example of this is, of course, Milton. Milton was in two minds about the ancient world. The

Puritan in him believed that its legends were false, that its gods were devils, that its philosophy was misguided, but the poet in him was irresistibly attracted by it and wished *Paradise Lost* to equal the work of Homer and Virgil. In *Paradise Regained* Milton made his great refusal and rejected antiquity, but in *Paradise Lost* he harmonized his vision of it with his own austere outlook. He turned to it whenever he wished to describe the beauty of Eve or of Eden, the claims of power and glory, the sweetness of music or of song. At times he found himself in difficulties. Having decided that Mulciber should build Pandemonium and so provide an opportunity for some noble lines on Doric architecture, he then lets himself loose on the architect and forgets for the moment that he is a fallen angel in the hosts of Hell :

> from Morn
> To Noon he fell, from Noon to dewy Eve,
> A Summers' day; and with the setting Sun
> Dropt from the Zenith like a falling Star,
> On *Lemnos* th' *Ægœan* Ile. (P.L.I 742-746)

Then Milton pulls himself up and says that the Greeks related this 'erring', but the damage has been done, and the enchanted light of Olympus has shone on Satan's master-builder. So too Satan himself, who has caused so much trouble and debate, has done so largely because Milton has put into him much of Odysseus and of Aeneas. Milton's classical training told him that his heroic poem must present a warrior and a leader, and such Satan is, to the great confusion of morals and religion. Milton is typically English in his contradictory and paradoxical attitude towards the classics. In theory he should have rejected them altogether, but without them he could not write his great poem as he knew that it ought to be written. To them he owed its most glittering glories and above all its sense of the majesty and dignity of man even in his corruption and his fall. The antique world, with its acceptance of human worth and its delight in the senses, is an essential corrective to English austerity. It made Milton what he was; it gave their finest moments to Tennyson and Arnold. But for it they might have lost themselves in sermons and have failed to find what was noblest in their creative gifts.

I would maintain, then, that the strength of the classical education in England and its peculiar qualities are due to this close association with fine literature and especially with poetry. Our scholarship helps us to form our literary taste and enables our writers to extend their range and perfect their art. The spiritual experience which we get from great literature is not a thing that we can lightly throw away, and if we allow the study of the classics to decay, we shall impoverish our national life to an incalculable degree. An educational instrument so important as this cannot be treated as a mere luxury and should not be confined to a leisured few. All who can derive profit from it should be able to do so, and we may be confident that it will sharpen their wits and enliven their sensibility. In a broken world we are fortunate that we have kept our classical inheritance, and it will fall to us to set a lead in the renewal of classical studies. We must see that they regain some of their old power to shape the imaginative life of man and to give him that trust and that pride in himself which they brought into the world and have preserved through centuries for it.

IV

THE MEANING OF A HEROIC AGE

[*The 37th Earl Grey Memorial Lecture, delivered at King's College, Newcastle-on-Tyne, 9 May 1957*]

MANY PEOPLES cherish the legend of an age which, in the splendour and the scope of its achievements and in the prodigious qualities of the men who took part in them, is thought to eclipse all that comes after it. For the Greeks this was an age of heroes, and though the word ἥρως originally meant no more than 'warrior', it soon assumed other more august associations and implied a special superiority in human endowments and endeavours. A similar notion is to be found in a number of other peoples, and though it appears in different forms, it remains fundamentally constant. In western Europe, where it once had an enormous vogue, it has long ceased to be more than a subject for antiquarian enquiry, but in the Slavonic world it is still part of popular belief, even though for the Russians it centres round Vladimir Monomakh of Kiev, who reigned 1113-1125, and for the Southern Slavs round the destruction of the old Serbian kingdom by the Turks at Kosovo in 1389. In Asia traces of it can be found, overlaid by priestly distortion, in the Old Testament, and, under accumulations of myth and theology, in the Indian *Mahābhārata* and *Rāmāyana,* but over a vast area from the Caucasus to Polynesia it is cultivated as a national inheritance and known to everyone both high and low, while in some parts of Africa it is of so recent a growth that it has just had time to take root and may still be expanding. Such legends are kept alive by song and saga, which are passed by word of mouth from generation to generation and make a people conscious of its unity and its past. Though tales of a heroic age contain much mythical material and must not be treated as history, they are based on actual people and actual events. The question before us is to ask what this belief in a heroic age really means, why and how it comes into existence, and what significance it has for the peoples who believe in it.

63

If we look at such an age through the songs or sagas which tell of it, its first and most distinctive characteristic is the quality of the men who compose it. They are regarded as superior to all other generations in their physical strength, their courage, their endurance, their control of their bodies, their willingness to sacrifice themselves for honour and fame. Sometimes, like certain Greek heroes, they are half-divine in origin; there is often something unusual or miraculous in their birth. But this is incidental and almost irrelevant, no more than a tribute to their eminence by trying to explain it as a matter of breeding. They differ from other men not in having fundamentally different qualities but in having the same qualities on a far grander scale. Tradition may canonize them as exemplars of manhood to be imitated, but it assumes that in the last resort they cannot be rivalled. The Greeks explained this by saying that they possessed a higher degree of inborn power, and indeed it is this which makes a hero, wherever he is to be found. This power may recall and in some respects resemble that of the gods, but it has a much narrower scope, and instead of being applied to all kinds of action, it is concentrated on the most testing kind, which is war. Heroes realize their full natures, and display their surpassing gifts, in fighting. Great warriors are honoured in most societies at most periods of history, but the essence of a heroic age is that it fosters a whole generation which is unusually equipped by nature for war and finds its satisfaction and its reward in it.

In making war the central focus of such an age popular tradition is confirmed by independent testimony. The Siege of Troy, which is the climax of the Greek heroic age, was a real event, to which the burned ruins of the site VII A on the hill of Hissarlik still bear witness. The Germanic heroes belong to the great movement of peoples, which began with pressure from the East by the Huns in the time of Ermanaric in the fourth century A.D. and ended with the transformation of Europe after the disintegration of the Roman Empire. In the sixth century Welsh princes, like Urien and his son Owain, fought valiantly for the remnants of their old dominions against the Saxon kings of Bernicia and Deira, and there is no good reason to doubt that King Arthur fought against the heathen from beyond the sea in defence of the old religion and the lands of its adherents. Though Charlemagne did not make conquests so vast as legend ascribes to him, he was by far the greatest commander of his age, and his power was acknowledged from the Vistula to the Ebro. The heroes whom Russian tradition gathers round Vladimir Monomakh belong to the first resistance to the Tartars; and the disaster of Kosovo, where Tsar Dušan perished with all his chivalry, was the tragic culmination of the struggle between the Serbs and the Turks.

In Armenia the sturdy figures of David and Mher embody the tough defence which this isolated country put up against the forces of Islam in the tenth and eleventh centuries. The portentous warriors of Kalmuck legend, who ride forth from their tents on inaccessible mountains, look like distant versions of Chinghiz Khan and his descendants. The Achins of western Sumatra recall, however dimly and inaccurately, long wars first against the Portuguese of Goa and then against the Dutch of Malacca. There is ample evidence that the connection of a heroic age with war is justified by fact. Even when we know too little of the circumstances to find any historical basis for legends, we may legitimately suspect that such a basis exists. The Kara-Kirghiz Manas, who invades China and takes Peking, may be the reflection of some Turkic chieftain remembered only in oral tradition by a people not given to written records, and the mysterious Narts, of whom the Ossetes of the Caucasus tell many stories, may be a far-off version of the Scyths, whose warlike ways were known to Herodotus, and who vanished from history in the flood of desperate nomads from the east.

Though tradition is justified in assuming the existence of heroic ages, its idea of them is not what we ourselves might expect. In some important matters it does not conform to what we know to have been the actual case, and, so far from confirming history, it seems almost to flout it, not merely in details, which are inevitably distorted by time, but in such central features as social organization and habits. The Greek heroic world, as Homer sang of it, has indeed many attractions other than those of the battlefield, and whether in Troy or in Ithaca, in Agamemnon's camp or in the household of Alcinous, Homer presents a picture of life as he imagined it to be and as we might easily accept it. But now that we know something of the Mycenaean world from the inside through its own documents, we see that Homer's vision of it was in some ways unlike the reality. The decipherment of the Mycenaean records has shown that the civilization of Cnossus, Mycenae, and Pylos does not conform to our earlier notions of it, which we owed largely to Homer and which did not seem to be at variance with the evidence of the sites uncovered by Schliemann and his successors. First, as we know from its careful documents, it was a highly organized, even bureaucratic society. The tablets show that meticulous inventories were made of all kinds of possessions, that military orders were given in writing, that there was an elaborate system of land-tenure, which differentiated between royal, private, and common holdings, that the word *basileus*, which means 'king' in Homer, meant little more than a minor princeling under a superior *wanax,* and that the *wanax* himself need not have been the same as the *lawagetas,* 'leader of the people', who commanded troops in war. The Mycenaean organization was in fact closer to that of the Hittites than to anything we hear of in Homer, who reflects a simpler and less ambitious order of things. The Mycenaeans used writing as an instrument of organization on a large scale for quite trivial matters, but Homer mentions it only once in a mysterious context for a correspondence between kings.[1] Its almost total absence from his picture of the heroic world shows how inadequately he was informed about it. Secondly, though Homer often dilates with pride on the wealth of his heroes and clearly thought its level high by the standards of his own time, the evidence for Mycenaean wealth suggests that it was in fact much higher. For instance, Odysseus and Alcinous each keep fifty women to work in their houses,[2] and there is no hint that this is not princely, but the Pylos tablets, which come from a single place and a very short period, give the name of 645 slave-women, together with some 370 girls and 210 boys.[3] Homer's respect for the fabulous wealth of the past falls short of the reality. Whatever tradition gave him, it did not give him accurate information on the social and economic structure of Mycenaean life.

Something similar may be seen in the treatment of Theoderic, king of the Ostrogoths. The fullest assembly of the legends which clustered round his name is to be found in the late *Thithreks Saga of Bern,* but this is itself based on earlier materials, and Theoderic has already a place in the Anglo-Saxon *Deor* and the Old High German *Hildebrand.* His position is remarkable because neither in character nor in achievement does he resemble the other leading figures of Germanic traditon. The chief monuments of his rule were not victories but aqueducts, baths, and palaces, a system of law based on that of Constantine, a flourishing, if somewhat artificial, literature, theological controversy, and religious persecution. These are not the usual qualifications for a hero, but there is no doubt of Theoderic's heroic status. The reason for it must be his defeat of Odoacer, who had not only dethroned that *magni nominis umbra,* Romulus Augustulus, the last emperor of the West, but shown in his own fiery career the merciless instincts of a man who revels in war. To destroy such a man, even by treachery when he was a guest at a banquet, may have been a title to heroic honours, but in giving them to Theoderic popular imagination displayed a one-sided and partial view of his achievements.

The difference between heroic ages as they are presented in legend and as we reconstruct them from historical documents indicates a real

---

[1] *Il.* VI 168 ff.

[2] *Od.* VII 103, XXII 421.

[3] L. R. Palmer, *Achaeans and Indo-Europeans* p. 5.

difference of approach and outlook. History is concerned with them as political situations and parts of a general process of human change; legend is interested mainly in their dominant personalities and their more sensational events. History tries to take a synoptic view of them from which nothing significant is missing; legend concentrates on a few highlights of a kind to thrill and exalt audiences who like to hear of men and doings above the ordinary run. But, allowing for these differences, we must not assume that legend is wrong at all points. Its interpretation of the tremendous past is based on sound instincts. In the first place, it assumes that events so staggering can only have been carried out by a superior breed of men. Biologically, no doubt, this is absurd, but psychologically it has a measure of truth. The violent impetus which flung the Goths and Vandals across Europe or the Mongol cavalry to Korea and Hungary, or took the Achaeans to Egypt or the Maoris to New Zealand, does indeed indicate a most unusual self-reliance, a belief that almost nothing is impossible for men who have the courage and the will to attempt what they want. What this means in practice can be seen from our earliest document of the Turks, the inscription carved on monoliths near the river Orkhon, a tributary of the Yenisei, by Vilga-kagan in the eighth century. It records with pride the doings of the Turks since they became a people and reveals the irresistible spirit which inspired them :

> 'Such was the union of tribes that we won, and such the power that we displayed. O Turkish chieftains and people, listen ! So long as the heaven above and the earth below have not opened, O Turkish people, who can destroy your rule ?'[1]

The emergence of such a spirit suggests the snapping of many inner ties and obstructions, and though this may be common enough in individuals, it is certainly not common in a whole people. It may well owe something to new horizons revealed by nomadic movements and to the discovery that unforeseen and unfamiliar needs can be met by determination and resource, and it undeniably implies a break with many traditions which have held a people in a stiff frame of custom and convention. But whatever may account for it, it breeds an infectious confidence and thrives on success. The belief in a heroic age is a recognition of this fact, and has history to support it.

In the second place, heroic ages, as we know them from history, represent a crucial and dramatic stage in the emergence of the individual from the mass. In truly primitive societies his life is so closely intertwined with that of his fellows that he does not count for much in his own right. Even if he is conscious of himself as a distinct being,

---

[1] S. E. Malov, *Pamyatniki drevneturskoi pis'mennosti* p. 39.

and of course to some degree he is, he is hampered by all the fears that infest a world thought to be in the control of gods and demons, whom only the shaman or the witch-doctor is qualified to placate. To escape from these bonds is indeed a notable achievement, but at least the men who saw that they could rely on their own strength and skill rather than on omens and oracles must often have been justified by success. This is most obvious at a low level of development, and can be seen clearly in the emergence of certain African tribes, like the Zulus, from insignificance to power, but it lurks not very far behind the conviction of irresistible strength with which the Huns or the Turks swept across continents. It establishes a principle, which is by no means universally recognized and is often regarded as preposterous presumption, that men must trust in their own powers, and through this it gives a new meaning to the claims of the individual.

The hero of legend relies on himself. He may occasionally dabble in magic or display supernatural gifts, but what counts is his essentially human nature and his full use of it. No doubt this happens because magic is after all an unreliable instrument, and, since it cannot do all that it pretends, it must sooner or later yield before the pressure of enlightened and experimental experience to a belief in less sensational but more trustworthy powers which a man can exert of his own will. This emancipation comes only by effort and struggle, and among the stiffest obstacles which a heroic society has to overcome are the pretensions of priestcraft and magic. In some places indeed the claims of the supernatural seem to have prevented the development of a heroic society. The absence of any such in Egypt, Babylonia, or Assyria, is due to the growth of theocracies and the ascription of all honours to a god-king, for whom his subjects live and die, who is the lord of everyone and everything, and who takes to himself the credit and the glory for what his servants do. When such a king boasts of his victories, he may give thanks to his gods, but he gives none to his armies or his commanders, and the assumption is that the gods work for him alone, because he is their earthly counterpart and almost one of themselves. Such a system effectively stifles the growth of anything like a heroic society with its belief that what matters is the pre-eminence of a whole class which shares both responsibilities and renown. It offers in its place the concentration of power and glory in a single figure, who may indeed be of more than heroic proportions, but is certainly not the centre of a group, however small, such as would form the nucleus of a heroic society.

This difficulty is overcome only when the pioneers of a heroic outlook bring the forces of priestcraft under some kind of control and assimilate them into the new conditons. There is more than one way of doing this. The Zulu Shaka, who was a sharp-witted and sceptical critic of religious practices, was not above making use of them if he thought that they would strengthen the morale of his troops, but he also saw that his witch-doctors were dangerous when they claimed powers even greater than his own. So he laid a trap for them, which proved that they were cheats, and was then able to have the approval and the assistance of his army in killing them.[1] Attila solved the problem by arrogating supernatural authority to himself. A herdsman found an old sword buried in the grass, and brought it to the king, who declared that it was the sword of the war-god, which had been honoured by former rulers of the Huns but had been lost long ago, and that with it in his possession he would triumph over all his enemies, and that no one had any right to dispute his claim to divine powers.[2] By such means the ruler creates conditions in which the heroic spirit can realize its ambitions and establish a new kind of society.

If a people escapes from the perils and temptations of theocracy, it may be free to develop in a direction in which men are judged by their possession of certain human qualities and given ample opportunities to use them. The process by which a heroic society comes into existence means something like a revolution in social conditions and the assumptions which protect them. How this happens at a primitive level can be seen from two relatively modern examples.[3] At the beginning of the nineteenth century, when the Tonga Islands first became familiar to Europeans, they were under a military organization which had the main characteristis of a heroic age. It was of recent origin and came into being because young men, who had returned from serving abroad as mercenary soldiers, seized power and set up their own system with themselves in control at the head of it. So too at the beginning of the present century in northern Uganda the Lango were organized on military lines. Each village was under the captain of a company, and several such captains were under a petty chief. The chiefs owed their position to prowess in war, and were in fact constantly at war with each other. The system had, some fifty years earlier, replaced another which was freer and and easier and more peaceful. Like the system in Tonga it had been established by men who had served abroad as soldiers of fortune, but it was largely directed by a single leader called Akena, who on his return from foreign service made himself master of his own land. No doubt the similarities between these two cases are largely fortuitous, and there is no reason to assume any necessary connection

---

[1] E. A. Ritter, *Shaka Zulu* pp. 99-104.
[2] Priscus p. 314; 2.
[3] H. M. and N. K. Chadwick, *The Growth of Literature* III pp. 732-3.

between the establishment of a heroic society and the return of mercenaries, but what seems to be indispensable is the sharp realism of the military outlook which sees through many pretences and puts its trust in its own well-tested methods.

Neither legend nor history is very enlightening on how a heroic age begins. While legend tends to ascribe its start to some more or less miraculous cause, like the appearance of a generation which has the blood of gods in its veins, history shrinks from making any sharp distinction between it and other societies which delight in war. Yet even in history there is a real difference between a truly heroic society and other societies which give much time and trouble to war, and this difference turns on the vastly increased attention paid to it, the energy and enterprise thrown into it, and the special outlook which it promotes. In some cases this intensification of a military idea is due simply to the need for survival in lands where subsistence is never easy and conquest becomes a necessity; in other cases, as with the Achaeans and the Huns, the perfecting of a military system and the adoption of new weapons or tactics open up prospects of living more luxuriously and more easily by predatory methods at the expense of richer and more established societies; in still other cases, as in Wales, a people, which has been used to peaceful ways, is driven by foreign invaders to take to war as a normal routine. But in each case what counts is the organization of a society on a military basis for military ends, and the subordination to this of other aims, whether secular or sacred, which have hitherto been held in equal, if not superior, esteem. Legend takes this for granted, and its vision of a heroic age is of an age primarily concerned with war, not as a means to mere survival but as a field in which certain qualities may be realized to the full and win their proper reward of honour and glory.

A heroic society which begins on a small scale may be content to operate over a small area, but it may equally expand to an enormous size and have all the appearance of a far-flung empire. In so doing it maintains the same methods as at its humblest beginning. There is little fundamental difference of principle or method, though there is a prodigious difference of scale, between the military organization of Tonga or Uganda and that of Chinghiz. In both a small, special class of men comes to power through its determination and cohesion and clarity of purpose. They may at the start be no better than bandits or cattle-thieves, but they keep together and know what they want. In such a group or gang one man may predominate over the others by his superior will or courage or intelligence and become its leader. When Chinghiz was still an obscure horse-raider, called

'Tämüjin, he acquired such an ascendancy over his companions that they gave him the title of 'khan' and said to him :

> 'If in the day of battle we disobey your orders, take away from us our vassals and our servants, our wives and our women, and abandon us to the desert. If in time of peace we disregard your counsels, send us away from our men and our servants, from our women and our sons, and abandon us to the land which has no master.'[1]

From this small circle of devoted followers Chinghiz built his army and his empire. Though he claimed to have peaceful intentions and to wish to encourage trade, war was his paramount passion, and for it he shaped his organization, and his powers over his subordinates were far greater in war than in peace—a consideration that in fact counted for little, since he was never for long at peace. Round such a nucleus he formed his armies and recruited reinforcements from the many tribes whom he broke in battle or frightened into alliances. His formidable genius in war meant that he did on a gigantic scale, over nearly the whole of Asia, what would otherwise have been confined to a limited territory, but in his methods he kept the simplicity of a chieftain who commands a small group of captains and knows that he can trust them to carry out his orders.

In every heroic society the chief and his associates work closely together, and it is to this degree aristocratic, though the chief may have the titles and the prestige of kingship. From his point of view the seizure or the maintenance of power demands the service of men hardly less eminent than himself, to whom he must give his complete confidence and not grudge position and fame. Without them he would never attain his full ambitions, and without him they might never rise from obscurity. Legend is emphatic on this point. A heroic age is one in which the ruler is surrounded by remarkable men who go their own ways in considerable freedom but remain, even if with reservations and misgivings, under his command. This is true in different degrees of Agamemnon's kings, of the paladins of Charlemagne, of the knights of Vladimir and of King Arthur. It is no less true of those who serve formidable Asiatic princes like the Kalmuck Dzhangar and the Kara-Kirghiz Manas. The rulers command in battle, but they could hardly win their full successes without the help of men almost as redoubtable as themselves. It is this co-operation of ruler and his supporters in a single military caste which provides the essential structure of a heroic age as posterity sees it. Respect for individual prowess has been extended from a single man

[1] P. Pelliot, *Histoire secrète des Mongoles* p. 156.

to a company of men, who may not have his position or his authority, but are his equals in worth and honour and by contributing to his glory gain their own.

In this assumption legend does not go astray. Heroic societies are in fact organized for war and have their own aristocracy of valour. The leader cannot exist without his warriors, or his warriors without him. When Tacitus says of the Germans, 'the princes fight for victory but the companions fight for the prince,[1] he emphasizes the unity which sustains such a system and the loyalty which is indispensable to it. No matter how pre-eminent the king himself may be in battle, or how avid his thirst for glory, he cannot do without devoted and courageous captains. Even Attila had his *logades,* who were chosen largely for their military capacities, guarded his person, conducted his missions, governed portions of his empire, and commanded sections of his army.[2] Chinghiz was able to conquer enormous territories and to hold them after conquest because he had commanders whom he could trust absolutely to carry out his orders far away from his presence. Shaka was an implacable and ruthless disciplinarian, but he not only felt some affection for his generals but even at times sent them in command of expeditions while he himself remained at home. Such captains see in their leader the embodiment of the qualities which they most prize, and admire him all the more because he shares their risks and hardships. They have too among themselves such a solidarity as befits men who are engaged in the same undertakings and act from similar motives. They are proud of their superiority to other men and feel that they deserve special honour. So the Russian *Tale of Igor's Raid,* which celebrates an event of 1185 and was written two years later, closes on a note of praise to all who took part in it :

> Glory to Igor, son of Svyatoslav,
> To the brave bull, Vsevolod,
> To Vladimir, son of Igor !
> Long live the princes and their men
> Who fight for Christians against infidels !
> Glory to the princes and their men !

This is how members of a heroic society see themselves. Posterity takes them at their own value and may even improve upon it.

Legend, then, is not entirely wrong in its conception of a heroic age. If it differs at many points from the interpretations of historians, it emphasizes something which is undeniably important—the emergence of a group of individuals into power and eminence,

[1] *Germania* 14. 1.
[2] E. A. Thompson, *Attila and the Huns* pp. 163 ff.

especially in war. But it remains remarkable that such a conception should come into existence and have so definite a character and so strong an appeal. We cannot but ask *why* this happens. Granted that such ages, as legend tells of them, can usually be identified with actual historical counterparts and have certain characteristics in common with one another, why are they held in special regard and thought to contain a superior breed of men whom subsequent generations cannot hope to equal? It is not enough to say that an age is thought to be heroic just because of its dramatic achievements. These are indeed indispensable, but they are not in themselves enough to create a legend of this kind. There are many ages which might well qualify to be called heroic, but have not in fact been so. The reason lies not so much in the character of the age itself as in the view which posterity takes of it and in the psychological factors which shape this. It rises from some change in political conditions, when public attention is turned from a depressing or unsatisfactory present to what has gone before and thinks of it with admiration and longing. Such a change may come in various forms, but it always promotes a belief in the past as more adventurous and more glorious than the present. In the process much that we think important in the past may be neglected, and what matters is precisely the sense of a fuller life, of a less restricted world, of richer opportunities for adventure and glory.

The first and commonest type of such a change is conquest. The Welsh memories of a heroic age were fostered by the loss of most of their old territories to the Angles and Saxons. The poems of Taliessin and Aneirin are contemporary records of this age and show how well qualified it was to be celebrated in song and story, how firmly it embodied the heroic outlook and quest for honour. The monk Gildas might denounce it for its addiction to war and songs, but his word carried little weight with a later generation confined to narrow frontiers and threatened by relentless enemies. The efforts and the sacrifices of the time passed into legend, and the legend was of an age notable for a heroic breed of men. The old Russian world perished at the battle of Kalka in 1228, when the Russians were annihilated by the Mongols under Jebei and Subodai, and the monkish author of the *Chronicle of Rostov,* who was no more friendly than Gildas to heroic ideals, recorded dryly :

'There took place the slaughter of the wicked for our sins, and there took place the victory over the Russian princes, the like of which had never taken place since the beginning of the Russian land.'

This disaster was followed by the fall of Kiev in 1240, and the long, melancholy domination of Russia by the Mongols. Under their alien masters the Russians looked back to a time when their princes and champions had repulsed all invaders and maintained a high style and a courtly dignity. No less catastrophic was the defeat of the Serbs by the Turks at Kosovo in 1389, and its results were even more enduring, since the Serbs did not again become a free nation until the nineteenth century. Soon afterwards Armenia was divided between the Turks, the Mongols, and the Mamluks; and its people, which was never again to be its own master, found consolation in the recollection of the long struggle which in its great days it had sustained against infidels. If in these cases conquerors from Asia promoted heroic traditions among their victims, in Asia itself the situation was reversed with the Russian conquests of the sixteenth and subsequent centuries. The Turkic peoples, no less than their old adversaries the Mongols, cherish a belief in a heroic age, which preceded the arrival of the Russians and had for its setting the steppes and the mountains of Asia, when they were still open to exploitation by daring nomads. In defeat and humiliation these peoples have been comforted by the thought that they were once the uninhibited masters of their destinies.

The Greek belief in a heroic age was in its inception not very different from these cases, but it was shaped by special factors. The Mycenaean civilization collapsed about 1200 B.C., though the citadel of Mycenae survived, isolated and impoverished, for some fifty years. The catastrophe was caused by invasions from the north by the people later known as the Dorians, but it may well have been accelerated by the prodigious efforts which the Achaeans had made in such enterprises as the attack on Egypt and the siege of Troy, and which cost them more than they could afford in lives and resources. On the Greek mainland a vast destruction brought the Mycenaean world to an end, but tales of it survived in such places as Athens and Pylos and were taken with them by colonists who fled to found new cities in Asia Minor. These men looked back, with ample justification, to a time when the Achaeans had indeed been masters of Aegean lands, and preserved with tenacious loyalty the memory of a glorious past. The names of its heroes and the outline of their doings were passed on by a long succession of oral poets, of whom Homer was among the latest. The Greek conception of a heroic age may have begun on the mainland after the Mycenaean collapse, but its survival was largely the work of Ionians, who knew that their original home lay across the sea, and were for that reason eager to keep their ancestral ties with it.

In these cases conquest or disaster turned the minds of the defeated to a time when they had been free and victorious, and the legend must have begun to grow soon after the collapse of the age which it canonized as heroic. The sense of political failure was enhanced by the decline, usually rapid and often sensational, in material conditions. The ages which were now honoured had enjoyed wealth such as was no longer the lot of the living. This wealth had been gained by strong government and the opportunities which it gives to trade, by booty gathered in war, by skilled handicrafts encouraged by princely patrons, by the possession of fertile lands now lost. The Britons, driven from their rich plains to the mountains of Wales, had to adapt themselves to the demands of a sterner and narrower life. The Russians, who, in the heyday of Kiev, had maintained a brilliant and individual outpost of Byzantine civilization, got no encouragement from their Mongol masters and had neither the security nor the financial resources to maintain their art and architecture. Such art and learning as survived in Serbia were confined to a few isolated monasteries. The Turkic and Mongol peoples, accustomed to unlimited openings for theft over most of Asia and a large part of Europe, had nobody left to rob but one another. In the dark age of Greece the decay of civilization was rapid and universal. The fine arts of fresco, metalwork and ivory-carving came to an abrupt end, and, what may seem almost incredible to us, even writing vanished for over four hundred years, perhaps because it had been the monopoly of a small professional class, whose duties meant nothing to the new, illiterate conquerors. It is no wonder that these peoples looked back with nostalgic admiration to a past when they could cherish vast designs and enjoy an appropriate splendour in their external circumstances, and that sometimes, despite all their sense of an impoverished present, they failed to grasp fully how prosperous and how civilized the past had been.

A second type of change, less dramatic but hardly less disruptive, comes when a people leaves its familiar home and moves to distant lands. So the Norsemen who sailed to Iceland and Greenland cherished as a most precious heirloom the legends of their continental home. So the Angles and Saxons confined their heroic legends to events which took place before they crossed the sea to Britain. Legends were almost the only tie between colonists and the lands which they had never seen but cherished as the cradle of their race. With time the historical basis of these legends might become dimmer and their events confused, but there was no diminution in the honour in which they were held. No less illuminating is the case of the Kalmucks, who in the eighteenth century trekked from their home in the Altai on the borders of Mongolia to the Caspian basin and brought with them not only tales of the magnificent Dzhangar and his companions but precise and picturesque details of mountains, lakes, rivers, and shrines in central Asia. Such migrations need not necessarily imply material impoverishment like that of conquered peoples, but they mean a violent break with the past, and such a break provokes a glorification of it.

A special case of a legend fostered by migration may be seen in the sagas with which the Maoris commemorate the astonishing voyages, which between c.825 and c.1350 brought them over 2,000 miles from Tahiti to New Zealand. That this period is regarded as a heroic age is clear from the difference of spirit between the treatment of it and that of later events, which are no less fully handled but lack the same distinction and nobility. In this case the heroic age is that of the actual migrations, which began when Kupe, starting with two canoes from Ra'iatea in the Society Islands, returned after circumnavigating both North and South Islands, and ended when the crews of the seven canoes, known as the 'Great Fleet', went by way of Raratonga in the Cook Islands and settled in North Island. These stories are carefully treasured not only for their spectacular adventures but also for the consummate seamanship and the proud personalities of the men who took part in them. Their spirit and vicissitudes are well illustrated by the story of Whatonga. About 1125, when competing in a canoe-race at Tahiti, he was swept out to sea and eventually driven ashore at Ra'iatea. His grandfather, Toi, started in search of him, saying :

> 'I am departing to search for my grandchildren. If anyone arrives here in search of me, tell them that my canoe is directed to New Zealand ... Perhaps I shall stay there, perhaps I shall return. If I do not reach there, I shall have descended to the bottom of the great belly of Lady Ocean.'[1]

Toi reached New Zealand and, after almost incredible chances, was joined by Whatonga, who settled there with him. In the petty feuds which form so large a part of the history of the Maoris after their settlement, they had good reason to exalt the migrations to the enviable grandeur of a heroic age.

A third type of change comes when a political system, which seemed to be firmly and strongly built, disintegrates. The movements of peoples on the frontier lands between Europe and Asia from the fourth to the sixth century are so obscure that it is hard to fasten any theory on to them, but they may explain a legend known to the Ossetes that the fabulous Narts insisted on fighting against Angels and Archangels and were punished by a famine which destroyed

[1] Chadwick, *Growth* III, p. 248.

them. If the Narts are indeed a legendary version of the Scyths, this story would be an attempt to account for their disappearance in the hurly-burly of huge migrations. Their memory was preserved in secluded valleys of the Caucasus by a small and insignificant people who claimed connection with them and may indeed be their forgotten and impoverished heirs. A more spectacular case can be seen in the French legends which cluster round Charlemagne. He was indeed portentous enough to attract them, but they gained strength from the vast difference between him and his successors. The rapid dissolution of his empire after his death, and the chaos which this brought, meant that the Frankish emperor was seen as a superhuman figure who carried his conquests to the limits of the known world and was able to do so because he and his peers belonged to a superior breed of men. The decline of power and security may well incite visions of the past, which exert all the greater influence because it seems difficult indeed to recover what once was gained with apparently irresistible ease.

Something similar to this lies behind the legends which cluster round the figures of the great European migrations, and especially round Ermanaric, Attila, and Theoderic. All three were connected with resounding catastrophes or huge changes. The death of Ermanaric meant the end of the old Germanic system in central Europe; the death of Attila was followed almost at once by the disintegration of his empire; the rule of Theoderic was the manifest sign that the main migrations had come to an end. The events of their lives were indeed dramatic enough to win them a special place in the memory of men, but the inclusion of them, with their allies and their victims, in a single heroic age was a tribute to more than mere drama. What came after them contrasted ingloriously with these enormous events, and as Europe settled into the Dark Ages, it might produce notable figures, but it lacked the sense of limitless possibilities which had allured and inspired the men of the migrations. This sense of diminished and contracted opportunities was in part due to the fall of the Roman Empire. While it lasted, the barbarians felt that they had not only adversaries worthy of themselves but unlimited loot within their grasp. But once Rome had failed, the sense of a prodigious struggle and of incalculable rewards faded, and with this came the conviction that men were no longer what they had once been and that a glittering splendour had perished from the earth. The Germanic peoples cherished the memory alike of their heroic ancestors and of the no less heroic men who had fought against them, but all this bore little relation to their own lives or to the laborious poverty to which they were now reduced.

A fourth type of change is more psychological than political and is paradoxically connected with religion. In some countries the heroic vision of existence has been condemned by a priestly caste, but has survived in wilful defiance of it and even been strengthened by it. The heroic age of Ireland does not end in any overwhelming catastrophe, but fades away in local and personal feuds. The conception of it seems to have been stimulated, with an agreeable perversity, by the introduction of Christianity. Once the Irish accepted a creed which denounced their earlier martial propensities and their delight in war for its own sake, they reacted against their new prohibitions and thought how splendid and delightful their old ways had been. They looked back with pride and envy to the time of Conchobar and CuChulainn and Fergus, when men were not hampered by Christian scruples but indulged their manly instincts without fear of priestly rebuke or danger to their immortal souls. With an engaging but understandable inconsistency, they believed that, though they might now have become a people of saints, they had once been a people of heroes, and were proud of it. Indeed the antagonism between the two systems of behaviour added savour to both, and the recollection of a heroic age brought colour into a life that might otherwise have been drab and unadventurous. Some people might recognize the insoluble character of the conflict and make St Patrick denounce the old heathenish ways, but others compromised by telling that he drove into battle on a chariot and was, to all appearances, himself a hero. In such an atmosphere the cult of the Irish heroic age survived happily and was cherished by men who had in theory long rejected its ideals but still hankered for its splendours.

The situation in Israel was not absolutely dissimilar. The early records show that at first the Hebrews were led by prophets, such as Moses, who are comparable to the shamans and medicine-men in other pre-heroic societies, but in the Song of Deborah, composed about 1200 B.C., there are forecasts of a heroic outlook which sets a high value on warlike prowess and recognizes the achievements of whole groups of fighters :

> Zebulun and Naphtali were a people that jeoparded their lives unto the death in the high places of the field.[1]

The song still shows traces of priestly domination, but some two hundred years later, when David laments Saul and Jonathan, the heroic spirit is undiluted and undeniable :

> From the blood of the slain, from the fat of the mighty, the bow of Jonathan turned not back, the sword of Saul returned not empty.[2]

[1] Judges 5.18.
[2] II Samuel 1. 2.

In its judges and its first kings Israel had something that might have formed a heroic society, but even in its heyday its leaders were never free from priestly interference and opposition, and after the death of David the priests and prophets increased their claims and condemned the assertion of personal independence by anyone except themselves. In Israel the heroic age died before it reached maturity, and though the prophets often outbid the kings in the bloodthirstiness of their patriotism, they prevented the growth of a truly heroic society free to make its own decisions and to live for its own honour. The failure of David's successors to control the priestly castle meant that the cult of the individual was superseded by a theocratic outlook, ably enforced by religious sanctions and implacable menaces. The traditional stories were embalmed in lessons of moral theology or distorted to the discredit of their protagonists. But even the priestly editors and authors could not quite eliminate every hint of a heroic outlook, and there must have been many for whom these stories had a more immediate and more intimate appeal than anything promised or threatened by the priests. It is not unreasonable to infer that the belief in a Hebrew heroic age was consolidated soon after David's death not exactly by hostility to priests and prophets but by a lurking conviction that life held other and more alluring prizes than those which they offered, and that there had been a time when these had been easier to win and held in higher renown.

A variation of this type of situation can be seen in India. Beneath the vast layers of lore in the *Mahābhārata* and the *Rāmāyana* lies the genuine tradition of a heroic age, which reached its apogee about 1000 B.C. and meant as much to later generations in India as the tale of Troy in Greece. The kernel of each poem is a great battle, and the antagonists seem to have been men whose forbears had come to India not many centuries before and may perhaps be related to the people for whom about 1500 B.C. Kikkulis of Mitanni wrote, in a language akin to Sanskrit, the treatises on horses which have been found in the Hittite capital of Boghazkoy. The poems themselves are much later, but embody old material, which looks as if it had been preserved by oral traditon, since they abound in the formulae which are characteristic of this art. The Indian heroic age ended with the rise of the Brahmans to power, and the emergence of its legend was surely due to the desire of the warrior-caste, from which the kings were drawn and which was separate from the priests, to establish the notion of a great age whose ideals they still admired and imitated. The priests mangled the traditions by turning them into sermons and holy books, but the foundation of heroic stories survived. In

India, as in Israel, an unfriendly priesthood helped, despite itself, to secure the preservation of a tradition of which it never approved.

In these different ways, and for these different reasons, the legend of a heroic age is established and takes place in a national tradition. The several kinds of need which it answers are all related to the sense of honour and to the conviction that the reward of noble actions is glory. The belief in glory as an end of life is implicit in any belief in a heroic age, and when later generations recall the past, they feel that they bask in the reflection of its glory. But before this can happen an important obstacle has to be surmounted. The praise which a single hero claims for himself or receives to his face in his lifetime or over his body after death is more personal and restricted than the notion that a whole class or a whole people is equally glorious. This comes only when a ruler is able to make his companions feel that they are almost part of himself, that they are so closely connected with his achievements that his glory is also theirs. This happens easily enough in military circles and is not confined to societies which have earned the name of heroic. Even in ancient Egypt, where personal glory was gravely mistrusted, c.2375 B.C. a commander of Pepi I allows his soldiers to sing of their united prowess. In such cases the gap between the individual and his people is bridged by a common sense of power and the conviction that both are at work in a single cause. But this is no more than a preliminary. It exists only for the present and is not interested in the past. It may provide the material from which a heroic age is made, but the actual notion of a heroic age begins with the application of it in a new direction with a new purpose.

In this the determining factor is a much enhanced sense of the past. In primitive societies such a sense may exist, but within narrow limits and usually for family or social reasons, as the kings of Uganda have wise men who know their genealogies for twenty-three generations, or the aboriginal Larakia of Australia, now living far from the sea, sing of maritime lands which belonged to their ancestors. Such traditions are needed to justify claims to power and titles or to keep a people aware of its identity when it has been driven from its former home to wander in unwelcoming deserts. They imply no real sense of the past as something which can be recalled to life in its fullness and variety. Even when the cult of the dead promotes stories about them, the outlook is not much wider but confined to a recognized range of subjects. But when heroic legend takes up the past, it does so in a different spirit. It sees it as in some sense akin to the present, but more vivid and more dramatic. This may seem natural enough to us, but it implies a notable advance in human thought, a transference from the immediate to the distant, from the actual to what has partly

to be imagined, from the visible scene to a world invoked by words.
Stories of it have their own detachment and independence and serve
no more special purpose than to give an exalted pleasure. They are
hardly to be found among really primitive peoples, and the state of
mind which they reflect marks a striking advance in the use of human
faculties. The change comes when praise and lament are replaced by
narrative, which is concerned with men not known to the singer and
his audience but remembered from the past and made to live again
through the arts of song and speech. Of course such a change implies
a great deal more than an impulse to believe in a heroic age, but that
too it fosters, as it turns the imagination to the domain of Memory,
the mother of the Muses, and through her devices confers a special
prestige on a generation which has for other reasons already established itself in popular regard.

An example of how this happens can be seen from comparatively
recent times. In the second and third decades of the last century
Shaka united the different Nguni tribes into the formidable Zulu
monarchy, whose armies conquered a large part of south-eastern
Africa. In his own life-time, he was, like other African kings, honoured with praises, and we have an example in a song which his
soldiers sang to him in 1826, not long before his death:

> Thou hast finished, finished the nations,
> Where wilt thou go forth to battle now?
> Yes! where wilt thou go forth to battle now?
> Thou hast conquered the kings,
> Where wilt thou go forth to battle now?
> Thou hast finished, finished the nations,
> Where wilt thou go forth to battle now?
> Yes! Yes! Yes!
> Where wilt thou go forth to battle now?[1]

Shaka saw himself so clearly as a hero, that he thought even this
praise inadequate, and indeed at this stage he so overshadowed his
captains that he was still isolated in his glory, and there was as yet
no conception of a heroic age. But after the British conquest of 1879,
the Zulus were forced by their new status to look back upon his rule
as a glorious time when their armies carried all before them and men
sacrificed their lives gladly for an ideal of manhood. Shaka's glory
spread to the men who had served him, and his reign was in retrospect exalted to a heroic age, whose events were turned into saga
and drama. A striking case of this is the play *Dingana,* written quite

[1] J. Shooter, *The Kafirs of Natal* (1857) p. 268; E. A. Ritter, *Shaka Zulu* pp. 303-4.

recently by a Zulu, H. I. E. Dhlomo.[1] It begins with the murder of
Shaka by his brother Dingana, and Shaka's only appearance is at
the start, when he speaks his dying words :

> 'You kill me, my brother ! You will not reign long ! I see white
> swallows and strange, from a far country, coming to reign over
> you ! I shall be avenged. Jeque, my body-servant, remember me !'

The play shows how Jeque does indeed remember his murdered
master and is not content until he has avenged him by the death of
Dingana. Though Shaka appears only for a moment, his spirit
dominates the play, and his formidable temper has passed to his
loyal friends, who risk every danger to avenge him, and even to his
murderer Dingana, who has something of his pride and aloofness.
The memory of events which took place a hundred or so years ago
has crystallized into a heroic legend, in which the chief characters act
and speak with a high distinction and are thought to belong to a
different order of beings from that of the present day.

The power of a belief in a heroic age may be seen from the in-
direct but undeniable influence which it has on men and events,
even when it has become a distant memory. This is not merely
because it provides thrilling stories which are absorbed in childhood
and remain with a man through his life; it is rather that the notion
of it is so vivid and so firm that the imagination instinctively feeds
on it and is unconsciously moved by its spirit and its example. Just
as the belief in it is commonly formed after some defeat or disaster,
so the memory of it may be stronger among people who suffer
from a sense of deprivation or inferiority or servitude. To them it
brings confidence and hope. They feel that, if they have been free
and brave in the past, freedom may be won by bravery in the future.
So the Welsh in the long lean years of English encirclement and
enmity looked for comfort to their old heroes and dreamed that
deliverance would come through them. The *Presage of Britain,*
composed about A.D. 900, foretells how, led by their ancient leaders,
Cadwaladr and Cynan, the Welsh will attack the English and
destroy them :

> For the English there will be no returning.
> The Gauls will return to their comrades.

---

[1] I am indebted for my knowledge of this remarkable work to Mr W. R. G.
Branford, who generously sent me a type-written copy of it and gave me information about the author. Dhlomo, who died at the age of fifty-three on 23rd October,
1956, wrote his plays in English. Others were *The Girl who killed to save*, which told
of the girl Nonquause, who had a vision which is said to have inspired the 'suicide'
of the AmaXhose tribe about 1856, and *Ntsikana,* who early in the nineteenth
century foretold the conquest of his country by the whites.

The Welsh will arise in a mighty fellowship—
Armies round the ale, and a throng of warriors—
And chosen kings who kept their faith. . . .
The (English) race will be called warriors no more,
But bondmen of Cadwaladr and his hucksters.[1]

When in the eleventh century the story of Roland sprang into a special prominence, it was used to inspire the French to new efforts, as when Taillefer sang it to the Norman barons at Hastings, or a century later Turoldus refashioned it as exalted propaganda for Henry II and the House of Anjou. In the grip of Russian and Turkish brutality the Armenians have found consolation in the thought that in his cave Mher watches over them till the end of the world. As the poet Avetik Isaakyan says :

> Until that day
> The cave hides Mher.
> He sits on his strong horse,
> In armour,
> Lightning in his right hand,
> A shield in his left hand,
> A helmet on his head.
> He listens to the world around him,
> He listens in silence, in darkness,
> All his soul is in his listening;
> His ear
> Is turned to his people.[2]

When in 1912 the Serbian troops entered the field of Kosovo, they fell on their knees, said prayers, and kissed the ground, as if at last a hideous wrong had been righted and a heart-breaking decision reversed. After the Revolution of 1917 Russian peasants were easily persuaded by local bards that their new leaders resembled the warriors of Vladimir while the Tsar and his generals were modern reincarnations of Tartar ogres. A heroic tradition is seldom a cosy bedfellow. Not very long ago, among the Yakuts of the river Kolyma in northern Siberia, blind women used to sing of their hero Djennik, who fought against the Russians in the seventeenth century, and to dwell with much professional and loving detail on how his enemies were flayed alive.[3] When in 1945 the Achins of Sumatra fought for independence and locked the Dutch planters into deep refrigerators

---

[1] Translated by H. I. Bell, in T. Parry, *A History of Welsh Literature* p. 14.
[2] *Poeziya* (Moscow 1956) I p. 288.
[3] I. V. Shkvlovsky, *In Far North-East Siberia* p. 209.

before throwing their frozen corpses to the crocodiles, they felt that they were acting in the true tradition of the ancestors. And who knows what secret memories of vanished glory may not today be cherished, with all the ardour of injury and bitter resentment, by some Bantu peoples as they see even their present liberties restricted and their humble status still further lowered? The belief in a heroic age has its engaging side if it is not too near to us, but at close quarters it can indeed be disturbing and formidable.

We must judge such a belief not from a civilized outlook but in retrospect as a stage in the development of human society. Some peoples, like the Chinese, have done altogether without it, and fashioned their own remarkable culture by other means. Other peoples have never reached it because they have stayed congealed in a world of tribal terrors and tabus or yielded to the claims of theocratic absolutism which insists that everything should be done for its own glory and that it alone is worthy of honour. But in many parts of the world a heroic outlook has played a decisive part in history and done much to liberate mankind from primitive prohibitions and deterrents. Its chief use has been to discredit superstition by proving that a man can do more by his own efforts than by pretensions to magic. By this it draws attention to the individual, gives him a place of honour at the expense of the gods and their agents who hamper or oppress him, and establishes an impressive case for his recognition in his own right for his own sake. The ways by which man has emerged from primaeval savagery are indeed devious and strange, but he would hardly have emerged at all if he had not at some time seen that he can perform more than is expected of him, and rise above his circumstances, and almost above his nature, by a discharge of forces hitherto unrecognized and unused.

V

MEDIEVAL LOVE-SONG

[The John Coffin Memorial Lecture, delivered before the University of London on 28 November 1961]

THE LYRIC poetry of modern Europe springs suddenly on our notice about the year 1100. Yet we have no right to assume that before this date songs hardly existed. There were the Latin poems of the Dark Ages, and there were other secular and vernacular songs, like that which the monks of Ely sang in the time of King Canute. There were even songs about love. In the eleventh century short refrains in a primitive Spanish were written in Hebrew or Arabic script and attached to Hebrew and Arabic love-songs. They were composed in Moorish Spain, and were undeniably European, a forecast of what was to come later and ample evidence for short, lively songs about love. Similar songs must have been composed in most countries, but on the whole they were not thought sufficiently serious to be written down, and it is likely that they were not much noticed by the ruling classes. The ardent temper which found its daydreams reflected in heroic epic may even have despised as unmanly too much attention to love, and certainly, when it is forced to deal with it, does so either perfunctorily, as the *Chanson de Roland* deals with Roland's betrothed 'la belle Aude', or as a disturbing and destructive passion, justly exemplified in Guthrun and Brynhild. But when vernacular song appears in a new form in the work of Guillaume IX, Duke of Aquitaine (1071-1127), it already renders to love some of the dignity of a cult and gives it pride of place in the ceremony of song. Of his ten surviving songs three are concerned with love and treat it in a spirit which is quite unlike that of the Mozarabic songs or of any other early songs known to us. This reckless, feckless adventurer, with his unscrupulous schemes and his lamentable failures, wrote songs of a delicate freshness and an untrammelled joy. The main features of the love-song, which was to spread so luxuriantly over western Europe in the next two centuries are already visible in his work. It is unlikely that he invented either the form or the spirit of medieval love-song, and indeed at one place he hints that it has established rules which he obeys. But he is its first known practitioner, and with him the love-poetry which has played so leading a part in European literature for nearly nine hundred years is firmly set on its remarkable course. Despite his manifold faults and follies Guillaume was a true poet, who understood the new spirit and responded finely to it.

This art, conveniently called Provençal, used the *langue d'oc* as its language, and its poets were by no means confined to Provence. Its home was all France south of the Loire, and it was there that it found its swift and fruitful development. Within a few years of Guillaume's death it was expanded and enriched by such gifted men as Jaufré Rudel, who took part with Louis VII in the Crusade of 1147; Bernart de Ventadour, who was favoured by Eleanor of Aquitaine and died in 1194; Arnaut Daniel, to whom Dante pays the princely tribute that he surpassed everyone in 'versi d'amore' (*Purg.* xxvi, 118); and Bertran de Born (1140-1207), whom Dante praises in the *Convito* (iv, 11) for his courtesy and liberality, but, with inflexible impartiality, assigns to one of the lowest circles of Hell for setting the Young King against his father Henry II (*Inf.* xxviii, 134 ff.). The thirteenth century did not produce figures quite so eminent as these, but a succession of vigorous and skilful poets was maintained and included such men as Sordello of Mantua, who in the intervals of a turbulent life wrote songs not in his native Italian but in the *langue d'oc*, as if he felt that his own vernacular was too gawky for the finer flights of song. These poets by no means restricted their songs to love. They sang also about their injuries, their griefs, their hates, their political quarrels, but to love they gave their fullest attention and their most disciplined powers. They differed greatly from one another in temper, technique, imagery, outlook, and even in their opposing theories about the relative merits of clarity and obscurity in poetry, between the claims of the *trobar clus* and the *trobar leus* and the possibility of a compromise in the *trobar ric*. They did not form a movement in the sense that they had a programme or agreed aims, but, despite their differences and their disputes, they fall into a coherent group. Their similarities are far more marked than their dissimilarities, and their practice, seen in its historical perspective, reveals an ideal of poetry which was characteristic of them and of almost nobody else before or since.

The extraordinary, the unique quality of this poetry is its rigid conception of love. It takes the least calculable and most capricious of the passions and expects it to conform to a strict type. The lover not only falls in love at first sight but remains faithful to his beloved through all his days. She is for him the embodiment of perfection, physical, intellectual, and moral, and his dominating desire is to be worthy of her. All his efforts must be directed to giving her pleasure and gaining her regard. To win a smile or a word from her is for him an untold happiness, and even without them he counts himself fortunate if she takes any notice of him or marks his presence by the smallest sign. His love for her is so sacred a matter that he speaks of her under an assumed name, and he is wise to keep to himself any thought of their relations in case they should be profaned by vulgar tittle-tattle. His beloved is not his wife, and his love does not call for fulfilment in marriage. Nor does he wish that it should. She stands outside the round of his common activities almost as a presiding deity. To be worthy of her he must be the embodiment of chivalrous manhood, courteous, modest, gentle, and brave. Her being becomes the centre of his own, and through it and for it he endeavours to be all that he ought to be in her eyes. He is her vassal, her knight, and her servant, and he submits himself to all her wishes without question or complaint. This love is a philosophy, a religion, and a code of manners. In theory it is the love of one soul for another and moves on so exalted a plane that without her encouragement his life is cold and empty and purposeless. So far it is indeed Platonic in a sense that Plato himself would have understood, but by a surprising paradox it breaks away from him in its acceptance and its approval of physical relations. They are spoken of with restraint and caution, but they are certainly desired and make the relation between the lover and the beloved stronger and even in their own sphere more exalted, since they imply that the lover has received a gift which is beyond all price and which he can never adequately repay. This rarefied, exacting conception of love is already present in Guillaume of Aquitaine and reaches its height in Jaufré Rudel, Bernart de Ventadour, and Arnaut Daniel. But even those who set themselves the most rigorous standards in it differ very little from the rest. Courtly love, as this poetry embodies it, is a most unusual invention of the human spirit, and for some two hundred years the love-songs of western Europe were dominated by it.

The origins of this doctrine are still a subject for debate and surmise. Though Ovid was read at the time, it can owe next to nothing to him. It may perhaps owe something to Latin translations of Plato, but it is hard to believe that these were familiar, even at second-hand, in courtly circles or indeed that they existed by 1100. It has been claimed that it learned much from Arabic poetry composed either in Moorish Spain, which was in easy reach of southern France, or in Syria, where it attracted the attention of the first Crusaders. In this there is indeed a kind of idealism which

encouraged poets sometimes to pride themselves on refusing the
favours of their mistresses, as if this were a form of *adab* or good
manners, but this is just what the Provençal poets do not do. It may
have some remote connexion with the arrival of the Cathars from
the East in the beginning of the eleventh century, and its freedom
in sexual matters may have been excused by the Manichean conception that the body is so unimportant that it may be permitted
any licence, but the songs give no hint of such a doctrine and indeed
attach importance to bodily pleasures as a manifestation of spiritual powers. Courtly love has more affinities with Persian epics, like
those of Nizami (1140-1202), in which lovers perform stupendous
feats of prowess for ladies whom they hardly know and seldom see,
or even with such a work as the Georgian epic, *The Knight in the
Panther's Skin,* written between 1196 and 1207, in which the two
heroes are victims of ideal love and obey its most exacting demands
in honour and courtliness and courage. Yet these poems are later
than the first appearance of courtly love in France and may even
have been touched by western ideas. Any or all of these influences
may have done something to shape the western notion of it, but it
remains different from them in its feudal setting and its peculiar
idealism, and whatever it owed to foreign sources, its special character
looks like the natural product of an age in which chivalry had
taken a new prominence and inflamed new ideas by forcing men
to conform to its unprecedented respect for women. Though it
embodies much of which the Christian Church disapproved, it is not
avowedly anti-Christian and at times uses an imagery which seems
to come from Christian worship, but it is certainly un-Christian in
its disregard of marital rules and prohibitions, and its substitution
of another, incompatible ideal for them. The discord is revealed,
though hardly solved, in the treatise *De arte honeste amandi,*
which Andreas Capellanus wrote about 1185 for the circle
of Marie of Champagne. In it he gives a full, sympathetic,
and even admiring analysis of courtly love as it was pro-
pounded by the highest ladies of the land, and garnishes it with
appropriate quotations from Ovid, only to turn against it in his
final chapter on the ground that God holds all such love in abhorr-
ence and punishes its practitioners with 'the flames of ever-burning
Gehenna'. But to such menaces the singers and their patrons turned
deaf ears.

We might feel that in this uncompromising attachment to an
ideal there is an element of artificiality, of obeying a convention
which does not come naturally to most men and attempts to defy
their wayward instincts by keeping them on a straightforward diffi-

cult path. Yet though love is the strongest of the passions, it often suc-
cumbs to an idea or an ideal of what it ought to be, and at different
periods takes different directions, as if it needed some guiding goal
to give it confidence and justification. What various forms it can
take may be seen from the diverse notions of it which prevailed in
classical Greece, Augustan Rome, France of the *grand siècle,* and
Victorian England. In all of these societies it played a central and
inspiring part in serious poetry, and in each it developed its own
idiosyncrasies and its special claims. By a curious paradox the undifferentiated force of passion, which seems likely to follow a wilful,
unpredictable course, takes colour and shape from its surroundings
and adapts itself easily and sincerely to what is expected of it in them.
When a man falls in love, he is so carried away, and so conscious that
he has lost his usual bearings, that he needs some direction to guide
him, and often he finds it in current notions of what love ought to
be, since after all these represent the experience of other men like
himself in a like case. This is what happened to the Provençal poets.
They responded with their full and eager natures to a creed which
gave a new eminence and a paramount place to love without in any
way detracting from its excitements or its satisfactions. They made
the best of both worlds by assuming that love was not so much permissible as obligatory, and at the same time by avoiding the indigni-
ties which discredit the emotions when they are allowed to run wild
and riot. What was forbidden by the Church had not only its own
order and discipline but gained a novel glory from the majestic
philosophy with which it was now clothed and presented as the
noblest aim of man. It is not after all surprising that poets responded
to such a challenge and such a chance. Even if service to this ideal
did come easily to everyone and made exacting demands, this does
not mean that poets were acting a part when they sang of it,
or merely pretended that it was the noblest school of behaviour
known to them. They had a clear notion of what it meant, and they
were prepared to exert themselves to the utmost in getting the best
out of it. Their honesty reveals itself not in any accounts of love in its
raw state but in their ambition to create something nobler out of it,
in their conviction that the lady of their desire is worthy of love for
far stronger reasons than any immediate passion for her and is an
embodiment of virtues which a man of honour cannot but admire
and emulate and adore. The strength of this philosophy is that it
redeems and sanctifies the flesh by making it serve an impeccable
ideal of humility and self-sacrifice, and that it heals the quarrel between the body and the soul by making the body the instrument
by which the soul gains dominion over a man's whole being and

directs his thoughts and actions towards a goal which has a celestial solemnity and resplendence.

This love-poetry, which established itself so swiftly and so firmly in southern France, soon began to exert an increasing influence in most parts of western Europe. What could be done with such effect in the *langue d'oc* could be done also in other languages, and by the middle of the twelfth century other countries had begun to produce their own versions of it. It appealed to princes and their courts, who felt that the cult of chivalry called for something less violent than *chansons de geste* and less crude than the buffoonery of wandering *jongleurs*. The new love-songs appealed to the courtly classes in more than one way. Their technique, with its astonishing elaboration and dexterity, its unfailing ingenuity in devising new patterns for stanzas and rhymes, was well-suited to an age which admired ornament and cunning workmanship for their own sake and welcomed as a new refinement their appearance in verse. Moreover the new songs made a brave and adventurous attempt to interpret an important aspect of chivalry to those who were most committed to it. If women were to preside over tournaments and other knightly relaxations, it was tempting to give them an exalted resplendence and to emphasize their place of honour in a courtly world. There were good reasons for the new style spreading so widely and so rapidly as it did. By 1150 it had begun to make its mark in the German-speaking lands of the Rhine and the Danube, and there for a century it maintained a noble distinction. In northern France it was more slowly acclimatized, but had found a prominent place by the end of the twelfth century, when a charming example is attributed to Richard Coeur de Lion's minstrel, Blondel. In the *magna curia* of the Hohenstaufen Emperor Frederick II, at Palermo and other places in Sicily and southern Italy, poetry flowered abundantly under his inspiration from 1220 to 1250 and amongst its many achievements invented the sonnet. It was not long before northern Italy caught the spirit of his enterprise, and its lessons were applied by Guittone d'Arezzo (*c*.1225-*c*.1294) and Guido Guinizelli (*c*.1240-1276). In the Iberian peninsula, where the language of lyric song was Galician, Provençal modes had a vogue, especially in Portugal, throughout the thirteenth century. Even in England, where the ruling classes spoke Norman French, about 1250 there is a sudden outburst in the vernacular of what looks like spontaneous song in such pieces as 'Alysoun' and 'Lenten is come with love to toune', which are in fact products of a highly accomplished art in the Provençal manner. What had begun in southern France became a truly European movement, and France did what she was to do more than once in later centuries by setting a standard of poetry which so

caught the imagination of other countries and inspired such emulation in them that to write in any other manner looked dowdy and
provincial.

This resounding success was won at the expense of a vernacular
poetry, which might not belong to a high social level but was by no
means disreputable, and lost its glamour when the new style won
the day. In Provence there were various dance-songs, in which the
leader sang the main part, while the rest of the company joined in
the refrain, and the subjects were of a traditional kind, the complaints of unhappy wives, the laments of love-sick maidens, the
disputes and quarrels between lovers, and their separation by the
dawn. In northern France similar songs existed and took a special
form in the *chansons de toile,* which women sang over the loom with
a conscious, if unambitious, technique of composition. In Germany
a lively art, close to folk-song in its conventional imagery of falcons,
hawthorns, and linden-trees, its unadventurous metres, and its con-
finement of a poem to a few lines, had been taken up and polished
and enriched in courtly circles without losing its old freshness and
popular character. In Italy and Sicily there were various dance-
songs and folk-songs, which survived by devious or subterranean
routes until the fifteenth century. In Portugal there was an art of
song quite unlike anything that existed elsewhere, composed in
variations on single themes, largely concerned with love and delightfully limpid and fresh and melodious. It had been adopted in courtly
circles and had a lively career in them until it reached its heyday
with King Dinis the Labourer (1271-1325) and then passed out of
currency. In England the difference between the new style and the
old may be seen by a comparison of 'Alysoun' with 'Sumer is icumen
in'. The latter is by no means as artless as it looks, and its adaptation
to music betrays a high ingenuity, but it is too outspoken and too
close to the soil to have been touched by Provençal idealism. Except
in Portugal, where it had a hard and not very successful struggle,
Provençal song displaced its more popular rivals and drove them into
the lower levels of society. The Emperor Henry VI wrote in the old
style, Frederick II in the new, but the victory was never complete,
and in the end this was all for the best.

In all the countries where the new love-song flourished, it both
maintained much of its first Provençal character and made variations
on it in new directions, and it adapted the needs of rhyme and stanza
to suit the characters of other languages or gave to traditional local
themes an enhanced grandeur in a courtly setting. Yet, despite superficial differences, what counts is the tenacity with which love-song,
once it is set on its formidable, uncompromising course, maintains
its ideals and its dominating temper. The centre of this system, we

might almost say philosophy, is that the sublimest moments of a
man's life are when he is in the presence of his lady. Then he is not
only most himself but also his best self, not only alive as nowhere and
never else, but vastly more alive than other men who have no like
experience. That is why, when he is not in love, he feels that he ought
to be, and tries to be, and why he welcomes, in countless songs, the
arrival of spring as the season of love. This theme occurs so frequently
that we almost cease to notice it, but it is by no means idle. The
courtly cult of love is closely bound to the spring when men and
women ride in the country or walk in the garden, but it is also connected with the return of life to all living things. The first flowers,
the leaves on the trees, the songs of birds are a summons to love
and a testimony that it is right and natural. They are nature's
answers to the harsh injunctions of the Church against any union
outside marriage, and the courtly poet gladly accepts them as such.
The theme is already present in Guillaume of Aquitaine, and a
characteristic specimen of it comes from Rinaldo d'Aquino (fl. 1228),
who brings the main elements together in graceful harmony :

> Confortami d'amare
> L'aulimento dei fiori
> E'l canto de li auselli.
> Quando lo giorno appare,
> Sento li dolci amori
> E li versi novelli
> Che fan sì dolci e belli e divisati
> Lor trovati a provasione;
> A gran tençone stan per li arbuscelli.

.   .   .

> Love is brought unto me
> In the scent of the flower
> And in the birds' blithe noise.
> When day begins to be,
> I hear in every bower
> New verses finding voice :
> From every branch around me and above,
> A minstrels' court of love,
> The birds contend in song above love's joys.
>
> (D. G. Rossetti)

The spring, which begins by being a summons to love, soon becomes
a symbol of it, of the life which it brings and the impulse to song

which it inspires, and one of the lover's chief aims is to maintain and
live up to this spirit. Through it he feels himself in harmony with
nature and bursting with vitality like her own. Behind such songs
lies a half-forgotten or half-unconscious belief that the spring really
summons men and women to love, as it was thought to do in Roman
times when, perhaps about A.D. 300, the *Peruigilium Veneris* was
composed with its invitation and challenge to all men, whether they
have loved or not, to love on the morrow. This spirit, so assertively
present in medieval song, makes the cult of love a ceremony, which
imposes special duties and responsibilities and rules of honour.

The entirely satisfying reward which love offers to a man and
which he himself seeks so ardently and purposively is the unmixed
joy which he feels in the presence of his lady. Once he is with her,
and knows that she accepts his devotion and his service, he asks for
nothing more. He may cherish other, less abstract ambitions, but for
the moment he is so enthralled by her that he does not speak of them
and may not even think of them. Just as she inspires him to behave
with the full scope of courtesy and to dedicate all his actions to her
approval, so he is convinced that she enables him to do what she
wishes and provokes him also to song. If he proclaims his pre-
eminence in song, as such poets often do, it is not so much a compli-
ment to himself as a tribute to the exalting inspiration of his mistress,
and this is precisely what Bernart de Ventadour, the most spontan-
eously lyrical of the Provençal poets, says with some assurance :

> Non es meravelha s'ieu chan
> Mielhs de nulh autre chantador,
> Que plus mi tra'l cors ves amor
> E mielhs sui faitz a son coman.
> Cor et cors e saber e sen
> E fors'e poder hi ai mes;
> Si·m tira ves amor lo fres
> Que ves autra part no m'aten.

.   .   .

> No wonder is it if I sing
> Better than every minstrel else,
> For more than them love me compels;
> I am his thrall in everything,
> Body and soul and sense and wit,
> And all my strength and force beside;
> Such is love's rein to which I'm tied,
> That I give heed to naught but it.

This is the authentic, directing mood of medieval love-song, and may be found in almost any poet in any country from Guillaume of Aquitaine to the last troubadours and minne-singers. At no other time in European literature, with its vast array of love-poetry, has this particular system been in favour. Usually the spirit of love blows where it wills and carries the poet with it to all manner of strange places, but in medieval song everything radiates from this point of exalted and confident joy, and without it nothing would happen.

At the opposite pole to spring and love are winter and loveless-ness. If a man is neglected or deserted or despised by his lady, he feels that his whole life has lost its meaning, and he compares his state with winter, when the flowers are dead and the birds have ceased to sing. The fountain of his song dries up, and, if he sings, it is no longer because he must but because it is a sign of his refusal to admit defeat, of his fidelity in spite of everything to his mistress, of the pride which still abides in him from her first smile on him. He cannot but beseech his lady to restore her favours. To abandon all hope of her, still more to leave her for someone else, would be a base dereliction of honour, and he cannot admit, except under the gros-sest provocation, that he is capable of it. The result is that, while there are many songs which complain of neglect or coldness, there are very few which are final farewells. A typical example of a lover's complaint is that of Heinrich von Morungen :

Frouwe, wiltu mich genern,
So sich mich ein vil lützel an.
In mac mich langer niht erwern,
Den lip muoz ich verloren han.
Ich bin siech, min herze ist wunt :
Frouwe, daz hant mir getan
Min ougen und din roter munt.

.   .   .

Lady, wouldst thou save me, give,
Give but one little look to me ;
No more can I endure to live ;
I needs must perish utterly.
My heart is wounded and I pine ;
Lady, so they would have it be,
Mine eyes and that red mouth of thine.

The courtly poet is content with very little, but this little must come from the highest source, from the lady whom he adores and without whose approval he withers and fades. His life passes between extremes, between the springtime of love satisfied and the winter of defeat and frustration and darkness.

In both these extremes there is an element of abstraction, of living up to a duty, of behaving as the chivalrous code commands. The poet accepts these rules not only because his poetry relies on this ideal for its inspiration but because they give him something to live for. But of course the ideal is not a mere ideal; it has its intellectual strictness, but it is rooted in human nature and can hardly work unless it has all the drive of authentic passion behind it. A man cannot force himself to fall in love, but at least, if he does, he can cultivate and train his passion and make the best of it by thinking of it in a certain way. This is what these love-songs do. They assume that human beings are likely to fall in love, and they insist that, if they do, they must make the best possible use of it, and this is not beyond their powers. That the system works is clear from many examples. Perhaps the most immediately attractive of these songs are those which tell of the moment when a man falls in love. The sudden, unforseen enhancement of his whole being which this brings passes into song which needs few preliminaries or explanations and can afford to speak frankly about its subject. Such themes existed long before our kind of song, and when courtly singers took it up, they followed a popular tradition, even if they used many new and ingenious devices to enforce their appeal. So Colin Muset (fl. 1250) sings from sheer delight at falling in love, and though he uses a very simple measure, which many love-poets of his time would have thought unduly humble, he knows well how to keep his poem lively and stylish and shows a mature skill as he leads up to his overwhelming shock of joy when he first saw his beloved :

> Lez un rosier s'est assise
> La tras bele et la sennee;
> Ele resplant a devise
> Com estoile a l'anjornee;
> S'amors m'esprent et atise
> Qui enz el cuer m'est entree.

. . .

> I saw her sit by a rose-tree,
> Her, the most beautiful and wise;
> Her radiance, for all to see,
> Shone like a star before sunrise.
> With love for her I flame and flare;
> She's found my heart and entered there.

Muset's emotions are drowned in delight, and his hope turns into confident assurance that he will win his lady. He concentrates on the enchanting moment and centres all his ten stanzas on it. So too one of the few songs of this kind from England catches the same absorbing, ecstatic joy, and, though it makes use of a refrain, which is more a popular than a courtly device, it shows its full acquaintance with the high style in its rich enlacement of rhymes and sustained brilliance of effect. The poet has obviously and frankly fallen in love and is swept off his balance by the revelation that this love is quite unlike anything that he has hitherto known :

> An hendy hap ichabbe yhent;
> Ichot from hevene it is me sent;
> From allē wymmen mi love is lent
> Ant lyht on Alysoun.

The shapely, intricate balance of the verses adds power and passion to the poem. The poet has been caught by the full onslaught of love, which occupies his whole being and drives all other thoughts from his mind.

Since love provides such joy, it is eagerly sought, and the search may take unusual forms. The man who wishes to love at the highest level may be so hard to satisfy that no woman known to him can give him all that he demands; so he forms an ideal picture of what a woman ought to be, and falls in love with it. This calls for no mean powers of imagination, but it is at least an understandable conclusion from the conceptions of ideal love with their insistence that such a love is first and foremost between one soul and another. Something of this kind underlies three poems by Jaufré Rudel, whose love for a mistress in a distant land provoked a delightful legend. His anonymous biographer tells that, without ever having seen the Countess of Tripoli, Rudel fell in love with her from what pilgrims from Antioch told him. In order to see her he joined the Crusade, but fell sick aboard ship and was brought in agony to Tripoli, where the Countess nursed him until he died in her arms. There need not be much truth in this tale, which looks like a construction built from Rudel's own poems. But these are strange enough. He began with a less exalted passion, but it came to a painful end when he was caught with his lady and humiliated. This turned his mind to love of another sort, and he writes poems about a woman far away, with whom he is rapturously in love. It is not clear that he has ever seen her, and though she is a real woman, she is for him the embodiment of an ideal. His dream is that when, if ever, they meet, she will love him, and in comparison with her no other woman counts for anything :

Ja mais d'amor no·m jauziray
So no·m jau d'est' amor de lonh,
Que gensor ni melhor no·n sai
Ves nulha part, no pres ni lonh;
Tant es sos pretz verais e fis
Que lay el reng dels Sarrazis
Fos hieu per lieys chaitius clamatz !

. . .

In love I'll never find delight
Except in this love far away.
No better, gentler lady might
I know, or near or far away.
So perfect and so pure is she
That for her I would captive be
And to the Saracens be sold.

This carries devotion to its limit, and no other poet is quite so ruthless with himself as Rudel, who sacrifices all immediate advantages
to an imagined presence. But his position is in full accord with
accepted assumptions of courtesy and obeys a consistent rule of
conduct. He means every word that he says, and yet at the end of it
he knows that it is no more than imagination, and ruefully admits
that, if he ever meets his lady, she will pay no attention to him :

Mas so qu'ieu vuoill m'es atahis.
Totz sia mauditz lo pairis
Que·m fadet q'ieu non fos amatz.

. . .

But what I wish forbidden is.
Curse him who pledged himself to this,
That I shall find my lady cold.

The vision which means everything to Rudel is broken by his grasp
of reality, but even that does not persuade him to abandon it.

To fall in love is not always to win love in return, and the stresses
and struggles of frustration occupy much of medieval love-song.
In setting to work the lover must observe certain rules if he is not
to be rejected by his lady and despised by everyone else. First, he
must maintain silence, if not about being in love, at least about
whom he loves, and he must on no account disclose her name, be-

cause, if he does, it will cause her pain and make her reject him. Secondly, he must appeal to her not by boasting about himself or proclaiming his own worthiness, but by showing how tenderly he feels for her. His best, almost his only course is to invoke her gentleness, in the hope that she will be moved by his humble devotion. But in doing this he must not diminish his dignity or make himself unworthy of her. He claims her love not as a right but as a supreme favour, which transforms his whole being. He is at full liberty to say how strongly he desires her and how her coldness makes his life a misery, but even in this he must maintain his proper style and tread a delicate path between self-abasement and pride. Though he asserts his unworthiness, he also asserts that, with his lady's guidance, it will be corrected and his finest qualities set to work. In the end what he asks for is a noble compassion, which unites a true confidence in him with commiseration for what he suffers in being deprived of her love. A graceful case of this can be seen in a song which is one of the few successful examples of its kind in Portuguese in that it is composed in the new manner with no reliance on the old. Written by João de Lobeira in the thirteenth century, it puts its central message into its refrain, whose irresistible melody warns us that, though many of these songs are built on a majestic scale with a stately movement, this is not always necessary, and, if the occasion so calls, they can burst into lighter and more airy strains :

> Leonoreta,
> Fin roseta,
> Bela sobre toda fror :
> Fin roseta,
> Non me meta
> En tal coita voss' amor.

'Leonoreta, perfect rosebud, lovely beyond every flower; perfect rosebud, let not my love for you put me in such distress.' The protest is charming and touching, but it is also dignified. Lobeira places his lady on a pinnacle of praise and is not shy or ashamed of appealing to her generosity.

The sincerity of these lovers is easily tested by the candour with which they speak of their failures. Starting with the loftiest aims, they could not always hope to be successful in them, and though they might beg their beloveds to take pity on them, there were inevitably moments when they were forced by circumstances to be severely honest with themselves and to ask whether they had really done so well as they thought or claimed. This arose not so much in defeat as in uncertainty whether the poet was faced by success or failure. His hopes might foster illusions in him, but when he looked bravely at them, he might see that they deceived him. So Bernger von Hornheim (fl. 1196) describes with admirable candour both his deceiving fancy and his disillusionment in it :

> Ich mac von vröiden ertoben ane strit :
> Mir ist von minne so liebe geschehen.
> Swa waere ein walt beidiu lanc unde wit,
> Mit schoenen bluomen, den wolte ich erspehen;
> Da möhte man mich doch springende sehen.
> Min reht ist daz ich an vröiden mich twinge.—
> Wes liuge ich gouch? Ich enweiz waz ich singe.
> Mir wart nie wirs, wil der warheit ich jehen.

. . .

> Maybe in my joy I'll go out of my mind :
> So sweetly delights from my lady befall.
> Were there but a wood, long and deep and entwined
> With beautiful blossoms, I'd see through it all;
> There might a man watch me leap in my glee.
> No, it is right that I bridle my mirth.—
> I lie, like a fool, and my song's of no worth :
> Truth to confess, it was ne'er worse with me.

Bernger is in love and dreams that all will be well, but his sceptical intelligence sounds an alarm, and he cannot but listen to it and face the melancholy truth.

Even when a lover has gained his lady's approval and basks in the life-giving light of her favours, he is not free from his troubles. She expects so much of him, and he himself rates his obligations so highly, that any small divagation from the strictest standards may make him despise himself and feel that she also despises him. Above all he fears that envious rivals or common spies and gossips will calumniate him to her and make her think the less of him. The theme of spies and slanderers, which exists also in Moorish poetry and poetical theory, as in Ibn Hazm's *The Ring of the Dove,* is surprisingly common in medieval love-song and is certainly no literary trick. Such characters were part of the social structure of the time, and it is easy to see why. These songs were composed in courts and castles for princes and nobles, and since everyone knew almost everything about everyone else, we can well believe that the *lausengiers,* of whom the troubadours so often complain, were lurking about to cause trouble for its own sake or their own profit. Even so tough a man as Bertran

de Born is moved to violent protestation by the suggestion that someone has spoken ill of him to his lady. Rather than be unworthy of
her in the least respect, he would sooner have his falcon torn from
him in pieces by hawks, lose his whole fortune at dice, and share his
castle of Altafort with other lords who are at perpetual war with
him. There is no humiliation which he will not undergo to prove his
loyalty, and he rises with fine indignation to his climax :

> Ma dompna·m lais per autre cavalier
> E pois, no sai a que, m'aia mestier;
> E falha·m vens, quan serai sobre mar;
> En cort de rei mi baten li portier;
> Et en cocha fassa·l fugir premier,
> Si non menti cel que·us anet comtar.

.   .   .

> Let my love leave me for another knight,
> Nor let me find how to escape my plight;
> When I am oversea, let the winds fail;
> Let the king's lackeys drub me from his sight,
> In press of battle let me take first flight,
> If they lie not who tell of me this tale !

Bertran is gravely disturbed that he is thought to have fallen short
of the highest standards of honour, and is prepared to go to the
limit in proving that he has not.

True love, as these songs celebrate it, is tested by separation and
absence, and here too it conforms to rules which are entirely consistent with the main philosophy of devoted service. On the one
hand the lover must be heart-broken, and in many songs his grief
is indeed touching in its prospect of an impoverished and lightless
existence; on the other hand separation demands that he must
maintain undiminished his love and loyalty to his lady. Though he
feels that the winter has come again, yet the thought of her warms
his heart, and nothing must take it from him. Separation became a
real and poignant issue with the Crusades when it might last for
years, and the *chansons de croisade* illustrate how seriously parting
and its obligations were taken and how bravely courtly love stood up
to the strain. If it was normal and natural for poets to speak of their
own plight, there were times when they saw it from the woman's
point of view, and one of the most charming of these songs is by
Rinaldo d'Aquino, who makes a girl lament the departure of her
lover. In it he reverts, at least in his situation, to a theme of folk-

song, and this allows him to seek a graceful simplicity, but his art is none the less in the high Sicilian fashion. The girl's predicament must have been common enough at the time. As she sees the ships in the harbour hoisting their sails and laments that her beloved is going with them, she prays to God to look after him, and such a concession is allowed because the occasion is a Crusade and the girl is a simple girl. Then with a trope that is both ingenious and touching, true alike to the head and to the heart, she says :

> La croce salva la gente
> E me face disviare :
> La croce mi fa dolente,
> Non mi val Dio pregare.
> Oi croce pellegrina,
> Perchè m'hai sì distrutta?
> Oi me lassa, tapina,
> Ch'i'ardo e 'ncendo tutta !

. . .

> The cross saves everyone,
> But leads me from the way :
> By the cross I'm undone,
> In vain to God I pray.
> O pilgrim cross, say, why
> Have you destroyed me so?
> Afire and flaming, I
> Am worn out by my woe.

The song is unaffectedly true to life, and yet it maintains the right tone and keeps the right rules. The deserted girl's feeling for her lover is implicitly a mirror of what he feels for her, and the theme of the lovelorn maiden takes a new significance with the choice words and the lilting measure.

This song illustrates how much high love-song gains in humanity and pathos when it borrows from a humbler and less courtly art. Our poets may have looked down upon this other poetry as lacking the polish and the style which they honoured, but they found it uncommonly useful in extending their range. The authentic themes of medieval song were so few and pitched at so high a temper that poets must often have felt a need to have some respite from them, to find something less refined and more earthly, less remote and more dramatic. This need they satisfied by drawing themes from

folk-song and making the best they could of them. This had the incidental advantage that, instead of writing directly about themselves,
they could introduce a small element of drama by making someone
else speak. Just as in the earlier songs women often speak in the
first person about themselves, so now men wrote such songs and
through them spoke indirectly of their own feelings from a different
point of view. This happened even in Provence, though some of the
first simplicity is lost when the woman's confession becomes an
oblique tribute to her man, who speaks through her. But that it
could introduce a new warmth and wealth into songs that might
otherwise be too abstract is clear from a song by Walther von der
Vogelweide :

> Under der linden
> An der heide,
> Da unser zweier bette was,
> Da mugt ir vinden
> Schone beide
> Gebrochen bluomen unde gras.
> Vor dem walde in einem tal,
> Tandaradei,
> Schone sanc diu nahtegal.

. . .

> Under the lindens
> On the heather
> There was our double resting-place,
> There might you find them,
> Both together,
> The broken blossoms and the grass.
> By a coppice in a vale,
> Tandaradei,
> Sweetly sang the nightingale.

Walther, more than any of these poets, felt the restrictions of the
form and was most enterprising and ingenious in his efforts to pass
beyond them. Here he takes a familiar theme from folk-song and
gives to it the ease and gaiety of his own accomplished art.

Secondly, songs in which a man and a woman, preferably lovers,
both take part are no less ancient a form, known both from Greek
and from Latin. A fine example of this comes from northern Italy in
the thirteenth century and was written by Ciacco dell' Anguillaia,
who may be the same as the Ciacco whom Dante places in Hell for

gluttony (*Inf.* vi. 52 ff.). The lover and his lady conduct an interchange of stanzas, in which he presses his claims on her, basing them on his prowess in action and his willingness even to die for her. She rejects them as irrelevant, and mocks his readiness to die by saying that she will say masses for his soul. In turn he rejects this as being useless, and all seems well set for a quarrel, when he changes his tactics and promises her his service in true humility, and then all is well. The song is both lively and life-like and makes a nice distinction between what the lover thinks of himself and what his lady demands of him. A more adroit, if less searching, treatment of the dialogue is that in which Ulrich of Lichtenstein (*c.*1227-1275) makes a lover and a lady debate what love is. The lover, speaking in the high-flown language of courtly love, stresses its strength and its rewards, while the lady archly affects ignorance of the whole matter and protests her deep interest and curiosity. Then the song comes to a surprising close :

> Vrouwe, da soltu mich meinen
> Herzenlichen als ich dich,
> Unser sweien so vereinen
> Daz wir beidiu sin ein ich.
> Wis di min, so bin ich din !
> 'Herre, des mac niht gesin.
> Sit ir iuwer, ich bin min.'

> Lady, let our spirits mingle,
> I in you and you in me;
> Let the two of us in single
> Being both together be.
> Each to other let's be true !
> 'Sir, that I will never do.
> I am mine, let yours be you.'

The old songs between men and women usually end in a declaration of love, and in making his new song do the opposite Ulrich pursues an ingenious variation, and his song is all the gayer for the echoes which it awakes of folk-songs on similar themes.

These examples show what benefits courtly love-song gained when it reinforced its themes from a stock which its own triumph had largely dispossessed and discredited. It made them live up to its own high level of accomplishment, but in them it found a less exacting matter than it normally found obligatory. How useful this popular art could be is brilliantly exemplified by Walther von der Vogelweide, who has a far wider range of themes and a closer contact with ordinary feelings than any other troubadour or minnesinger. Indeed, though Walther owes much of his art to courtly song, he passes far beyond its boundaries and prepares the way for a much more capacious poetry. The characteristic love-song of the twelfth and thirteenth centuries appeals through qualities which Walther certainly possessed but did not indulge on a large scale. Its most eminent exponents strike a note which is very much their own and has a peculiar brilliance and exaltation. If some songs are of no real interest, that is because the ideal of courtly love cannot be expected to inspire every poet with the same force or conviction, and anyhow among so many songs some are bound to be second-rate or second-hand. It is true that this art lacks many qualities that we take for granted in poetry and feel to be necessary to it. Its imagery, despite resplendent exceptions, tends to be stereotyped and repetitive, largely because it has to suit an abstract language, in which vivid, pictorial images, like those which glitter through the love-songs of Moorish Spain, would upset the balance and spoil the exalted tone. Sometimes too a poet may be so taken up with displaying his virtuosity that he does not pay sufficient attention to giving body and variety to his matter. The accepted themes, despite the resourceful agility of their treatment, may seem to be confined to too narrow a quarter of experience. Yet this is just where the strength of courtly love-song lies. Because it concentrates its powers on a small point, it is able to make the most of it and to convey with a singular fidelity the ecstatic joy which is its glory and its justification. To build everything round such an aim calls for an extraordinary self-command, and the wonder is that so many poets were able to exert it and sustain it without slackening their enterprise or losing their individuality. For this end were fashioned the intricate technique with its rich range of ingeniously shaped stanzas, the dexterously sustained rhymes, the maintenance of a demanding but indispensable tone. By its carefully calculated means love-song secures both purity and strength—the purity of aim which seeks an authentic ideal of generosity and devotion, and the strength which gives to otherwise remote and elusive ends a recognizable place in a world of flesh and blood. The artifice and the formality which medieval love-song needed to rise above the level of popular song challenged poets to choose their words with a fine discrimination and to extract the utmost from the situation into which they had been led by the compelling discipline of love. This is by no means the only way to treat love, and only at this period has this treatment been predominant and almost universal. But just because the poets believed in it and sang of it with full conviction and a deep sense of their artistic responsibilities, their words have a peculiar freshness, which testifies to the unexpected effect which an essentially intellectual theory may have upon the most wayward of the passions.

By 1300 this art was moribund. In southern France the cult of courtly love had been dealt a cruel blow by the Albigensian Crusade of Simon de Montfort, but even in other parts of Europe the decay of the chivalrous outlook meant that its love-songs were doomed. The richest legacy fell to heirs whom the poets themselves would not have found entirely to their taste, and was turned to the transformation of courtly into Christian love. Present already to some degree in Guido Guinizelli and shyly asserting itself in some songs of the Crusades, the new spirit was indeed different from that which inspired courtly song, and yet it owed an incalculable debt to it. Though Dante put Frederick II and Bertran de Born in Hell, and was sufficiently suspicious of Arnaut Daniel and even of Guinizelli to place them among the carnal sinners in Purgatory, he learned something from them all, and his own presentation of ideal love in the *Vita Nuova* was the final, logical, almost inevitable conclusion of the notions which, two centuries earlier, had sprung upon an admiring world with Guillaume of Aquitaine. Its first pioneers did not try to claim that this ideal was Christian, and at times both they and their later adherents suggested that it was not common but they believed that it was the highest good attainable by man and that the enjoyment of it was indeed a blessed state. Dante made this belief the starting-point for his own bold speculations, but, true to his lifelong vision of Beatrice, raised it to an even loftier level by transmuting it into the most exalted form of transcendent love.

VI

DANTE AND SORDELLO

ON THE lowest slope of the Mount of Purgatory Dante and Virgil, seeing that night is coming on, decide to make enquiries about the best way of ascent. They mark a solitary figure looking towards them and approach it :

> Venimmo a lei : O anima Lombarda,
> Come ti stavi altera e disdegnosa,
> E nel mover degli occhi onesta e tarda !

> Ella non ci diceva alcuna cosa;
> Ma lasciavane gir, solo sguardando
> A guisa di leon, quando si posa.
>
> (Purg. VI 58-59)

. . .

> We came to it. O Lombard spirit, how
> Disdainful and majestical thou wast !
> In moving of thine eyes how stately and slow !

> No word to us approaching it addrest,
> But let us go on, watching only there
> In likeness of a lion couched at rest.
>
> (Binyon)

When questioned by Virgil about the way upward, this figure replies by asking about the strangers' country and life. On hearing the word 'Mantua' he leaps up and embraces Virgil, and reveals that he is Sordello of the same city. At this dramatic point Dante suddenly breaks his narrative to devote seventy-six lines to a blistering denunciation of Italian discords and lawlessness. After this he picks up the tale and makes Sordello and Virgil exchange information about their respective places in the after-world. Sordello then guides the two poets to the Valley of the Negligent Rulers, where with appropriate comments he points out the chief inmates and adds some hard words about their sons. When during the night Dante and Virgil are transported to Purgatory proper, Sordello remains behind :

Sordal rimase, e l'altre gentil forme. (*Purg.* IX 58)

.   .   .

Sordello and the other noble natures stayed. (Binyon)

He has played his part and is not mentioned again.

Sordello is a prominent and engaging figure of his time, at once poet and man of affairs.[1] Born towards the beginning of the thirteenth century at Goito, near Mantua, he entered the court of Count Ricciardo di San Bonifazio, Lord of Verona, where he fell in love with his master's wife, Cunizza da Romano, and about 1223 eloped with her to the court of her brother, the terrible Ezzelino, at Treviso. Soon afterwards he abandoned Cunizza and made a secret marriage with Otta di Strasso. This meant that he had to flee from Treviso and the fury of his wife's relatives, and no doubt explains why about 1229 he left Italy for the south of France, whence in due course he visited the courts of Provence, Toulouse, Roussillon, and Castile. About 1245 we find him at the court of the Countess Beatrice, daughter of Raymond Berengar, Count of Provence, and wife of Charles of Anjou. From 1252 to 1265 Sordello's name appears in several treaties and records, which show that Charles held him in high esteem and entrusted him with important tasks. He followed Charles on his Italian expedition against Manfred in 1265, but seems to have been captured by the Ghibellines before reaching Naples. At any rate, in September 1266 he was a prisoner at Novara; but Clement IV persuaded Charles to ransom him, and in 1269 he received as a recompense for his services five castles in the Abruzzi near the river Pescara. Nothing more is recorded of him; but, since in the same year the castles passed to other owners, the probability is that he died at this time, being by now an elderly man.

Sordello was also a poet of distinction and renown. Of his poetry there survive twelve *chansons,* four *partimens,* two *tensons,* eight *sirventés,* fifteen *coblas,* and a didactic poem in 1327 lines called *L'Ensegnamen d'Onor.* His shorter poems may lack the royal gaiety of Guillaume of Aquitaine or the accomplished grace of Bernart de Ventadour or the virile passion of Bertran de Born, but they have their own merits. He is an accomplished metrist, who knows how to lace rhymes into elaborate patterns; a stylist, who avoids phrases which are too trite or too recondite; a man of the world, who relates his poetry to his own varied experience. We can understand that Dante might think well of him, since, unlike other troubadours, who combine protestations of ideal love with desires which are more

---

[1] The poems are edited by C. de Lollis, *Vita e Poesie di Sordello di Goito* (Halle 1896), which also gives the documents concerning his life.

earthy, he is a thorough idealist. Whatever his actual conduct may have been, his poetry is consistently high-minded and chivalrous. He tells his lady that he does not wish to taste of any fruit whose sweetness will turn to bitterness (xxi 23-4), that no knight loves his lady unless he loves his own honour equally (xxv 17-19), that he will never reveal to any honest woman his true feelings about her (xxiv 49-50), that every loyal lover is sufficiently recompensed if he is honoured in himself (xxvii 1 ff.). He builds his cult of love on personal honour and is quite consistent in his conclusions. It is not surprising that in the interchange of verses between him and Peire Guillem, Peire says that he has never known anyone like Sordello, since he disdains what other men make it their ambition to win (xviii 13 ff.).[1] In Sordello's system the man of honour must love a woman as honourable as himself and be as sensitive for her reputation as for his own. If Sordello is not in the highest rank of troubadours, he is certainly among the most distinguished of those who came from Italy and sufficiently original and powerful to have attracted Dante's attention by his poetry.

It has been claimed that Dante regards Sordello as himself a member of the class of negligent rulers and that this determines his place in Purgatory. So R. W. Church says : 'He is placed among those who had great opportunities and great thoughts—the men of great chances and great failures.'[2] Something of the same kind seems to have been in Browning's mind when he wrote his remarkable *Sordello*. For Browning Sordello is a fascinating failure, who might have been a true forerunner of Dante but through some defect of character or conviction failed to realize his proper destiny. It is true that Browning does not follow history very closely and that his Sordello is largely an imaginary figure; yet he too regards him as one who had great gifts and chances but failed to take advantage of them :

> one who was chiefly glad
> To have achieved the few real deeds he had,
> Because the way assured they were not worth
> Doing, so spared from doing them henceforth—
> A tree that covets fruitage and yet tastes
> Never itself, itself.

Church and Browning can hardly be right about Dante's treatment of Sordello. The only possible evidence that he is one of the negligent

---

[1] Cf. A. Jeanroy, *Poésie lyrique des Troubadours* (Paris 1934) II p.167
[2] *Dante and other Essays* p. 228.

rulers is that Dante and Virgil leave him with them when they ascend
to Purgatory proper, and that is by no means conclusive. On the
other hand, there are good arguments against this view. First, if
Sordello were himself one of this company, his language about its
other members is unsuitable, especially in Purgatory, for one who
has himself been guilty of the same fault. Secondly, he was never in
so exalted a position as the kings and princes whom he criticizes. He
belonged to a section of society eminent enough in its own way
but not charged with imperial or regal responsibilities, and Dante
would hardly have classed him with the Emperor or with the Kings
of France and England.

In fact, it is quite clear where Dante places Sordello, and his
reasons for doing so are of some interest. When Dante and Virgil
meet him, he is outside Purgatory proper and says of his position :

> 'Loco certo non c'è posto :
> Licito m'è andar suso ed intorno;
> Per quanto ir posso, a guida mi t'accosto.'
>
> *(Purg.* VII 40-42)

.   .   .

> 'No set post is prescribed us', answered he.
> 'It is permitted to go up and round :
> Far as I may, I will companion thee.'
>
> (Binyon)

Sordello's place indicates that he is one of the late repentants, who
have died violent deaths. Apparently Dante knew something about
him which is not mentioned in the brief Provençal biographies. Nor
is this surprising, since such biographies are very feeble affairs and
draw most of their information from the poems. There is no difficulty about Dante knowing of an event which took place in 1269
and must have made a stir at the time, since Sordello was a man
of mark and note. The passage not only settles where Dante places
Sordello, but also indicates that he knew more of him than his
poems. At the end of a varied life Sordello died a violent death, and
to this Dante implicitly refers. That Dante had various sources of
information is clear from a passage in *De vulgari Eloquentia,* where
in discussing the need for an *illustre vulgare* he considers the Bolog-
nese dialect but, after admitting its merits, comes to the conclusion
that it too is not fitted for the highest purposes of poetry. He illustrates his point from Sordello :

Dicimus ergo quod forte non male opinantur qui Bononienses asserunt pulcriori locutione loquentes, cum ab Imolensibus, Ferrariensibus, et Mutinensibus circumstantibus aliquid proprio vulgari adsciscunt; sicut facere quoslibet a finitimis suis conicimus, ut Sordellus de Mantua sua ostendit, Cremonae, Brixiae, atque Veronae confini; qui tantus eloquentiae vir existens, non solum in poetando sed quomodocunque loquendo patrium vulgare deseruit. (I 15)

.   .   .

We say, then, that they are probably not far wrong who assert that the people of Bologna speak a more beautiful tongue because they take into their own speech something from their neighbours of Imola, Ferrara, and Modena; even as we have concluded that anybody does who borrows from his neighbours; as Sordello shows in the case of his native Mantua, which is next to Cremona, Brescia, and Verona; and he, who was so distinguished a man of eloquence, not only in poetry but in every kind of speech, abandoned his native dialect.

This example supports Dante's contention that Italian dialects were not suited to the grand style; Sordello tried first to write in his own vernacular but abandoned it, presumably for Provençal. We know nothing of his work in Italian, since it is doubtful whether a poem claimed for him is really his,[1] but Dante knew not only his Italian poems but other works, presumably not in verse, or at least knew his reputation as a writer or a speaker. In this, as in other respects, Dante was better informed about Sordello than we are.

On one matter Dante shows a remarkable restraint. He must have known about Sordello's elopement with Cunizza and is not likely to have approved of it. Of course, if he said nothing about it, no question would arise; but he comes near to referring to it in the *Paradiso,* when Cunizza, being placed in Venus, explains that she is rightly placed in the star of love and that her former sins no longer distress her :

> 'Cunizza fui chiamata, e qui refulgo,
> Perchè mi vinse il lume d'esta stella.

> 'Ma lietamente a me medesma indulgo
> La cagion di mia sorte, e non mi noia,
> Che parria forse forte al vostro vulgo.'
>
> (*Par.* IX 32-6)

.   .   .

[1] Jeanroy *op cit.*, I, p. 430.

'Cunizza was I called; and here I glow
Since I was conquered by this burning star.

'But for the cause of this my lot I owe
No grief, but shrive myself in happiness;
Hard saying, may-be, to your crowd below.'

(Binyon)

Here Dante is a little artful. He would know that any mention of Cunizza would stir his readers to expect some mention of Sordello, but he says nothing of him. Instead, he tantalizingly makes Cunizza speak of her devotion to another troubadour, Folquet de Marseilles. Dante's silence on Sordello in this connection suggests that he has weighed his faults with his virtues and decided that the virtues win.

Yet, though Dante admired Sordello and may well have approved of his love-poetry, what he most liked seems to have been the courageous expression of political and moral convictions in which Sordello more than once indulged. In the *Purgatorio* Sordello's first function is to provide a starting-point for Dante's passionate outburst on the woes of Italy. The abrupt transition is surely dictated by Sordello's own views on such matters and especially by what he says in *L'Ensegnamen d'Onor,* where he sets out his notions of chivalrous behaviour and his theory of *pretz* or worth. It is by no means the only poem of its kind, nor the best. It is quite legitimate to prefer the *Romans di Mondana Vita* of Folquet de Lunel or the *Four Cardinal Virtues* of Daude de Pradas; and, of course, if Dante himself knew these other poems, he may well have thought them better. But that is no reason for arguing, as some have,[1] that Dante would therefore pay no attention to Sordello's poem, still less that he did not know it. Since he seems to have been well acquainted with Sordello's writings, we can hardly doubt that he knew this piece. Once he decided to make use of Sordello in the *Divine Comedy,* he would naturally seize on any relevant elements in his outlook and especially on those expressed at some length in *L'Ensegnamen d'Onor.*

Though the chivalrous ideal set forth in this poem is commonplace in comparison with that of the *Vita Nuova* or even of the *Convito,* with which it has more in common, it certainly says much of which Dante would approve and very little of which he would disapprove. Just as in his shorter poems Sordello makes the ideal love of a woman an important element in his whole conception of honour, so here he bases his philosophy, and especially his notions of *pretz* and *onor,* on the inspiration and challenge which such a

[1] H. J. Chaytor, *The Troubadours of Dante,* p. 175.

love gives. His course is somewhat sluggish and circuitous. He dilates on the love of God and the origin of evil before he reaches the rules of behaviour. He does not at first say much about women or love, but that is because he keeps them in reserve As he draws to his close, he expands upon the relations of women and their lovers and tells how they should bear themselves and what conversation they should hold. Then in the last paragraph he pays a tribute to his own lady, Agradiva, who inspires all that is best in his life. In this poem ideal love is a system of worth and honour; and though Sordello does not draw such bold conclusions as Dante would, he is a consistent apologist for the cult of love as a system of life.

In *L'Ensegnamen d'Onor* Sordello proves himself worthy of Dante's respect as a critic of life and politics, whose philosophy is of the kind which Dante himself held and developed. In this we may see Dante's reason for placing his outburst on Italy immediately after Virgil and Sordello have greeted each other as fellow Mantuans. This covers a deeper kinship between them, and Dante draws the moral:

> Quell 'anima gentil fu così presta,
> Sol per lo dolce suon della sua terra,
> Di fare al cittadin suo quivi festa;
>
> Ed ora in te non stanno senza guerra
> Li vivi tuoi, e l'un l'altro si rode
> Di quei ch'un muro ed una fossa serra.
>
> (Purg. VI. 79-84)

.   .   .

> That gentle spirit was thus quick to acclaim
> His countryman and hail him there for friend
> Merely at the sweet sound of his city's name;
>
> And now their days in thee the living spend
> In quarrel, and each one doth the other wound
> Of those whom one wall and one moat defend.
>
> (Binyon)

Italy is equally dear to Virgil, to Dante, and to Sordello. From his knowledge of Sordello's work Dante advances from the friendly warmth of the greeting to a fierce denunciation, in which he not only says much with which Sordello would agree but even seems to follow with his own vivid variations certain topics with which Sordello deals in his poem.

If we compare Dante's outburst with Sordello's *L'Ensegnamen d'Onor,* we notice several points of similarity, which suggest that

Dante has a good reason for his abrupt change of subject. There is, it is true, a vast difference of manner between the two poets. While Sordello is dry and abstract and theoretical, Dante is vivid and personal and illustrates individual issues with homely or colloquial images. But behind this difference there are considerable resemblances of thought and outlook. Indeed each point made by Dante can be paralleled by something said by Sordello. Dante begins by denouncing the disobedience prevalent in Italy and proclaiming the need to let the Emperor rule; Sordello (543 ff.) also lays down the need for an ideal of service and blames those who shun what is right or accept what is not. Dante blames the German Albert for deserting his duty and calls down judgment from heaven on him; Sordello (589 ff.) says that a common failing of the great is to be interested in themselves instead of in those whom they rule. Dante ascribes imperial negligence to the avarice of Albert and his father; Sordello (506 ff.) expatiates on the obligations of wealth and the need for generosity. In his denunciation of Florence, Dante says that its people have no justice in their hearts, though its name is often on their lips; Sordello (601 ff.) inveighs against those who condemn the faults of others and pay no attention to their own. Dante blames the Florentines for refusing public burdens; Sordello (555 ff.) regards such service as owed to both God and man. Finally, Dante denounces the improvidence which means that what is spun in October does not reach to mid-November; Sordello (489 ff.) regards forethought as the first duty of all rulers. Thus Dante's principles of government, as revealed in his denunciation of Italy, may be illustrated almost line for line from Sordello's poem.

This does not mean that Dante necessarily had Sordello's *L'Ensegnamen d'Onor* before him when he wrote this passage or even that he knew it so well that he was able to adapt its thoughts to his own. But it suggests at least that he knew it and agreed with it and saw in it sufficient justification for making the meeting with Sordello the occasion for a denunciation of Italy and its rulers. It is of course true that other poets expressed ideas very like Sordello's and that, if he had wished, Dante could have made use of them. But he does not, because Sordello, being a fellow townsman of Virgil, is ideally suited to stress the need for Italian unity and the horror of its present discords. This was enough to give Sordello priority over other politically minded poets and to justify the place which is given to him in the *Divine Comedy*. The passage is introduced with great skill, both formally and essentially. After the moving character of the meeting between the two Mantuans, what follows comes with an impressive and dramatic shock of contrast, but the similarity between Sordello's views and Dante's justifies the intrusion of a theme which might otherwise do undue violence to the narrative.

In this passage Dante agrees with Sordello on some general principles of politics, though he gives them a particular application which Sordello does not. Later in the *Purgatorio,* when Dante is again concerned with political personalities, he follows another model from Sordello and shapes it to his own purpose. In Canto VII 83-136 Sordello points out the various negligent rulers who are seated on the grass in the wonderful valley and comments on them and on others who are not present. Here, we can hardly doubt, Dante had in mind Sordello's most famous poem, the *planh* which he wrote on the death of Blacatz and which is so important that it must be quoted in full :

Planher volh En Blacatz en aquest leugier so
Ab cor trist e marrit, e ai eu ben razo,
Qu'en lui ai mescabat senhor et amic bo,
E quar tuit l'aip valen en sa mort perdut so.
Tant es mortals lo dans qu'ieu non ai sospeisso
Qu'onca mais se revenha, s'en aital guiza no
Qu'om li traga lo cor e qu'en manjo·l baro
Que vivon descoratz, pais auran de cor pro.

Premier mange del cor, per so que gran opsl'es,
L'Emperaire de Roma, s·el vol lo Milanes
Per forsa conquistar; car lui tenon conques
E viu deseretatz malgrat de sos Ties.
E de seguentre lui mang'en lo Reis franses,
Pois cobrara Castela qu'el pert per nescies :
Mas si pes'a sa maire, il no manjara res,
Quar ben par a son pretz qu'el no fai ren que·l pes.

Del Rei engles me platz, quar es pauc coratjos,
Que mange pron del cor; pois er valens e bos
E cobrara la terra per que viu de pretz blos,
Que·l tol co resi de Fransa, quar lo sab nualhos.
E lo Reis castelas tanh qu'en mange per dos,
Quar dos regismes ten ni per l'un non es pros :
Mas s'il en vol manjar, tanh qu'en manj'a rescos,
Que si·l maire o sabia batria·l ab bastos.

Del rei d'Aragon volh del cor deja manjar,
Que aisso lo fara de l'anta descargar
Que pren sai de Marselh'e e d'Amilhau; qu'onrar
No·s pot estiers per re que posca dir ni far.

E apres volh del cor don hom al rei Navar,
Que valia mais coms que reis, so aug contar.
Tortz es quan Dieus fai hom'en gran ricor pojar,
Pos sofracha de cor de pretz lo fai baissar.

Al comte de Toloz'a ops qu'en manje be,
Si·l membra so que sol tener e so que te;
Quar si ab autre cor sa perda non reve,
No·m par que la revenh' ab aquel qu'a en se.
E·l comes Proensals tanh qu'en manje, si·l sove
Qu'om que dezeratatz viu gaire no val re :
E si tot ab esfors si defen ni·s capte,
Ops l'es manje del cor pel gran fais que soste.

Li baro·m voldran mal de so que ieu dic be;
Mas be sapchan qu'ieu·ls pretz autan pauc comilh me.

Bels Restaurs, sol qu'ab vos pusca trobar merce,
A man dan met cascun que per amic no·m te.

.   .   .

Blacatz is dead. In this plain descant I intend
To weep for him, nor care a jot if I offend;
For in him I have lost my master and good friend,
And know that with his death all princely virtues end.
It is a mortal loss, which nought can ever mend;
In truth I so suspect, unless his heart we send
To the great lords to eat. To hearts they can't pretend!
But then they'll have enough of heart to make amend.

First let the Emperor eat. Full need of it is his,
If he would crush by force the rebel Milanese
And force his conquerors to do what he decrees;
Despite his German guards he has no fiefs or fees.
Then let the French king eat, and may-be he will seize
Castile again, which he lost by his idiocies;
But he'll refrain if his good mother disagrees;
Honour, we know, forbids that he should her displease.

I bid the English king, who is so ungallant,
Eat of the heart; then he'll be bold and valiant,
Win back the lands whose loss proclaims him recreant,
All that the French king took, knowing him indolent.

Next the Castilian king enough for two will want;
Two realms has he, but ev'n for one his heart's too scant.
If he would eat, let him be secret and not flaunt;
He'll feel his mother's stick if she learns of his vaunt.

Then of this heart must eat the king of Aragon;
So shall he wash away the shame which he has won
At Marseilles and Milhau; of his lost honour none
Can he recover now, whatever's said and done.
Then unto Navarre's king I bid this heart be shown,—
Better as count than king in my comparison,—
Great pity 'tis when God exalts dominion
For princes who then bid all name and fame be gone.

Next, the count of Toulouse is in sore need of it,
If he recall what lands he has, of what he's quit,
To win his losses back a new heart he must fit,—
The heart that he has now will mend them not a bit.
Last the count of Provence will eat, if he admit
That the disinherited are honoured not a whit;
Yes, let him do his best himself to benefit;
So burdensome a load he bears that he must eat.

For all these well said words I'll win the great lords' hate,
But let them know I'll pay their knocks back with like weight.

Sweet Comfort, if I find your favour in the end,
I'm little vexed by those who scorn to call me friend.

This unusual poem shows the robust originality of Sordello's art
and makes it easier to understand why Dante forgave him his sins
and gave him an honourable part in the *Divine Comedy*.

In the well-regulated world of Provençal poetry Sordello's *planh*
has a peculiar place. It has precedents in such pieces as Cercamon's
lament for Guillaume of Aquitaine in 1137, or Bertran de Born's for
Henry II's son, the 'young King' in 1183, or those of Jaucelm Faidit
and Guiraut de Borneil for Richard Coeur de Lion in 1199. The
lament was an ancient form and followed conventional lines, in
which the poets usually complain that with the passing of a great
man courtesy, valour and chivalry have vanished from the earth.
They do not usually seize the occasion, as Sordello does, to say unpleasant things about the living. But historically he is justified in
this, because the *planh* is closely related to the *sirventés*, which is

what Provençal poets use when they wish to criticize their lords and masters or to pass political judgments. Sordello must have known this, and his *planh* is close to such poems as that written by the younger Bertran de Born against King John in 1204, in which he mocks him for the loss of Poitou and Guyenne, accuses him of betraying his armies, and generally derides his failure. Sordello's originality lies in finding in Blacatz's death an opportunity to say what he feels about the rulers of Europe. If the form allowed some latitude, he took full advantage of it and made the most of it.

Blacatz, whose death Sordello laments, is not unknown to history. He was seigneur of Aups near Draguignan and is mentioned in several documents after 1194. Himself the author of ten surviving poems, he was also a friend and benefactor of poets, who was praised for his goodness and generosity. Sordello seems to have come into contact with him at the court of Guida, daughter of Henry I, Count of Rodez, before 1240. She has been thought to be the 'Belh Restaurs' to whom he addresses several poems, including the *planh*,[1] and she is associated with Sordello in the parody of it written by Bertran d'Alamanon. Though in 1240 Sordello is known to have been at Montpellier, it looks as if he wrote the *planh* when he was back with Guida and addressed her in it because she too had been a friend of the dead man. The freedom with which he speaks is an instructive comment on the conditions of the time, when a small court like that of Guida could flaunt its hostility to all the great powers of Europe.

In gathering his kings and princes Sordello throws his net wide. In turn he denounces the Emperor Frederick II, Louis IX of France, Henry III of England, Ferdinand III of Castile, James I of Aragon, Thibaut I of Navarre, Raymond VII of Toulouse, and Raymond Berengar V of Provence. It is not impossible to find a date for the poem.[2] The death of Blacatz seems to have coincided with a considerable crisis in western Europe. In 1242 Raymond VII of Toulouse formed a league of southern potentates in the hope of shaking off French suzerainty and received assurances of help from the kings of Castile and Aragon. At the same time Henry III of England set sail for France on 9 May with the ambition of regaining the lands lost by his father. On 23 July he was defeated by Louis IX at Saintes, and though his army remained for some time in France, it had no prospect or hope of success. Despite this Raymond tried to make a treaty with Henry and eventually did so by the end of August. Then in October all went wrong. The Count of Foix deserted the allies; the Kings

---

[1] C. Fabre in *Annales du Midi* XXIV (1912) pp. 153-184 and 321-354.

[2] A. Jeanroy in *Annales du Midi* XVI (1904) pp. 311-329; H. J. Chaytor *The Troubadours and England*, pp. 80-85.

of Castile and Aragon held aloof from action; and on 20 October Raymond submitted to Louis. It is a sorry tale, and Sordello takes full advantage of it.

Of Sordello's eight rulers five were involved in the revolt, and each is mocked for his failure, Henry III, quite accurately, for lands lost to the French king, not so much what John had already lost but Saintonge as far as the Gironde; Ferdinand III for his cowardice in failing to help Raymond VII; James I for still not being master of Marseilles, which ought to have been his on the death of Raymond Berengar IV, and of Milhau, which once belonged to his house but was still in the hands of Toulouse with the connivance of Louis and the Pope; Raymond VII of Toulouse for his failure to regain lands lost earlier to Louis; and Raymond Berengar V of Provence for gaining nothing by making up his quarrel with Toulouse and being forced into a reduction of his domains. The outbreak of 1242 was largely an attempt to regain territories recently lost, and when it failed, these remained with their recent owners and especially with Louis. To this list Sordello adds three other names, Frederick II, Louis IX, and Thibaut I, who fall into rather a different category. Frederick could hardly be omitted from a list of living monarchs, and Sordello, who himself came from Lombardy, delights in the Emperor's continued lack of success against the Milanese, whom he defeated at Cortenuova in 1237 but never subdued. Louis had indeed defeated his enemies in France, but Sordello condemns him for not making the most of his victory and taking Castile, to which he had a tenable claim through his mother, especially since Ferdinand's mother, Berengaria, was declared not to have been married to his father Alfonso IX of Leon. Finally, since Thibaut of Navarre, formerly Count of Champagne, is not known to have joined the coalition against Louis, Sordello probably derides him for his behaviour in the recent crusade, when he retreated before the Saracens and took ship home. These three additional names complete Sordello's picture of western Europe governed by poltroons. Although his actual occasion is the war of 1242, he passes beyond it to a wider survey and delivers his blows impartially to eight potentates.

Sordello's *planh* evidently made a considerable mark, since it was soon imitated or parodied by Peire Bremon, Ricas Novas and by Bertran d'Alamanon. It also became known in due course to Dante, who was evidently taken by the image of eating the dead man's heart. To this there seems to be no parallel in medieval poetry, except in poems obviously derived from Sordello's. It is conceivable that it comes from folk-song or folk-tale, since the troubadours were not averse from drawing on such popular sources, but even for this

the nearest parallel is no closer than a Greek τραγοῦσι, in which an
eagle summons other birds to eat of its vitals.[1] Dante's debt to the
planh may first be seen in the first sonnet of the *Vita Nuova*, where
the figure of love appears to him in a vision :

> Allegro mi sembrava Amor, tenendo
> Mio core in mano, e nelle braccia avea
> Madonna, involta in un drappo, dormendo.

> Poi la svegliava, e d'este core ardendo
> Lei paventosa umilmente pascea :
> Appresso gir ne lo vedea piangendo.

. . .

> He seemed like one who is full of joy, and had
> My heart within his hand, and on his arm
> My lady with a mantle round her slept,

> When, having wakened her, anon he made
> To eat that heart; she ate, as fearing harm,
> Then he went out; and as he went, he wept.
> (D. G. Rossetti)

Dante does not use the image of eating the heart quite as Sordello
does; Sordello insists that it will give strength to the feeble while
Dante suggests that his whole being is absorbed in that of his lady.
None the less, the two poems are sufficiently similar to justify the
conclusion that Dante has borrowed something from Sordello.

If this was the first impression which the *planh* made on Dante,
it was not the only one. When he came to write the *Purgatorio,* he
was interested not in the image of the heart but in the denunciation
of European rulers. If Sordello's poem surveys these about 1242, the
speech which Dante gives him covers forty years of history as seen
in retrospect from the ideal year of 1300. Dante uses the presence
of the negligent rulers for two purposes, first to comment on those
who belong to the class, then to say something, usually unpleasant,
about their sons and successors. The negligent rulers are the
Emperor Rudolf, Ottocar of Bohemia, Philip III of France, Henry
of Navarre, Peter III of Aragon, Charles I of Anjou, Henry III of
England, and William of Montferrat. Only on two of these does
Dante say enough to show why they are placed where they are. The
Emperor Rudolf is guilty of negligence :

[1] Passow, *Popularia Carmina Graeciae Recentiora*, p. 103.

... fa sembianti
D'aver negletto ciò che far dovea.

(*Purg.* VII. 91-2)

.   .   .

... has an air which owns
Neglect of those things which he should have done.

(Binyon)

In the previous canto he has shared with his son Albert the guilt of neglecting their lands out of covetousness (*Purg.* VI 97-105), and now Dante stresses the results of this policy in the condition of Italy, whose wounds Rudolf might have healed. Dante is also explicit about Philip III of France, who 'died in flight, dishonouring the lily',—a reference to Philip's fatal defeat in 1285 by Roger di Loria, the admiral of Peter III of Aragon. Dante may even had more than this in mind, since Philip had tried to seize Aragon for his son, Charles of Valois, of whom Dante had a low opinion because of his interference in Florentine politics (*Purg.* XX 71). So perhaps he here recalls that among Philip's other faults was favouritism to an unworthy son.

Though Dante does not explain why he claims the other kings and princes as negligent, no great difficulty arises. They have all in their way failed, presumably through some weakness of character, and their failure has led to discord or defeat. Whatever their personal virtues and charms may have been, and Dante is generous enough about them, they have none the less failed in their first duty, which is to rule and keep order. Ottocar of Bohemia has divided the Empire in his struggle with Rudolf of Hapsburg. The policies of Charles of Anjou ended in disaster when he was driven out of Sicily after the Sicilian Vespers, but before that he had caused havoc in Italy (*Purg.* XX 67 ff.; *Par.* VIII 73 ff.). Henry III of England, the only figure who appears both in Sordello's poem and here, 'il re della semplice vita', is another whose efforts to regain his lost lands have failed and have been followed by civil war. William of Montferrat tried to lead a league against Charles of Anjou, but could not control its members and, when Alessandria rose against him, he was put in a cage and kept in it until his death. Neither Henry of Navarre nor Peter III of Aragon, despite many chivalrous virtues and the admiration of their contemporaries, were really successful kings. The company is well chosen and excites little comment. Indeed the only possible criticism of it is that we may feel surprise at Charles of Anjou being so well treated. Elsewhere Dante says of him :

Carlo venne in Italia, e, per vicenda
Vittima fe' di Corradino; e poi
Ripinse al ciel Tommaso, per ammenda.

(*Purg.* XX 67-9)

.   .   .

Charles enters Italy; in his turn he sends
His victim Conradin to death; thereon
Thrusts Thomas back to heaven, for amends.

(Binyon)

The deaths of Conradin and Thomas Aquinas might seem to argue graver faults in Charles than negligence, but for some reason Dante condones them and sets Charles in reasonably virtuous company.

In his choice of negligent rulers Dante follows very much the same principles as Sordello in his *planh*. Each condemns rulers for not ruling and suggests that it is due to a failure of character. With Sordello the failure is simply cowardice; with Dante it is something wider, a failure to sustain responsibility, or something like moral cowardice. If Sordello thinks that a king's first duty is to hold all the lands which belong to his house, Dante thinks that it is to govern well what lands he has and not to promote discord. If Sordello insists in the case of Thibaut that elevation to kingship is no reason for lapsing into idleness, Dante throughout implies that rulers have great responsibilities and that the higher their position the more it demands of them. If Sordello regards war as the test of a man's worth, Dante at least regards defeat as a sign of weakness. Finally, it is noteworthy that, while Sordello does not shrink from deriding St Louis, Dante nowhere finds a place for him in the *Divine Comedy* or even mentions his name. This king, who seems to many to embody so much that is best in the thirteenth century, evidently did not appeal to Dante. Though Sordello and Dante differ in temperament, they judge rulers by much the same standards and have much the same ideas of what qualities they ought to possess.

If part of Sordello's speech is more generous than we might expect from a man of his character, that is no doubt because Dante wishes to be fair to men like Henry III, who was renowned for his piety, or Peter III, who was praised for his virtue and probity. But Dante was capable of scorn equal to Sordello's and was not afraid to show it when he thought it deserved. He ingeniously makes the sight of the negligent rulers an occasion to mention others who are not present, usually because they are still alive. Of these only two avoid unfavourable comment, Edward I of England, who is said to be a better man than his father, and the eldest son of Peter II of Aragon, who did not reign long enough to leave any definite reputation. The others mentioned are less worthy,—Wenceslas I of Bohemia, Philip the Fair of France, James II of Aragon, his brother Frederick II of Sicily, and Charles II of Naples. If the fathers' faults are pardonable, those of the sons are not. They are men of Dante's own time about whose characters and careers he is well informed and has usually something to say elsewhere in the *Divine Comedy*. So he speaks of Wenceslas :

> Che mai valor non conobbe, nè volle.
>
> (*Par.* XIX 126)

. . .

> Who never has known virtue and wills it not.
>
> (Binyon)

Philip the Fair, 'il mal di Francia', with his 'vita viziata e lorda', is accused of abetting simony (*Inf.* XIX 87), of ruining his country by debasing its coinage (*Par.* XXX 118), and of being a new Pilate in his treatment of the Church (*Purg.* XX 91). James II of Aragon is denounced for participating in the foul deeds of his uncle and brother and in making cuckold their family and its two kingdoms (*Par.* XIX 136-8). Frederick II of Sicily is attacked for avarice and baseness (*Par.* XIX 130); and Charles II of Naples is associated with him, when Dante says that Sicily weeps because they are alive (*Par.* XX 62), while the same Charles is blamed for selling his daughter (*Purg.* XX 80). If the fathers were no worse than feeble and indolent, the sons are vicious and bring disaster by their evil behaviour.

For this state of affairs Dante offers an explanation. It is, he makes Sordello say, usual for families to get worse as they continue :

> Rade volte risurge per li rami
> L'umana probitate : e questo vuole
> Quei che la dà, perchè da lui si chiami.
>
> (*Purg.* VII 121-3)

. . .

> Full seldom human virtue rises through
> The branches; and the Giver wills it so,
> That they to him for such a gift may sue.
>
> (Binyon)

In the *Paradiso* Dante reverts to the question of heredity and comes to a somewhat different conclusion, when Charles Martel explains that the fault lies rather with the assigning of tasks to men who are not naturally fitted for them :

> Ma voi torcete alla religione
> Tal che fia nato a cignersi la spada,
> E fate re di tal ch'è da sermone;
>
> Onde la traccia vostra è fuor di strada.
>
> *(Par.* VIII 145-8)

.   .   .

> But ye perversely in religion place
> Him born to gird the sword upon his side,
> And make him king who should a pulpit grace;
>
> Wherefore from the right road ye wander wide.
>
> (Binyon)

An age which had known both Boniface VIII and Henry III might well grant the truth of these words, and they are probably nearer to Dante's own final conclusion than the doctrine of natural decline which he gives to Sordello in the *Purgatorio*. Indeed this doctrine may well have been given to Sordello because it suits the outlook of one who says that Louis IX and Ferdinand III are weaker than their mothers and indeed implies that all his kings and princes are worse than their forefathers, whose lands they are too feeble to hold. The theory of degeneration suits Sordello's critical temper and is aptly attributed to him. If later Dante passes beyond it, that is only another sign that Sordello's views were much to his taste, but, with his usual gift for improving upon the lessons of his masters, Dante altered this theory and adapted it to another, more comprehensive view of history.

VII

SONGS OF DANCE AND CARNIVAL

IN THE latter part of the fifteenth century the highest honours in
Italian poetry fall to the writers of chivalrous epic, and though at
intervals story-tellers like Boiardo were driven by the urgency of
their passions or fancies into irresistible song, it was incidental,
if not accidental, to their main achievement. Many poets seem to
have found it difficult to escape from the manner so masterfully
imposed by Petrarch or to find any new thing to say or new way to
say it. Though among the people song continued its lively career,
in cultivated circles it seemed for the most part to have come to a
dead end. But at Florence circumstances and personalities combined to foster not indeed a new movement in lyrical poetry, but a
revival of old forms with a new curiosity and a new intention.
Though both Lorenzo de' Medici (1449-92) and Angelo Poliziano
(1454-94) may have felt that their gifts were best displayed in the
stately measures of *rime* and *stanze,* they also experimented with
something different which is no less characteristic of their age and
throws a revealing light on their tastes and talents. Their *canzoni a
ballo* and *canti carnascialeschi* are far removed from the vast,
crowded panoramas of chivalrous romance, but pursue in their
narrow limits a distinctive way of life. These two men, in whom a
passion for the Greek and Latin classics might have been expected
to stifle an appreciation of vulgar, vernacular poetry, found in it a
new source of strength, and with a notable dexterity turned its forms
to their own ends.

The *canzone a ballo,* as Lorenzo and Poliziano wrote it, is an
extension in a special direction of the *ballata,* which is itself
an ancient, indigenous, and popular form in Mediterranean lands.
In Provence the *balada* was not much taken up by the practitioners
of courtly song, but it had a respectable position, and enough

5

examples of it survive to show that it could be both popular and polished. Such songs as :

> Coindeta sui, si cum n'ai greu cossire,
> Per mon marit, quar ne·l voil ne·l desire,[1]

> .   .   .

> Lovely am I, and yet is grief my lot;
> My husband I desire not, and love not,

or

> Mort m'an li semblan que ma dona·m fai
> E li seu bel oil amores e gai,[2]

> .   .   .

> My lady's glances take my life away,
> And her fine eyes, so amorous and gay,

are certainly accomplished, but they are derived from a humble dance-song which had already a long history when they were written. Behind the Provençal *balada* and the Italian *ballata* lies an ancient form, in which a theme is first stated at the beginning and then stated again at intervals while variations are made on it. It was something of this kind which a Moorish poet called Mocádem, from Cabra near Cordova, is more likely to have discovered than invented about A.D. 900, when he composed the form called *zéjel* (*zekhel*) and brought into it words from the Romance language of his day.[3] The form survived and in due course caught the notice of cultivated poets in Latin countries. The *ballata* is the Italian version of it.

In the *ballata* the theme is stated at the beginning; then variations on it are given in the succeeding stanzas, after each of which it reappears. The reason for this lies in the circumstances of performance, on which we are well informed by a Latin poem of Giovanni del Virgilio, who describes what took place at Bologna on St John the Baptist's Day.[4] Men and women were drawn up in separate ranks, and then joined together in a dance. The soloist, whose task was to speak in the general character of the lover, sang a *recantus* or refrain, in which he struck the dominating note of the occasion and summoned Cupid to hear the entreaties of the

---

[1] A. Berry, *Florilège des Troubadours*, p. 6.
[2] Idem, p. 10.
[3] G. Brenan, *The Literature of the Spanish People*, pp. 26 ff.
[4] G. Bertoni, *Il Duecento*, pp. 206-7.

participants. The refrain was repeated by the whole company; then the soloist sang the first stanza, which was of unfulfilled love, and after it the company repeated the refrain. This happened at least twice more, and while the stanzas developed the theme, the refrain remained constant, and with its final appearance the song and the dance came to an end. This is the essential *ballata,* a combination of words and music and dance, performed in the open air at a popular festival and well suited to the amorous associations of Midsummer Day.

The *ballata* seems to have meant nothing to the poets of the *magna curia* of Frederick II, perhaps because it was too popular to suit their exalted ideas of courtly song, but in northern Italy it caught the fancy of poets before Lorenzo and Poliziano and especially of the masters of the *dolce stil nuovo.* Here was a song traditionally associated with love, cast in a neat and well-balanced shape, capable of transformation into something refined and sweet and gay. Guido Cavalcanti, Cino da Pistoia, and Lapo Gianni all made use of it, and Dante himself wrote at least six *ballate* and displays a delightfully happy touch in *Per una ghirlandetta.* Though any of these songs could have been performed in the traditional way, it is doubtful whether they were or whether they were intended to be. They are personal poems, for which a popular form has been chosen for its unaffected grace, rather as the first Minnesingers, like Der von Kurenberg and Dietmar von Aist, wrote love-songs in the old measure of the *trûtliet,* or the early Portuguese poets, who culminated in King Diniz, made brilliant variations on the ancient *cantiga d'amor.* Gifted Italians loosed the *ballata* from its old moorings to move as a work of art in its own right. In doing this they took some liberties with it and tended to vary the standard form. The refrain, which was indispensable to the full and proper performance, was not always repeated completely, but it was often thought enough to repeat its beginning or its end or merely to make the close of each stanza rhyme with the closing word of the refrain. None the less the *ballata* kept some of its essential characteristics as a song which reflected the spirit of a lively occasion and was well suited to any poet who liked to state a theme and then develop it in a graceful and orderly manner.

While the *ballata* was trimmed and polished in this way, it continued to have at the same time a popular vogue in its old shape and to be concerned with love less as an urgent personal necessity than as a natural and sociable pastime. Even so it was not confined to uncultivated songsters or a low level of society. It was popular in the sense that all classes enjoyed it and took part in it. Boccaccio reflects contemporary conditions, when in the *Decameron,* on the tenth day, the king tells Fiammetta to sing a song while the company dances, and her song, *S'amor venisse senza gelosia,* is a *ballata.* Franco Sacchetti (1314-1409), who was born of an old Florentine family at Ragusa and came to Florence in childhood, wrote *ballate* on the traditional model, which keep much of their native vigour and must have been performed much as Giovanni del Virgilio describes. From Sacchetti and his kind, no less than from less sophisticated performers, Lorenzo and Poliziano learned about *ballate* before turning them into *canzoni a ballo.* This popular art was much less restrained and less refined than that of Cavalcanti and his friends. It smacked of the soil and the streets, of bucolic pranks and primitive banter, of pungent ribaldry and unashamed appetites. No doubt Lorenzo and Poliziano were drawn to it just because it was a popular art; for they themselves came from the people and were bred on its songs. Their special achievement was to exploit both kinds of *ballata,* and though they kept them reasonably distinct, they gave to both a fine style and a deliberate elegance. With them the *ballata* resumed its function as a real song intended to be sung to the accompaniment of music and dancing.

This means that the *canzone a ballo,* despite its small scale and limited opportunities, has a certain dramatic element. In its brief compass it acts an episode and is, both in its origin and its development, a secular counterpart to the religious *laude,* which is constructed on a like scheme and uses a refrain for a like purpose. If *laudi* dramatized scenes from Holy Writ, *canzoni a ballo* dramatized scenes from the no less familiar gospel of love-making. Though the one was sacred and the other profane, both tended to use a simple metre with a lively lilt, especially the line of seven (or eight) syllables. This was regarded by Dante as not alien to the 'tragic style', but, perhaps with the Sicilian poets in mind, he felt that *si ad eorum sensum subtiliter intrare velimus, non sine quodam elegiæ umbraculo haec tragoedia processisse videbitur (Vulg. Eloq.,* II, xii, 6). It is just this elegiac quality which makes the line suitable for love-poetry, and that is why the masters of the *canzone a ballo,* fully aware of what they were doing, followed tradition in their attachment to it. Despite its dramatic qualities it remains a song. Just as popular *ballate* were composed for the festivals of the seasons, so these songs were composed, as Poliziano says, to be *carmina festis excipienda choris (Nutricia,* 764-5). Their performance was a festal rite, which had both its own rules and its own liberties. In some sense they offered an escape from reality into a world of make-believe, but only by clothing familiar things with a fantastic air, and they admitted almost any mood from ideal devotion to reckless gaiety or gentle pathos or sardonic satire. Just as the narrative-poems of Pulci

or Boiardo or Ariosto cover an astonishingly varied range of sentiment, so the *canzoni a ballo* are, in their own small way, a lyrical
counterpart to them and delight in a remarkable scope of tone and
temper.

The transformation of the *canzoni a ballo* into the *canti carnascialeschi* was the personal achievement of Lorenzo. In dedicating his
Tutti i Trionfi, Carri, Canti Carnascialeschi to Francesco de' Medici
in 1559 Anton Francesco Grazzini, known as 'Il Lasca', explains
that originally at Florence on the carnival of May Day masked
men used to accost women and sing a traditional song to them,
but Lorenzo changed this by extending the wearing of masks to
the wearing of fancy costumes and by substituting a variety of songs
for the single old song. That he gave serious attention to the change
is clear from his insistence that special music should be composed
for each occasion by *un certo Arrigo Tedesco,* that is Heinrich Isaac,
who was master of music at the chapel of San Giovanni. Lorenzo's
songs confirm this report. Each is composed for a new occasion,
and the classes into which Il Lasca divides them stand for differences
in their manner of performance. In addition to the ordinary songs
of dance and carnival there are the *trionfi,* in which mythological
figures take the chief part, and the *carri,* in which men and women,
dressed as chosen classes of craftsmen and the like, appear on cars
with their appropriate attributes. The simple old song was dignified
by a processional element, and more was made of its possibilities
as a masquerade. It must have kept some of the old formality, but
it was more gay and more stylish. Beneath the costumes and the
make-believe it kept the old spirit which insisted that the spring is
the time for frank declarations of love and for the consideration of
issues which arise from it.

We cannot determine how much Lorenzo and Poliziano learned
from each other in the composition of *canti a ballo,* but it is clear
that they shared a common interest and common aims. They were
united by their love of poetry and their belief that it could gain
fresh strength from the adaptation of popular forms. But their close
association does not hide considerable divergences of temperament
and manner between them. Each flung himself fully into these songs
and revealed much about himself in them, and each fashioned for
them his own style and technique. Lorenzo, the hard-headed statesman and adroit man of affairs, writes with all the robust vigour that
we should expect from his eager appetites and disdain of timorous
inhibitions; Poliziano, the learned scholar and the arbiter of taste,
picks his way daintily as he distils his experience into delicate
shapes and omits anything which is not strictly relevant to his main
point. Lorenzo succeeds through the impetus of his attack and the

irresistible candour of his revelations; Poliziano chooses his words with careful discrimination and is truly classical in the balance and ease and clarity which he gives to them. The two poets complement each other and show what different effects could be secured from a single, rather limited range of themes.

The most prominent, most admired, and most testing theme of this poetry is love. Ever since courtly song burst on the Mediterranean scene at the end of the eleventh century this had been the case, and the common choice was canonized by Dante when he proclaimed love to be the highest of all themes. Lorenzo and Poliziano accepted this without question, no doubt because it appealed to their personal inclinations, could hardly be avoided in a courtly society, and agreed with the practice of popular song. Their conception of love was not indeed as exalted as that of Dante or even of Sordello. They took a more human and less idealistic view of it, but they were no less aware of its claims and fascinations. For them the essence of courtly love is that the lover sets all his hopes on the *gentilezza* of his lady, and this binds him to her in a devotion which absorbs his whole being. This is indeed the spirit of the first Provençal troubadours, of the *magna curia* of Frederick II, of the great Minnesingers, but Lorenzo and Poliziano give it rather a different emphasis. Unlike Arnaut Daniel or Bernart de Ventadour, they are not greatly interested in the cult of love as a moral discipline, in which the lady evokes in her lover all the finest qualities and makes an ideal knight of him. They may take this for granted, but they do not say much about it. Their special concern is with a radiant, life-giving joy, which they find in love and which transforms experience and sets an exhilarating and enthralling enchantment on their every action. Each of them interpreted this in his own way and set the impress of his own temperament on it, but it remains the centre of their poetical theory and their translation of it into practice.

When Lorenzo writes a *canzone a ballo* about love, he throws his whole being into it. The dance becomes a central rite in love-making. He catches its exuberant ardour and makes his words swing in lively response to it. His mood is not relaxation or even pleasure, but a passionate concentration on the enthralling presence or prospect of love. The dance is a ceremony to which only initiates, only those who are really and truly in love, should be admitted :

> Chi non è innamorato
> Esca di questo ballo. (13, 1-2)[1]

. . .

[1] References to Lorenzo are from Lorenzo de' Medici, *Scritti Scelti*, ed. E. Bigi.

> Let him who is no lover
> Forthwith forsake our dances.

The rite calls for a special frame of mind, for emotions directed to a single end and entirely occupied with it, for a devotion in which jealousy has no place and modesty must be displayed not in the false restraint of cowardice but in the true expansiveness of generous intentions. The high sentiments, which in isolation might be a little arid and abstract, are transcended and transformed in joy, and there is none of that defiant disregard of other men which earlier poets like Bertran de Born and Arnaut Daniel pay as an indispensable tribute to the unique supremacy of their love. Each point is made firmly and finely, with emphasis and assurance. Lorenzo is certain that it is right for men to love in this way and wishes the movement of the dance to stir their lurking, shy desires into confidence and action. He himself displays this confidence with all the fervour of his abounding appetites and sets a lead for others to follow.

The joy which Lorenzo seeks through love is all-absorbing and leaves no room for anything else. Because it promises such rewards, the lover is ready to undergo setbacks and delays, knowing that in the end his joy will be all the richer for them. So Lorenzo tells of the magical moment when he finds himself in the presence of a woman whom he suddenly knows that he loves. He, who has lost his heart and not known what has happened to it, discovers that it is she who holds it, and to this his response is overwhelming gratitude :

> Ringraziato sie tu, Amore,
> Ch'io l'ho pure alfin trovato. (11, 3-4)
>
> . . .
>
> To thee, O Love, let thanks be given;
> For I have found my heart at last.

The fancy that the poet's heart has been lost and that, to his unbounded delight, he finds the thief, is in itself charming enough, but it gains in aptness and humanity from the surroundings in which the discovery takes place. The background of the dance, with its gallant company and its eager excitement, emphasizes the unique exultation of the lover and provides the process of which his sudden revelation is the climax.

The theme of gratitude for being in love must have been one which Lorenzo discussed with Poliziano; for Poliziano also makes use of it :

Io ti ringrazio, Amore,
D'ogni pena e tormento,
E son contento omai d'ogni dolore. (7, 1-3)[1]

. . .

For each pain that torments me
Thanks to thee, Love, I offer;
Now all I suffer in my grief contents me.

The main idea is the same, but Poliziano goes his own way with it. While Lorenzo presents sensations and emotions crowding in a crowded scene, Poliziano is wafted by his love to some ideal, almost Platonic paradise. His sufferings have earned him a place in it, and his chief delight is that he can look into the bright eyes of his beloved and know that she is gay, beautiful, and true. While love impels Lorenzo to see the immediate, present scene bathed in a fascinating light, and to find all that he desires in it, Poliziano's imagination flies to another world, where nothing matters but the beauty of his beloved. Lorenzo is busy with questions and hopes and anticipations, but Poliziano's whole being is absorbed in something akin to vision, in which there is no place for anything but celestial joy.

If love provides such moments of flawless felicity, it has also its failures and defeats, without which its victories would be less prized than they are. In the poetry of courtly love the well-worn theme of frustration wears a different look because it is pitched at a lofty level of sentiment and associated with a whole company of abstract notions which concern the worth and the end of life. The sense of deprivation, of undeserved rejection, of hoping against hope, is much more than an occasion for uncontrolled emotions; it makes its victim doubt the validity of much which he has hitherto assumed without question, and feel that he has been fooled and betrayed. He, who has believed love to be an incarnation of *gentilezza* and *cortesia,* now sees what deceit and hardness of heart can lurk in it. Though Lorenzo passed rapidly from one passion to another, there is no need to think that he was not somehow engaged in all. His strong hold on reality saves him from exaggerating his sorrows, and his self-command and self-knowledge give power to his complaints. He attains an impressive dignity when he abandons the seven-syllable line, so well suited to enthralled delight, for the eleven-syllable, whose aptness for grave themes was approved by Dante—*cum tragice poetari conamur, endecasillabum propter quandam excellentiam in contextu vincendi privilegium promeretur (Vulg. Eloq.,* II, xii, 3). All that the dance means to Lorenzo when he is happy

[1] References are to Poliziano, *Rime,* ed. P. Mastri.

forsakes him in his distress, and he writes with a frank and urgent
seriousness :

> Io non credevo al tuo falso sembiante,
> E ben ti conoscevo in altre cose :
> Ma de' begli occhi lo splendor presante
> E le fattezze sì belle e vezzose,
> Fecion che l'alma mia speranza pose
> In tue promesse; e morte n'acquistai. (7, 15-29)

. . .

> I never did believe in your false face,
> I knew you well in every other thing,
> But your fine eyes shone with so bright a grace,
> Your features were so sweet and cozening,
> That to your promises my hopes would cling;
> My soul believed them; and for this I die.

Though the lines were written for a *canzone a ballo,* we accept
them as a personal revelation. Lorenzo faces his failure by analysing
his state and allows himself no excuse. His candour cannot be
denied, and he convinces us that he means every word, that the
lines have been wrung out of him by his frank recognition of his
plight. This is the way in which a man, whose intellect is as strong
as his passions, may take his failure, and there is nothing factitious
or stagy about it.

Poliziano also knows the bitterness of defeat and sees it as a denial
of the best prizes which life has to offer, but he treats it in a different
spirit with a different art. He masters his emotions and turns them
into song, and that is why he keeps the seven-syllable line, which
Lorenzo rejects for such a theme, and through it reveals his unim-
paired confidence in himself and his cause. He asserts his own right
to live and to love, to be himself and not to be treated as the helpless
victim of a heartless rejection. His love has not quite turned to hatred,
but it refuses to be despised without saying something hard in return.
He sets out the situation in deft, everyday words, and short, stabbing
phrases, and at each stage proclaims the force of his resistance :

> Ecco l'ossa, ecco la carne,
> Ecco il core, ecco la vita :
> O crudel, che vuo' tu farne?
> Ecco l'anima smarrita.
> Perché innovi mia ferita,
> E del sangue mio se' ingorda?
> Questa bella aspida sorda
> Chi verrà che me la incanti? (9, 29-36)

' ' '

> Here's the flesh, and here the bone,
> Here's the life, and here the heart :
> What's your purpose, cruel one?
> Here death rends my soul apart.
> Why renew my wound and smart
> Can my blood your frenzy slake?
> Ah, that deaf and lovely snake,
> What a spell she sets on me !

Poliziano's terse, dramatic language sharpens his point and makes it deadly. He had none of Lorenzo's gravity or restraint. If his lady shows no *gentilezza* to him, he shows little to her. With a keen eye for a striking effect, he concentrates on a single mood and makes all he can of its possibilities. He is kept to his task by his acute recognition of his mistress as she really is and of his own feelings about her. It is this distillation of his emotions which keeps his poem at the level of song. The two poets illustrate the different ways in which emotions can be treated in poetry. Lorenzo is still in the grip of them, and their conflict, sincerely and strongly recorded, gives depth and richness to his words; Poliziano has reduced them to a unity which absorbs his whole being and enables him to assert himself and triumph over his disaster by the vigour of his defence.

This difference in poetical manner arose from a difference in temperament, and was accentuated by it. Lorenzo had in him a vein of melancholy, which was not present on the same scale or in the same quality in Poliziano. It is of a kind that comes often to men of robust appetites and bounding vitality, who in the intervals of effort and indulgence are assailed by nagging misgivings that time passes and they are missing their chances. Lorenzo felt this, not indeed as the black annihilation which made Greek poets declare that it is best not to be born, nor with an Elizabethan sweetness which makes despair itself a pleasure. For him it was a conviction reached by active experience and matured by intimate meditation. He saw it not merely as his own private doom but as a curse which dogs the young and beautiful. In his verse he looks about him at beautiful women who behave as if they were unaware of the future and its menaces, and he addresses them not, as Horace would, with ugly forecasts of decaying beauty, but with compassionate understanding :

> Donna, vano è il pensier che mai non crede
> Che venga il tempo della sua vecchiezza,
> E che la giovinezza
> Abbi sempre a star ferma in una tempre.

Vola l'etate e fugge;
Presto di nostra vita manca il fiore :
E però dé' pensar il gentil core
Ch'ogni cosa ne porta il tempo e strugge.

Dunque dé' gentil donna aver merzede
E non di sua bellezza essere altèra :
Perché folle è chi spera
Viver in giovinezza e bella sempre. (2)

. . .

Lady, vain is the thought that dare not say
That with the years old age will surely come,
And youth has no sure home
In which to bide for ever in one stay.

Time's on the wing and flies;
Soon from our life the blossom must depart :
This thought must therefore stir the gentle heart,
That everything is snatched by time and dies.

Let gentle ladies give their thanks for this,
And in their beauty not be arrogant;
Foolish are they who want
Always to live in youth and loveliness.

No doubt Lorenzo implies the lesson that, since this is so, we should
enjoy ourselves while we can, but he does not say so, and his mind
is occupied by this tyrannical, melancholy foreboding. In this mood
he reveals something deeply and firmly rooted in his nature, and
that is why the slow, solemn movement of the lines is admirably
suited to his theme. Elsewhere indeed he has an answer to this
trouble, but here he is concerned with the trouble itself, and his
poem has its own grave and compassionate strength.

Poliziano was no less aware of the brevity of youth, but faced it
in a less troubled, less brooding spirit. To convey the delights of
youth as he saw them he shaped an effective imagery in which a
garden in springtime stands for youth and its opportunities. He sets
out the theme with his usual attention to what is strictly relevant :

I'mi trovai, fanciulle, un bel mattino
Di mezzo maggio in un verde giardino. (3, 1-2)

. . .

On one fine morn, maidens, I found my way
To a green garden in the month of May.

The garden comes from medieval romance and allegory, and in front
of it lie the magical gardens of Ariosto and Tasso, but Poliziano
presents it so simply that we do not think of its literary associations
and accept it without ado as a fit image for the beauty of youth and
the glory of love. He develops its implications neatly and prettily.
In it there are flowers of every kind and colour, and he begins by
picking violets and lilies, only to see that the roses have a sweeter
scent, and he fills his bosom with them. The rose thus gets a more
distinctive character than usual and becomes the image of mature
love, which displaces earlier, less radiant affections. Then Poliziano
advances to his conclusions :

> Quando la rosa ogni sua foglia spande,
> Quando è più bella, quando è più gradita,
> Allora è buona a mettere in ghirlande,
> Prima che sua bellezza sia fuggita :
> Sicché, fanciulle, mentre è più fiorita,
> Cogliam la bella rosa del giardiano. (3, 27-32)

. . .

> For when the rose bursts from her tender sheath,
> When she is sweetest and her grace is spread,
> Then is the time to bind her in your wreath
> Before her glowing loveliness has fled;
> So, maidens, while she lifts her petalled head,
> Gather the garden's glorious rose that day.

Unlike Lorenzo, Poliziano does not mention old age or decay, but
concentrates on the sunlit moment of youth and love. He does not
even mention himself. His appeal is universal, and all the more
persuasive because it is based not on fear but on the unique opportunity of the present. He is concerned not to argue a case, nor even
to unburden his own thoughts, but simply to catch a mood and to
present it without any attraction but its own essential appeal.

In developing the courtly and romantic possibilities of the *canzone
a ballo* Lorenzo and Poliziano followed an aristocratic tradition
which believed in restraint and decorum and impeccable sentiments.
Parallel to this was another tradition with a very different temper.
Since *ballate* were sung at seasonal festivals, they had a strong

popular element of satire, gibes, and lubricious jocosity. Once they
were performed by a 'king' and a 'queen', of whom the first was the
love, the second the beloved. The illusion was maintained by gala
costumes, a crown of flowers on the 'queen's' head and a certain
simple formality in the whole occasion. But the 'king' soon lost what
small dignity he had and became the jealous and hot-tempered
husband, who tried in vain to keep the devotion of his wife the
'queen'. Such songs favoured a primitive licence and were a useful
way of mocking unloved husbands. An early example comes from
Poitou :

> A l'entrada del tens clar, *eya*
> Per joia recomençar, *eya*
> E per jelos irritar, *eya*
> Vol la regina mostrar
> Qu'el' es si amoroza.[1]

> .   .   .

> In the days of cloudless skies, *eya*
> That desire for joy may rise, *eya*
> And give pain to jealous eyes, *eya*
> Then the queen to all men cries
> That in love she's fallen.

The 'king' has become a figure of fun, who is derided and driven
out of the dance as one unfit for love. It is this spirit of ribald and
illicit love-making which lives again in some of the *canzoni a ballo*
of Lorenzo and Poliziano.

It is idle to pretend that in these songs either poet shows
his talents at their best. The question is rather why they wrote them
at all, and what they made of them. With Lorenzo the motive may
well have been partly political, since by such means he was able to
show that he understood the Florentines and shared some of their
less reputable tastes. No doubt Poliziano followed his example because they worked together, but also because he had his seamy
side which found satisfaction in this kind of poetry. Yet both men
may have felt a deeper need than these. Just as Provençal poets,
like Guillaume of Aquitaine, felt at times a need to abandon the
strains and stresses of selfless love for something crude and earthy,
so perhaps the two Florentines needed some violent corrective to
chivalrous devotion, which kept them in a strait-jacket and allowed
almost no deviation from its exacting rules. It must have been a
relief to turn things upside down and to make fun of the love which

[1] Berry, *op. cit.*, p. 18.

they must otherwise treat so seriously. This does not mean that we should attach much importance to these poems, which are only a by-product of their authors' activity. But in them both poets evolved a neat, colloquial style, which can say appalling things in a quiet, modest way. They have an element of low comedy and make something dramatic from such well-worn themes as wives who decry their husbands, or young women who fleece young men, or daughters who put into practice their mothers' all too worldly advice. Yet for the most part these songs fall flat because they lack the true Aristophanic ebullience. Their trouble is not so much that they have aged with time as that they are calculated rather than instinctive and snigger rather than laugh. None the less among them are a few pieces which show their authors in a new light and have a real claim to originality.

Poliziano is most successful when he keeps his humour in a quiet key and turns it into some small and engaging comedy. He wishes, for instance, to tell his audience of ladies that he suffers from something of which he cannot speak, and though we cannot guess what it is, we can admire the parable which sets out his situation :

> Donne mie, voi non sapete
> Ch'i'ho il mal ch'avea quel prete.
>
> Fu un prete (questa è vera)
> Ch'avea morto il porcellino.
> Ben sapete che una sera
> Gliel rubò un contadino,
> Ch'era quivi suo vicino
> (Altri dice suo compare) :
> Pois s'andò a confessare
> E contò del porco al prete.
>
> Il messer se ne voleva
> Pure andare alla ragione :
> Ma pensò che non poteva
> Ché l'avea in confessione.
> Dicea poi tra le persone :
> —Oimè, ch'i'ho un male,
> Ch'io noi posso dire avale—
> Et anch'io ho il mal del prete. (17)

. . .

> Once a priest—'tis really so—
> Killed a little pig to eat,

But at dusk, I'd have you know,
It was stolen by a cheat
Living in a nearby street;
—Others say he knew him well—
Of the pig he went to tell
In confession to the priest.

For this theft the good priest wanted
To resort to legal session,
But from doing it was daunted
Since he heard it in confession.
To his friends he made admission :
'Woe, by what a grief I'm hit;
I can never speak of it !'
I too suffer like the priest.

The skill of this poem lies partly in its tone, with its conversational ease and asides and comments, in which the situation is first set out with a flat and factual verisimilitude, and then made to reveal its inherent absurdity. The theme, reminiscent of Boccaccio, is economically and neatly handled. Priests were a legitimate subject for fun of this kind, and Poliziano laughs at himself when he compares his position with that of the frustrated confessor.

Priests are one thing, but the rites and ceremonies of the Church are another, and it is surprising to find Lorenzo using them as imagery for the cult of love. Something may be due to an ancient kinship between *canzoni a ballo* and ecclesiastical *laudi*. The original mime, from which both arose, must have been crude and primitive, and it is understandable that the secular arm should borrow themes from the sacred, but we should hardly expect this to be done so audaciously as Lorenzo does it. In one poem of his we almost feel that we are in the presence of some disciple of Baudelaire, who deliberately perverts the language of religion to the purposes of profane love. Lorenzo begins by stating his topic :

> Donne e fanciulle, io mi fo coscienza
> D'ogni mio fallo, e vo' far penitenza. (15, 1-2)
>
> . . .
>
> Ladies and maids, myself I pass my sentence
> On all my faults, and for them make repentance.

One of the most solemn rites of the Christian religion is turned to an unashamedly secular end. For Lorenzo then proceeds to enumerate his faults in love and models his manner closely on that of the

confessional as he speaks of his *peccati* and reaches his conclusion
in the language of contrition :

> Dico 'mia colpa', ed ho molto dolore
> Di viltà, negligenzia, e d'ogni errore :
> Ricordi o non ricordi, innanzi Amore
> Generalmente io mi fo coscienza. (15, 27-30)
>
> . . .
>
> I say the fault is mine; my grief is great
> For vileness and neglect and error's state;
> Remembering or not, with Love I wait,
> And for my every fault I make repentance.

The manner is that of Lorenzo's own *laudi,* and behind it lies a
long tradition of religious poetry which uses just this metre and
this language and whose early exponents would indeed have been
startled to see them put to such a purpose.

Yet after all there is nothing very surprising in a man of the
Quattrocento using the language of Christian devotion for illicit
love. It is the logical conclusion of the process which began in Provence when the idealized mistress was regarded as the source of all
virtue and worshipped with self-abasing devotion. Christian mythology provided symbols for most conditions and occasions and was
so inextricably mingled with men's habits of thought that they
would not always stop to ask whether it was appropriate or permissible. If it could be applied to one kind of love, it was easy and
not entirely unreasonable to apply it to another, especially if this
evoked its own reverence and imposed its own obligations. Lorenzo
approaches his faults in love with what looks like real contrition and
we must take him at his word. His poem is certainly not a blasphe-
mous parody. Its significance is rather that he feels his faults as a
lover to resemble his faults as a Christian and to call for the same
kind of treatment. The cult of love, as he knew it, exacted humility
and self-effacement and imposed a special state of mind. This was
in fact at war with some fundamental tenets of the Christian ethic,
but it was not so obviously at war with much of Christian feeling.
In this spirit Lorenzo feels that he must make confession of his faults,
and hopes that he will be forgiven for them.

Though the *canzone a ballo* encouraged its exponents to explore
the purlieus and even the slums of contemporary sentiment, it also
called for something gayer and brighter which appealed to the
Florentine love of visible show and splendour. That no doubt is
why Lorenzo elaborated the *canzone a ballo* into the *canto
carnascialesche.* It had always had an element of masquerade, and

when he accentuated this, he gave it new opportunities and extended
its range. The vivid costumes caught the eye and became inspiriting
incentives to love-making. Songs of carnival may begin by pretend-
ing that they are concerned with some condition or calling, but it
is soon clear that their chief concern is with love. Beggars have been
reduced by it to their present state; pilgrims have taken to solitude
because failure in love has made human society unendurable; mule-
teers are interested solely in their female patrons. The songs of carnival
were the progeny of the songs of dance and added a new spice by
making their occasions look more promising and more adventurous.

The most resplendent of the songs of carnival were the *trionfi*,
composed to present not trades or callings or classes, but popular
fables or classical myths, which embodied some theme of love.
Lorenzo's *Canzone delle Cicale* consists of a *contrasto* or debate
between girls and 'cicadas', who no doubt because of their unceasing
noise stand for the tittle-tattlers and gossip-mongers who spy upon
lovers and make their life a misery. The theme goes back to the
beginnings of Provençal song, where the *lausengiers* are stock
characters, who, from meanness and malice, work against lovers.
Lorenzo makes something fresh of them by allowing them to state
their own case. The girls attack them, and the *cicale* put up a good
defence by arguing that it is their nature to behave as they do, but
at least they give the girls a chance, when they tell them that their
best policy is simply not to be found out. Thus gives a more laugh-
able and less contemptible role to the shabby figure of the sneak.
The choice offered to the girls is not between love and virtue, but
between indiscretion and discretion. Even so they cannot submit.
They refuse to be secretive, since it is against their characters and
their principles. So they defy their critics and do not care what price
they have to pay :

> Or che val nostra bellezza,
> Se si perde per parole?
> Viva amore e gentilezza !
> Muoia invidia e a chi ben duole !
> Dica pur chi mal dir vuole,
> Noi faremo e voi direte. (3, 27-32)

> What's the worth of all our beauty,
> If words spoken can destroy it?
> Long live love and gentle duty !
> Death to hate, if good annoy it !
> Let them slander who enjoy it;
> We shall act, and you will chatter.

The girls are not frightened by the *cicale,* but act in the best traditions of *gentilezza,* which, being dedicated to the service of love, refuses to betray its ideals.

If this poem dramatizes a social aspect of love-making, another poem reveals its need for some kind of philosophy to counter Christian disapproval. In this Lorenzo presents as his characters the seven planets, and appeals to the taste for astrology which has obsessed many minds ever since it came from the East to Greece soon after 200 B.C. Lorenzo's planets begin, in the best classical manner, by proclaiming their power, for good and for ill, over human beings, animals, plants, and even stones. In the second stanza the range of their dominion is deftly and rapidly suggested, and Lorenzo enumerates some main types of human beings as astrologers classified them. So far he follows tradition. But at this point the poet of love asserts himself, and he turns his special attention to Venus, who is for him by far the most important of the planets and receives a notable tribute in the three remaining stanzas. Young men and women are summoned to forget their melancholy thoughts and follow her. The other planets are not even named but lumped together as the source of troubles and trials. It is wiser to follow Venus while we can. Part of the charm of the poem is that the weapons of astrology are turned against itself. Instead of a mechanistic system beyond human control we are presented with a field of choice in which the wise will certainly make the right decision. Venus becomes, if not a divine, at least a superhuman and supernatural power, and her cult receives the kind of authority that generations have given to the stars and their influences.

Poliziano did not, so far as we know, write songs of carnival in the strict sense, but in the *Favola di Orfeo,* which he composed for dramatic performance in 1479, when he was the guest of the Gonzagas at Mantua, he included a song which is very like a *trionfo.* It is the song of the Maenads with which the *Favola* ends, and it resembles a *trionfo* in its form, its reckless spirit, and its dramatic action. That Poliziano should end an unusually painful and tragic story with an uproarious song is indeed remarkable. Perhaps he felt that his episodes were so painful that they deserved a cheerful ending; perhaps after all he did not care very much for the poignant story and was determined to introduce something that he really liked. Whatever his motives, Poliziano gives a surprising turn to the story of Orpheus, which is abandoned and forgotten in a lively song on the powers of Bacchus. No Greek or Roman Maenads are dominated to this degree by wine. The Bacchants of Euripides have indeed their exultant and reckless songs, but their first concern is with the worship of their god. Poliziano, with his usual instinct for selection, goes for a single theme and makes the most of it.

The song reveals its excited character at the start :

> Ciascun segua, o Bacco, te :
> Bacco, Bacco, oè, oè !

. . .

> Bacchus, all must follow thee !
> Bacchus, Bacchus Hey ! Ohey !

As they sing the Maenads become progressively more drunken. The song is indeed a drinking-song, and during it the wine is passed round and the cups are filled. But it differs from most drinking-songs in being both exuberant and elegant. Too many of such songs are either shapeless and frothy or pompous and self-justifying. Poliziano writes an essential and ideal drinking-song—just what such a song ought to be, if it is also to be authentic poetry. At the end of it the Maenads are on the brink of collapse :

> Ognun gridi : Bacco ! Bacco !
> E pur cacci del vin giù :
> Poi col suoni farem fiacco.
> Bevi tu, e tu, e tu.
> Io non posso ballar più.
> Ognun gridi : eù, oè !
> Ciascun segua, o Bacco, te :
> Bacco, Bacco, eù, oè !

. . .

> Calling, calling 'Bacchus ! Bacchus !'
> Fill the cups with wine anew,
> Till we fall and sleep attack us,
> Drinking you, and you, and you !
> Everyone cry out 'Ohey !'
> Bacchus, all must follow thee :
> Bacchus, Bacchus ! Hey ! Ohey !

Poliziano embodies the Dionysiac spirit in its most elemental, most intelligible form. The art of the *trionfo,* transferred to the stage and given a new freedom of action and expression, enables him to transmute a common experience into brilliant art.

Poliziano gained in strength by detaching himself from the immediate scene and letting his imagination play in an independent world of poetry. He needed this distance to set his faculties to work, and when he had found it, he achieved an unusual distinction of style and manner. Always a lover of the vivid, precise word, he was able to make the best use of it when he was not disturbed by personal considerations and immediate needs. His masterpiece is perhaps the song which he composed for May Day, when the jousters entered the lists and, before competing, crowned their ladies with garlands. It is a song of spring and love and akin to a *canzone a ballo* in its spirit and its art. It concentrates on the inner meaning and the essential character of a resplendent occasion. Behind it lie many songs of spring, and with these it has something in common when it summons to love as an awakening of earth and all its creatures. But it also reflects a chivalrous festival, when gallants exert their manhood for the ladies whom they adore. In Poliziano's skilful art the two occasions become one, and the season of spring is inextricably that of glittering gallantry. Love is displayed through masculine feats of prowess, and all moves from a single centre. The song begins with a proclamation and a challenge :

> Ben venga Maggio,
> E'l gonfalon selvaggio !
>
> .   .   .
>
> Gladly let May come on,
> And her wild gonfalon.

Each stanza catches something new in the stirring of life in hearts and thews, in nature and in man. Poliziano convinces us that in the ceremonies of May Day the flowers and birds are not a background but part of the whole delighted ritual. The poem is true to its age in its high-pitched passions and its proud endeavours, its sense of supernatural powers present and at work, its formal elegance and its bursting, unflagging gaiety. In it Poliziano achieves his own kind of pure poetry, in which he makes everything contribute to an enthralling joy. This is his most special gift, and in its exercise he shows how, from his firm idea of what poetry is, he is able to distil some of its essential qualities and to see that every word contains them in as undiluted a purity as possible.

If this song shows Poliziano's powers at their fullest and best, Lorenzo's may be seen in the *trionfo* of Bacchus and Ariadne. In it he is most himself because he is inspired by powerful emotions and uses all his dramatic skill to give a lively and concrete form to them. The figures of Bacchus and Ariadne might have been used for an occasion of unclouded delight, but Lorenzo uses them to shape his own anxieties about the fleeting character of youth and the uncertainty of tomorrow. The unforgettable theme sets the tone at the start :

> Quant' è bella giovinezza,
> Che si fugge tuttavia !
> Chi vuol esser lieto, sia :
> Di doman non c'è certezza. (1, 1-4)

. . .

> Ah, how youth is beautiful,
> But it always runs away !
> Who so wills, let him be gay :
> Of to-morrow who can tell?

In the pageant that follows the allegorical figures are chosen with a keen eye for their relevance to the main theme. Bacchus and Ariadne may typify love at an almost celestial level, but even with them we suspect a faint hint that their love soon comes to an end. The Nymphs and Satyrs, creatures of nature and animal appetites, stand almost in antithesis to the leading figures and present love as something easy and irresponsible and not very serious. Then Lorenzo unexpectedly introduces Silenus and Midas, and with them presents contrasting ideas. While Silenus is an example of self-indulgent age, which still remains able to keep the happiness of youth, Midas wastes his years in a pursuit which does him no good and brings him no pleasure. As we look on these figures, we understand what it means to love in the present :

> Ciascun apra ben gli orecchi :
> Di doman nessun si paschi;
> Oggi sian, giovani e vecchi,
> Lieti ognun, femmine e maschi;
> Ogni tristo pensier caschi :
> Facciam festa tuttavia.
> Chi vuol esser lieto, sia :
> Di doman non c'è certezza. (1, 45-52)

. . .

> Listen well to what you're told,
> Care not what the dawn may bring.
> Everyone, both young and old,
> Men and women, laugh and sing,

Sorry thoughts abandoning.
All the time keep holiday;
Who so wills, let him be gay;
Of to-morrow who can tell?

This is close to the spirit in which the Greeks spent their happiest moments. Well aware of the limitations of mortality, they none the less believed that at certain times they partook of a celestial felicity and almost resembled the gods, that just because such moments are rare and life is fleeting, they must be all the more enjoyed while they last. Lorenzo is concerned with this, but his concentration on the moment is a little more deliberate and more conscious than that of the Greeks. His gaiety is achieved almost by an effort of will, by shutting his eyes to what lies before him, by flinging all his zest for pleasure into the immediate occasion. The poem gains from a hint of melancholy in the background, and shows Lorenzo as he really was when he turned his full attention to the delights that meant so much to him.

The songs of dance and carnival form but a small part of the complete works of Lorenzo and Poliziano, and they are not the most important part of them. Yet the best among these songs show their authors at their finest, and even the more mediocre have some interest for the historian of manners. They display that union of the medieval and the classical which was characteristic of the *Quattrocento* and accounts for much that is most attractive in it. The *ballata* and its progeny are indeed medieval not merely in their origin but in their special kind of formality. Greek choral odes have an elaborate and impressive formality, which is similarly due to the demands of accompaniment in music and dancing, but they are far freer to develop their themes. The *ballata* is limited to almost a single theme, and its task is to make variations on it rather than to move boldly into uncharted regions. On the other hand these pieces have a quality which is not to be found in the masters of medieval song and is certainly derived from classical examples. They have a new brevity and concentration, a gift for going straight to the point without preliminaries and asides, a feeling for the precise worth of words, a love of clear outline and striking effects. The medieval form is used to embody a classical temper, and the result is something new in Europe.

Just because love is an indispensable theme and has its own ritual and ceremonies, it creates in its adepts a dual system of thinking for which there is no parallel in Greece or Rome. Neither Lorenzo nor Poliziano shows in his poetry a unified personality. They accept eagerly the challenges of experience, and respond with all the ardour of their natures, but we do not feel with them, as we feel with Greek and Roman poets, that all moves from a single centre. Their inconsistencies may have been increased by the impact of the new learning on a traditional Christian outlook, but they were already inherent in the insoluble contradictions of courtly love. On the other hand their classical training gives a new depth to established notions of this love by stressing that, since all things are transitory, they must for this very reason be sought and enjoyed. This cleared and tidied the poets' minds and made them ask more purposively what their tastes and desires meant. Though in many ways they are the loyal heirs of a medieval tradition and maintain it with a sincere attachment, they bring to it a more inquiring and more searching spirit, a more discriminating and more intellectual art.

VIII

THE SIMPLICITY OF RACINE

[The Zaharoff Lecture, Oxford, 1956]

VERY FEW poets have fashioned a world which is at once so rich
and so strictly circumscribed as that of Racine. To us, who inevitably
judge most poetry by Shakespeare, he seems to come from another
order of being. Instead of bursting luxuriance, we find trimness
and formality; instead of experiment and innovation, the intensive
exploitation of a selected range of effects. Each poet had some fifty
years of dramatic art behind him, and each followed the main lines
marked out by his predecessors, but whereas Shakespeare continued
to the end extending the capacities of drama by exploring new territory, Racine narrowed them and confined himself to what he
believed to be its essential task. In his wish to surpass Corneille he
eliminated much to which Corneille owed his chief renown—his
heroic and chivalrous elements, his resonant maxims, his majestic
irrelevances, his moral disquisitions, his stage effects. Racine asked
himself what tragedy ought to be, and came to a firm answer, which
he followed from *Andromaque* to *Phèdre*. With unrelaxed determination he admitted nothing which did not agree with it. In the
desire to conform, which lay so deep in his nature, he obeyed the
main precepts of Aristotle with a piety beyond the emulation of
his contemporaries or the precedent of the Attic tragedians.

Though Racine owed his profound knowledge of human nature
to his observation of his contemporaries and especially of those
whom he saw at the court of Louis XIV, where a high style
and irreproachable manners were often a mask for formidable passions and unscrupulous ambitions, he did not copy them directly but
used them as material for his own realm of the imagination, in which
the fundamental workings of human nature could be displayed with
a special clarity and emphasis. The classic idea of tragedy, as it was
understood in his time, provided him with a ritual whose ceremonial

demands he observed with affectionate fidelity. The very strictness of the form appealed to his love of order and satisfied his desire to make every detail play an indispensable part in the main design, while the obligation to transpose his experience into distant spheres enabled him to maintain a majestic tone beyond the indignity of contemporary fashions and controversies. With this powerful convention behind him, he could create characters and situations which were at once particular and universal, and, by stirring many familiar chords in his audiences, force them to look on fundamental matters with a refreshed and sharpened vision. Just as the Greeks found the material for tragedy in a dateless, heroic past and were able through this to give a peculiarly vivid form to the problems which beset them, so Racine used the limitations of his art to isolate his subjects and make them more cogent and more impressive than if he had dramatized his own familiar world or made concessions to mere modernity. In selecting what he thought to be most dramatic in humanity Racine was able to do full justice to it by fitting it into a strict frame which allowed nothing but the most essential issues to be presented on the stage.

In this spirit Racine not only accepted the unities of time, place, and action but applied them rigorously to his tragedies and made them serve his central purpose. All his scenes are set indoors, in palaces which may be in Greece or Rome or Constantinople, but are equally indefinite and uncharacterized, differentiated by almost no suggestion of local colour or specific decoration. They hardly need any scenery on the stage, and too much of it spoils their authentic effect. Racine places his action at some distance from ordinary life on the principle that it adds reverence to the view.[1] If he usually secures this by choosing themes from remote ages like heroic Greece and imperial Rome, in *Bajazet* he makes a comparatively modern subject no less remote by setting it in the alien world of the seraglio at Constantinople. He does not need to vary the scenes of a play, since they are of no importance in comparison with what is said in them. What matters is that the dramatic action should be as concentrated as possible, and with this any change of scene would interfere. It means that most of Racine's catastrophes take place off the stage and are reported by witnesses. When Atalide kills herself before our eyes, it is but another tribute to the precarious and brutal conditions of Turkish life. It is more characteristic of Racine that he does not

---

[1] 'Les personnages tragiques doivent être regardés d'un autre œil que nous ne regardons d'ordinaire les personnages que nous avons vus de si près. On peut dire que le respect que l'on a pour les héros augmente à mesure qu'ils s'éloignent de nous: *major a longinquo reverentia*.' (*Bajazet*: Préface.)

follow Euripides in bringing the dying Hippolyte back on the stage and that Phèdre has already taken poison before she returns to speak her last words. He uses the unity of place to enforce his conviction that the first task of tragedy lies in its words, that these are more important even than its actions, since they reveal what happens in the hearts of his characters and should be hampered as little as possible.

The conditions of dramatic performance also forced Racine to observe the unity of time. Because he was compelled to confine a whole drama to less than two hours, he could not afford to waste precious moments on preliminaries and diversions. Everything must be relevant to a single end, and that means that he begins a tragedy with the sustained crisis which is its subject. In his opening words he always strikes a note of tension or alarm or anxiety, which shows his characters in the grip of their fatal obsessions, whether it is Agrippine fuming at her son's neglect of her, or Antiochus steeled at last to break with Bérénice, or Xipharès confessing his long-concealed love for Monime, or Agamemnon tortured by the oracle which tells him to sacrifice his daughter. Racine increases the emotional pressure as he proceeds, but it is already in strong blast when he begins. His plots are not unfolded with a Shakespearian elaboration but consist almost entirely of a single complex of events which sweeps all to the fatal end. The convention that the plot must be confined to one day suits this art, which deals only with the last stage of a process, when all the different stresses and conflicts come together in a crash of passion and doom. None of Racine's plots would gain from being spread beyond the conventional day, and indeed the shortness of time implied by his intervals is necessary to the breathless movement of his action, in which events crowd on each other in the relentless hurry of a crisis reeling to catastrophe.

The unities of time and place are demanded by the unity of action, and to no aspect of his art does Racine devote more vigilant care. In all his tragedies he makes every word and every situation relevant to a central theme, and this is always the relations between the members of a small group of human beings, who, by changing their positions with regard to one another, break the precarious balance on which they live, and precipitate disaster. The pattern of these relations is different in each play, from the complex movements of the quartet in *Andromaque,* each of whom is in love with someone who loves someone else, to the predominance in *Phèdre* of a single woman who drags everyone with her in her own ruin. Behind the leading figures are the confidants, whose main task is to draw out their patrons and to complete their interior monologues by apt suggestions, questions, and criticisms, and who act as mirrors to reveal what forces lie in wait to inflame and destroy. Only exceptionally do they have, like Narcisse and Oenone, an active part, and even then they are extensions of the chief characters, reflections of their desperate desires and instruments of their unconscious purposes. Racine conforms with exemplary fidelity to Aristotle's definition of the unity of action as

> a complete whole, with the parts of its action so closely connected that the transposal or removal of any one of them will alter and dislocate the whole. (*Poet.* 1451ª32.)

Racine secures this unity not only by making each situation rise with relentless necessity from what precedes it, but by basing the whole development of his plots on the personalities of those who take part in them. The march of events, which has so predestined an air, is determined entirely by the behaviour of human beings, who in obeying the commands of their imperious natures, come into conflict with one another and create havoc and disaster. Racine never allows any irrelevance, however alluring, to turn his eyes away from the plot.

This consummate art embodies Racine's highly individual vision of existence, his selection from experience and his transformation of it into a coherent and impressive form. In his own critical comments no word appears more often than 'simplicité', and though, by misinterpreting it, we can convict him of failure in something which he did not attempt, it stands for what is most characteristic and distinctive in his work. The simplicity which he seeks and attains is certainly not artless or unsophisticated or merely instinctive. Everything is carefully weighed and calculated; nothing is left to chance. Racine's simplicity is a form of simplification, in which he omits much that might seem relevant to us but does not seem relevant to him. He concentrates on what he considers to be the most forceful and most assertive element in humanity—the passions. These provide him with the driving power of all his plots and are set to work in the most dramatic and most economical way. If he simplifies, it is because he sees that the passions are responsible for all that is most exciting in human existence and form an incomparable basis for a convincing, lifelike art, for that 'vraisemblance' which he values almost as much as 'simplicité'. Few other dramatists see tragedy quite in this way or work with so firm and undeviating an idea of what it ought to be.

In his desire for this kind of simplicity Racine avoids much that we might expect to find in the presentation of societies far from his own. He was blamed for not making *Bajazet* sufficiently Turkish,[1] and he certainly had no love for the picturesque accessories which delighted Corneille. But he was not totally blind to some relevant aspects of historical or geographical atmosphere and gives alike to his Greeks, his Romans, and his Turks characteristics which are undeniably their own and almost peculiar to them. But he does this because it is indispensable to his plot. The sacrifice of Iphigénie, the reasons of state which impel Titus to reject Bérénice, the 'grande tuerie' which startled Madame de Sévigné in *Bajazet* arise inevitably from the worlds to which they belong. But Racine knew that any generous indulgence in local colour would spoil his most important effects. Having set his events in a separate sphere of the imagination, he could not break their isolation by adding details which would detract from its austere distinction. He had to keep the distance between his characters and the common scene, because otherwise he would not be able to display them in their authentic, unconcealed humanity. To make too much of their Greek or Roman background would be in some sense to dress them up, to give them delusive disguises, when what mattered was to show them in their all too human selves. Just as he avoided French subjects because they would inevitably suggest contemporary references which would interfere with his selective and concentrated art, so in his treatment of ancient or alien societies he eliminated any details, however attractive in themselves, which were likely to spoil the fundamental simplicity of his tragic vision.

Racine enhances this sense of distance by choosing his characters from kings and queens, their companions and their attendants. In this he not only followed the precedent of Attic tragedy but conformed to social distinctions as they were observed at the court of Louis XIV. But he had better reasons than these. If it is a main duty of tragedy to display how men fall from prosperity to disaster, their fall is the more appalling when they start with all that the world most honours. Such men and women have a detachment which makes them respond with unusual candour to the malice of events. In the closed circles in which they move there is ample room for them to be unrestrainedly themselves, to know one another with a remorseless intimacy, to speak with an unquestioning consciousness of their own superiority, and not to be afraid of unlocking their innermost thoughts. Yet in the midst of their pomp they are isolated

[1] 'Étant une fois près de Corneille sur le théâtre à une représentation de *Bajazet* il me dit: "Je me garderais bien de le dire à d'autres que vous, parce qu'on dirait que je parlerais par jalousie: mais, prenez-y garde, il n'y a pas un seul personnage dans le *Bajazet* qui ait les sentiments qu'il doit avoir et que l'on a à Constantinople; ils ont tous, sous un habit turc, les sentiments qu'on a au milieu de la France."'
(Segrais, quoted by Jules Lemaître, *Jean Racine*, p. 211.)

with the dangerous loneliness of those who are forbidden to mingle with the multitude. They stand exposed and unprotected in the grandeur of their heredity and their station. Because power offers opportunities of indulgence denied to ordinary men, they follow their ambitions and desires with an alarming eagerness and self confidence. In their uncurbed individuality corruption finds a ready prey, and feeds remorselessly on it. Racine's characters are so little broken to discipline that they plunge into the most desperate courses with no care for the consequences and are prevented by self-will, pride, and the voracity of their appetites from abandoning anything that they have begun. Tragedy justifiably deals with these privileged and uninhibited people, because they are free to pursue their own desires and through their exalted position present in sharp outline much that would be blurred in the pressure of common life.

The key to Racine's art is that character is destiny; that, by being what they are, men and women forge their own fates; and for him character means in the first place the passions. It is they which compel decision and action, which smash through the restraints imposed by society, and drive human nature to assert itself in primitive violence. Racine's persons have an extraordinary degree of reality, which is in no sense realistic or even familiar, since this is not the manner in which people ordinarily speak and act, but is none the less impressively real because it embodies something which everybody knows, and which is all the more striking because it has been simplified by discriminating insight and reduced to its indispensable essence. By eliminating all ornament or irrelevance or even idiosyncrasy from his characters Racine gives them an extraordinary degree of life, of convincing personality; for it is through their salient, ruling proclivities that we form our notions of people and think that we know them. This not only makes Racine's characters more 'heroic' in the sense that their motives are less confused and less hesitant that those of ordinary men and women, but also more real, since they have nothing but the authentic self, the irreducible element which remains when everything transitory or local has been removed. Despite all their capacities and their proud air of independence they cannot escape from the central laws of their being. They remain always and ineluctably themselves, and this is their glory, their pathos, and their doom.

Racine knows human nature too well to shape a character to suit a single passion, and prefers to show how one passion, however strong, may so foster others and be so infused by them that a new complex unity arises. Though he presents a whole galaxy of women in love, from the innocent Junie and the less innocent Monime to the furious and tormented Hermione, Roxane, and Phèdre, in none of them is love the only thing that counts. Junie has her tendency to fear the worst and to compromise with circumstances; Monime is not above jealousy and not always happy about the sacrifices which she is prepared to make for her beloved; Hermione is so deeply absorbed in herself that she loses her sense of reality in criminal irresponsibility; Roxane hardly distinguishes between her love of Bajazet and her love of power; Phèdre is racked by a conviction of defeat and guilt. Though Racine's men are notable for pride and ambition, these are countered in Acomat by worldly opportunism, in Mithridate by crafty suspicion, in Agamemnon by a father's affection. In Néron a cold-blooded egoism and a thirst for violent sensation are the more formidable because he conceals them in an accomplished talent for histrionic deceit. Racine disagrees with those moralists of his time who find the mainspring of behaviour in self-interest or self-regard; he knows that human nature is not so easily explained. His assumption is that, though a single passion may seem to be in command, it summons others to its service and reveals the complex unity which is the self.

Racine formed his characters on the psychological insight which his generation learned alike from the court and the confessional and which found such uncompromising exponents as La Rochefoucauld and Pascal. This taught that virtues and vices are more intimately allied than common decency is ready to admit and that nothing in human nature should really surprise us. This means that Racine not only is far more subtle than the Attic tragedians in his analysis of motives and vagaries of character but sometimes admits to tragedy psychological conditions which, but for his art in assimilating them, might seem to be below its dignity. He was fully awake to the paradoxes of behaviour and did not shrink from making them responsible for some of his most dramatic shocks. When Hermione hears from Oreste that, in obedience to her wishes, he has killed Pyrrhus, her immediate and obliterating reaction is contempt and hatred for him :

> Tais-toi, perfide,
> Et n'impute qu'à toi ton lâche parricide.
> Va faire chez tes Grecs admirer ta fureur.
> Va, je la désavoue, et tu me fais horreur.
> Barbare, qu'as tu fait ? Avec quelle furie
> As-tu tranché le cours d'une si belle vie ?

When Roxane, who has offered marriage and power to Bajazet, hears him falter in his acceptance, her whole temper changes to freezing hatred :

> Non, je ne veux plus rien.
> Ne m'importune plus de tes raisons forcées.
> Je vois combien tes vœux sont loin de mes pensées;
> Je ne te presse plus, ingrat, d'y consentir.
> Rentre dans le néant dont je t'ai fait sortir.

When Bérénice, who has denounced Titus for his heartless treatment of her and regarded him as a cowardly and dissembling traitor, sees that after all he acts from motives of the highest honour, she changes her whole outlook and speaks with the tenderest understanding :

> Mon cœur vous est connu, Seigneur, et je puis dire
> Qu'on ne l'a jamais vu soupirer pour l'empire.
> La grandeur des Romains, la pourpre des Césars,
> N'a point, vous le savez, attiré mes regards.
> J'aimais, Seigneur, j'aimais, je voulais être aimée.
> Ce jour, je l'avoûrai, je me suis alarmée;
> J'ai cru que votre amour allait finir son cours.
> Je connais mon erreur, et vous m'aimez toujours.

There is no need to show how these changes of heart and purpose take place; it is enough to display them in their full dramatic impact when they come, and then there is no doubt of their truth.

The quality of Racine's insight can be seen in his characterization of Néron. The plot of *Britannicus* turns on the crisis when the young emperor, who is thought to show promise of being a model ruler, suddenly reveals himself as a murderous monster. Agrippine is at the start aware of the danger, but others, notably Burrhus, are deceived by him. Racine takes a hint from Tacitus, who says that Néron hid his hatreds under deceitful flattery,[1] and shows how a man who is all too ready to deceive others deceives also himself. When Néron first appears, gloating over the abduction of Junie, he says, with apparent fervour, that he is passionately in love with her :

> Depuis un moment, mais pour toute ma vie.
> J'aime (Que dis-je aimer?), j'idolâtre Junie.

But we soon see from his horrible glee in making her suffer that he is moved not by love but by lust for some new and violent sensation. The man, who so lies to himself, lies with practised skill to others. When his mother has made her long appeal to him, he says that he will do all that she asks and speaks in words of affectionate reconciliation :

---

[1] In the Preface to *Britannicus* Racine quotes Tac. *Ann.* xiv. 56: *factus natura velare odium fallacibus blanditiis.*

Oui, Madame, je veux que ma reconnaissance
Désormais dans les cœurs grave votre puissance;
Et je bénis déjà cette heureuse froideur,
Qui de notre amitié va rallumer l'ardeur.

Racine leaves us to guess whether Néron has already decided to defy his mother and is lying to her or for the moment means what he says; and this is just the doubt which we feel with a man who is so corrupted by falsehood that he himself does not always know whether he means what he says or not.

It might be argued that, though Racine is invariably successful with his more violent characters, he is less successful with their victims, whose very innocence entails a certain lack of personality in comparison with the exorbitant passions and merciless claims of their persecutors. If this were true, it would illustrate W. B. Yeats's words that 'passive suffering is not a theme for poetry';[1] and indeed if Racine's victims went unresisting and uncomplaining to their doom, it would be too painful to endure. But he avoids this by giving to them a power of initiative which brings them to life and invests them with a tragic dignity. Andromaque has buried her heart with Hector, but he still lives for her in her son, and, when the boy's life is in peril, she shrinks from no stratagem or sacrifice to save him. Britannicus is only a boy, but, when Néron bullies and threatens him, he answers with a proud, defiant courage. Monime is in an impossible position, when both Mithridate and his two sons are in love with her, and at first she yields to his dominating insistence, but in the end she rejects him, though she knows that it may mean her death. Aricie is almost an unconsidered sacrifice in a general devastation, but she too has her moments of grandeur, when she stands by Hippolyte in his humiliation or defends his innocence to his frenzied father. In building his action on the passions a lesser poet might have found it difficult to arouse interest in these sane and unselfish characters, but Racine relies on more than the pathos of their lot or the contrast between them and their persecutors. By giving them their own pride and distinction he makes them live in their own right and brings them closer to us.

Racine's dramatization of the passions gains a new dimension from the clarity with which his characters speak. It is part of their grand manner, their distance from common men, their refusal to shirk issues or to be anything but themselves. Their lucidity implies a high intelligence and rises from their understanding of themselves and their circumstances. Racine makes great use of this and secures unique results from it. His characters display a searching insight into

[1] *The Oxford Book of Modern Verse*, p. xxxiv.

one another, and this is sharpened by the force of their passions. It is
Agrippine's desire to keep her hold on Néron which reveals to her
his innate savagery; Roxane's love for Bajazet which tells her that,
despite his protestations, he does not love her; Mithridate's self-
centred arrogance which betrays to him the love of Xipharès and
Monime. The passions provoke the discovery of truth because they
sharpen the intelligence on many matters which concern them. In
opposition to La Rochefocauld's maxim that 'l'esprit est toujours la
dupe du cœur', Racine shows how the heart, no matter how agonized
or how rotten, sets the intelligence to work with an increased lucidity
and penetration.

This formidable insight is also applied by the characters to themselves. Even Racine's gentler and less assertive heroines, when they
are called to make some supreme sacrifice, know exactly what it is
and why they make it. When Andromaque sees that the only way to
save her child is for her to marry Pyrrhus, she feels that this is none
the less an act of treachery to her dead husband, and that, once she
has done it, she must atone by killing herself. Faced by a situation
which might call for a dexterous display of casuistry, she follows
the dictates of her nature so scrupulously that she solves all her
problems by a single stroke :

> Mais aussitôt ma main, à moi seule funeste,
> D'une infidèle vie abrégera le reste,
> Et, sauvant ma vertu, rendra ce que je doi
> A Pyrrhus, à mon fils, à mon époux, à moi.

So Junie, terrified of the doom which Néron plots for Britannicus,
thinks not of her own safety, but of what she might have done to
save him. She has tried to warn him by signs, but knows that her efforts
have been fruitless. With courageous candour she blames herself for
not having dissimulated with more confidence and more success.
Though her own fate is sealed with that of Britannicus, she thinks
only of him and of what she might have done to help him. She
makes no mistakes about herself and does not shrink from condemn-
ing her own failure :

> Quel tourment de se taire en voyant ce qu'on aime,
> De l'entendre gémir, de l'affliger soi-même,
> Lorsque par un regard on peut le consoler !
> Mais quels pleurs ce regard aurait-il fait couler !
> Ah ! dans ce souvenir, inquiète, troublée,
> Je ne me sentais pas assez dissimulée.

In Andromaque and Junie affection, so powerful that it deserves the name of passion, enables them to see exactly what they are doing, without any obstruction either from forbidding self-control or from deluding self-pity.

A similar insight is displayed by those who are the prey of more violent and more destructive passions. They have at least no illusions about the nature and the demands of their desires. Agrippine deceives herself neither about the crimes which she has committed to make her son emperor nor about her own lust for glory and power; Agamemnon knows that in the last resort he prefers his own success in war to his love for his daughter; Phèdre sees both how strong and how wrong is her passion for Hippolyte. But this knowledge in no way impedes the course of passion. Racine's characters watch their own progress to destruction with an objectivity which never deserts them and yet can do nothing to save them; which stands apart from their tyrannous obsessions and yet is their helpless captive. We cannot but feel deeply for these men and women who are prevented by their own natures from helping themselves. Their dooms are the more appalling because they are dragged to them in full knowledge of what their actions mean and with a rational sense of responsibility for them. Living in an age which knew what self-examination is, Racine was able to turn it into a new force for tragedy by making his heroes and heroines spectators as well as agents in their own catastrophes.

Yet, though Racine endows his characters with this merciless insight and shows how it rises from the very force of their passions, he also shows how at a certain point it fails them and becomes an instrument in their fall. Though they remain almost clairvoyant in their knowledge of themselves, yet they make errors of judgement which hasten their ruin. They miscalculate the possibility of achieving their desires, and this is due to the violence of their passions, whether it is Oreste, who thinks that Hermione will yield herself to him if he does all that she demands; or Agrippine, that she can bring back Néron to her control by appealing to his affection and gratitude; or Antiochus, that Bérénice will accept his love if Titus rejects her; or Phèdre, that somehow she can seduce Hippolyte. The pathetic paradox of Racine's characters is that, though they know themselves and each other conspicuously well, they misjudge their ends. The very passions, which enable them to see so much with an unsparing clarity, blind them in the one thing which matters most to them; and this brings their ruin. They are so sure of themselves that they do not question their decisions until it is too late and there is no escape from disaster. Their doom is the more poignant because the intellectual penetration which gives them a singular distinction deserts them in their fatal crisis, and it is the cruellest of ironies when they fall through its treachery.

In this we may see Racine's bold and adroit adaptation of Aristotle's doctrine that the fall of tragic heroes should be due to some ἁμαρτία or error.[1] In this Aristotle seems to combine, or confuse, an error of judgement with a fault of character,[2] and this is natural enough in one who thought that right knowledge is an essential element in moral conduct. But he does not make his point very clearly and leaves the impression that a wrong judgement is in itself enough to create a tragic situation. Racine is not content to acquiesce in this uncertainty but consistently makes the fatal miscalculations of his characters rise directly from their passions, and thus builds his catastrophes on a satisfying and convincing scheme, which takes him far indeed from the practice of the Attic tragedians. With them the tragic action turns on the ignorance and the delusions of men, which grow and multiply until at last in the crash of disaster the victims learn that they can know nothing except their utter insignificance before the gods. Racine's characters are fully conscious of what they are doing, and their error is confined to one fatal blindness, but even then they dissect their feelings with unfaltering precision. Racine derives his catastrophes from the whole of a man's being and makes the intelligence almost as important as the passions, whether they sharpen it to see things with a peculiar clarity or delude it to work his ruin.

The notion that character is destiny excludes the play of chance. There are indeed moments when Racine allows coincidence to speed his action, but he does so only within strict limits. We cannot complain that Thésée arrives when he is rumoured to be dead, for it is in full accord with his unpredictable character; nor that Bajazet's love-letter to Atalide is found on her by Roxane's attendants after she has fainted, for it only hastens the revelation of what Roxane already suspects and is bound to know soon. In Racine chance plays an almost negligible part; for otherwise it would undermine his assumption that men act as they do because they are what they are. Though he naturally does not trouble himself with speculations about the freedom of the will, his characters are free in the sense which we usually give to the word: they make their own choices and in so doing act both from their emotions and their intelligence. They are not victims of some celestial savagery like the curse of bloodshed which ravages the House of Atreus or the doom to which the gods condemn Oedipus before he is born. Their faults are not in their stars but in themselves, and this makes it easier for us to participate in their aspirations and their anguish.

[1] *Poet* 1453ᵃ16.   [2] *Nic. Eth.* 1110ᵇ29; 1148ᵃ2.

In his seven tragedies from *Andromaque* to *Phèdre* Racine chooses his matter from societies which are in no respect Christian. Later, when he broke his twelve years' silence with *Esther* and *Athalie*, he forsook his former practice for a kind of drama which reflected a change of outlook both in his patrons and in himself. But *Esther* is in no strict sense a tragedy, and though Athalie herself is a worthy sister and successor of Agrippine and Roxane, the magnificent poem to which she gives her name is in effect a morality which demonstrates the triumph of God and His servants. If in his creative heyday Racine avoided any specifically Christian colouring, it may well have been due to the contemporary taste for classical and heroic subjects,[1] but, whatever the reason for it was, it had an incalculable influence on his art and brought special advantages to it. It meant that, despite his Jansenist education and the correct Catholicism of his patrons, he confined himself to a profane, pagan world, in which the lusts of the flesh and of the spirit determine and dominate the action, and, deeply though the fates of his characters may move us, they do so at a purely human level which rejects such consolations as religion might offer for their wounds. This suits something fundamental in the tragic vision of life, and Racine must surely have seen that the most authentic tragedy is based on a sense of irredeemable waste, of unresolved discords, of chaos at the heart of things, and that to advance any explanation or apology for these is to diminish their truly tragic character. For this reason perhaps he avoided not only any assumption that in the end all must be well but even any hint, such as we sometimes find in Shakespeare, that the ugliest catastrophes may be redeemed by love. Though Racine sometimes evokes pity, it is by no means his only or his chief effect, and with his more formidable characters he does not evoke it at all. In its place he offers sympathy in the sense that we enter into their souls and share their frenzies as if they were our own. What count with him are the intensity of passion and the emotional responses which it awakes. In this he resembles not Sophocles, who suggests that the most horrifying events must be accepted because the gods send them, but Euripides, who lets his catastrophes appeal to us in themselves without offering any solution or comfort, and is for this very reason 'the most tragic of the poets'.[2]

[1] 'C'était l'éducation religieuse en effet, qui avait créé, à côté d'elle, l'éducation classique et païenne. C'était des papes, des moines, les membres des ordres les plus austères, qui avaient fondé et légitimé pour Racine, à côté du monde chrétien, dont tous les héros ne pouvaient être que chrétiens, un monde à héros profanes.' (Jean Giraudoux, *Racine*, pp. 28-29).

[2] In calling Euripides τραγικώτατος τῶν ποιητῶν, Aristotle (*Poet.* 1453ᵃ30) refers to his taste for unhappy endings. But his main difference from Aeschylus and Sophocles is that he lets these endings speak for themselves without comment or explanation.

It is true that in his Greek plays Racine gives some part to the
gods, because he is compelled by his myths to do so. But not even
in *Iphigénie* is this more than a dramatic device for developing the
action. In *Phèdre* it is different, and Racine gives a new depth to
his drama when Phèdre, torn between the claims of life and of death,
shrinks alike from both :

> J'ai pour aïeul le père et le maître des dieux;
> Le ciel, tout l'univers est plein de mes aïeux.
> Où me cacher? Fuyons dans la nuit infernale.
> Mais que dis-je? Mon père y tient l'urne fatale.
> Le sort, dit-on, l'a mise en ses sévères mains;
> Minos juge aux enfers tous les pâles humains.

In this there is no need to see a transformation of Christian ideas into
Greek. Phèdre has good reason to fear the punishments which await
her after death, but these can be found in Tartarus as much as
in any Christian Hell. None the less we must surely feel that here
Racine does more than merely conform to ancient myth, that he
tries to give a new substance to it, that his images of the Sun and
Minos, of the light and the dark, are his way of stressing the implacable dilemma in which Phèdre finds herself. She cannot live, because
in her guilt she shuns the light of day; she cannot die, because she
dares not face what happens after death. Her position is tragically
human and familiar, and in dramatizing it so closely to Greek ideas
Racine displays his mastery of them and his ability to give them a
universal relevance.

In this scene Racine deals with issues of good and evil as Phèdre
sees them, and makes them perfectly consistent with her character
and her situation. If their treatment is more searching and more
revealing than we might expect, that is because he adds a new
domain to his objective art. It is therefore surprising that in his
Preface to *Phèdre* he speaks not as an artist but as a moralist :

> What I can guarantee is that I have done nothing in which
> virtue is set more in the light than in this play. In it the smallest
> faults are severely punished. The mere thought of crime is re-
> garded in it with as much horror as crime itself. In it the weak-
> nesses of love pass for true weaknesses. In it the passions are
> presented to the eye only to show the disorder of which they
> are the cause; and in it vice is painted throughout with the
> colours which make us know and hate its ugliness.

Racine is of course defending himself against the charge of stimu-
lating to vice, and he states his case strongly. Something of what he

says is true. Phèdre herself indeed shows the disorder which the
passions create. But the more we look at these words, the less do they
seem to be true of the play as a whole. Can Racine really mean that
the love of Hippolyte and Aricie is a true weakness rightly punished?
And what of Thésée, with the ruin of whose happiness the play
closes? Does Racine even hint that this is a fit requital for his past
loves and his passion for Phèdre? And even with Phèdre herself, is
it true that we are so impressed by the justice of her end that we see
in her a lesson and a warning? Even if Racine is more concerned
with moral issues than hitherto, he does not present them as a
moralist, still less on some facile theory, worthy of Miss Prism, that
'The good ended happily, and the bad unhappily. That is what
fiction means'. If he does, we cannot even answer with Cecily : 'I
suppose so. But it seems very unfair.'

In fact Racine's tragedies, including *Phèdre,* do not attempt to
prove any such lesson. The sufferings of the characters are by no
means in proportion to their deserts. Néron survives, not perhaps
happily but at least defiantly, his first excursion into murder, and
the innocent, whether Britannicus and Junie, or Bajazet and Atalide,
or Hippolyte and Aricie, are as often ruined as the wicked. If they
are punished for anything, it is for their virtues—Britannicus for
his outspoken resistance to Néron, Atalide for her self-denying
attempt to save Bajazet by yielding him to Roxane, Hippolyte for
his refusal to tell his father of Phèdre's attempt to seduce him. And
what are we to think of *Bérénice,* in which all three of the chief
characters are moved by the noblest motives and rewarded by broken
hearts? Some may perhaps take comfort from Mr T. S. Eliot's
judgement :

> To my mind, Racine's *Bérénice* represents about the summit of
> civilization in tragedy; and it is, in a way, a Christian tragedy,
> with devotion to the state substituted for devotion to divine
> law.[1]

That *Bérénice* is highly civilized nobody will deny, but even if we
admit that in it the state takes the place of divine law—and this is
both difficult in itself and unsupported by any evidence from Racine
—are we to believe that a tragedy is necessarily Christian because in
it the good suffer? Of course we might argue that in making their
several sacrifices Titus, Antiochus, and Bérénice have the consolation of knowing that virtue is its own reward, but, if that is so, it is
strange that Racine should close on a note of undisguised lament
when he makes Bérénice say :

[1] *The Use of Poetry and the Use of Criticism,* p. 41.

Adieu, servons tous trois d'exemple à l'univers
De l'amour la plus tendre et la plus malheureuse
Dont il puisse garder l'histoire douloureuse.

Whatever Racine may have felt about his characters, he did not distribute rewards and punishments among them according to their worth.

Racine indeed is too good a psychologist to divide his characters into two classes on any moralistic plan. He knows that good and evil are to be found inextricably compounded in the same person. Even his more obviously virtuous characters have serious faults. Burrhus may be a plain, blunt soldier, who prides himself on his hatred for any untruth, but he is unduly complacent about his training of Néron. Bajazet is undeniably ardent, courageous, and eager for renown, but there is an element of corruption in the facility with which, after his first failure, he succeeds in persuading Roxane that he returns her love. Moral judgements on Mithridate are perhaps out of place, since he moves in a sphere where what counts is not morality but honour, but on him also our feelings are divided; for while he is savagely jealous, suspicious, and cunning, we cannot but admire his superb self-confidence and his unquenchable spirit. Even Agrippine, who is on her own admission an accomplished criminal and shrinks from nothing to win and keep power, redeems her arrogance by her unsparing confession of her iniquities to her son and her terrible denunciation of him after the murder of Britannicus. If Racine had really wished his plots to demonstrate the triumph of virtue and the discomfiture of vice, he would have discriminated more decisively between them.

Racine's refusal to allow the design of his tragedies to be dictated by obvious considerations of morality is deeper than this. Even when he depicts characters who are by the standards of almost any age lost souls, devoured by ugly passions and reckless self-gratification, he somehow sees them from inside and makes us enter into their inner selves, when they might otherwise horrify and appal us. This is true above all of Phèdre, and no doubt accounts for Racine's own attempt to disown the obvious truth about her. However much we may condemn her in absence or in abstract, yet, when she is present on the stage or in the imagination, we are swept away by the force of her passion and her misery and do not stop to judge her. We do not even feel it necessary to excuse her on the ground that she is the victim of forces beyond her control; for we are too close to her, too tightly caught in her feelings, to think of making excuses or to respond to anything but the overwhelming anguish of her human state. In the end it may perhaps be a comfort that she makes amends by confession and death, but in the long crisis of her passion we do not anticipate or desire this. The same is true of Racine's other *femmes damnées,* of Roxane and Hermione. They may indeed frighten and horrify us, but there is none the less a fierce fascination in their unbridled temperaments, and we cannot but respond to their pride of life and their truth to their own natures. However violent and vicious these women may be, in the uncontrollable attraction and excitement of their imperious presences we do not pass moral judgements on them. So too even Néron, who turns the blood cold by his murderous selfishness, is still undeniably human in his desire to escape from the bonds in which his mother holds him and in his inability to defy her when he is alone with her. We rightly shrink in horror from him, but he is not ultimately alien to something that we know and understand.

If what Racine says in his apology for *Phèdre* is true neither of his other plays nor of *Phèdre* itself, we must try to find what he thought the essential function of tragedy to be, by what means he hoped to solve its disturbing discords and to explain our need for it. He gives a hint in the Preface to *Bérénice* :

> It is sufficient that the action should be great, that the actors should be heroic, that the passions should be aroused, and that everything should be imbued with that majestic sadness in which the whole pleasure of tragedy lies.

In the last words, in which Racine speaks not as a moralist but as as artist who has his own task to perform, he comes near to uncovering his secret. We may supplement them with a story reported by the Abbé de la Porte in his *Anecdotes dramatiques:*

> I have heard Madame de la Fayette relate, said the Abbé de Saint-Pierre, that in a conversation Racine maintained that a good poet could get the greatest crimes excused and even inspire compassion for the criminals. He added that it only requires a fertile, delicate, and discriminating mind to reduce to such an extent the horror of the crimes of Medea or Phaedra as to make them acceptable to the spectators, and even to inspire pity for the criminals.[1]

It is difficult not to believe that there is truth in this, since it amplifies and elucidates what Racine himself says about *Bérénice;* and surely the most important words are 'a good poet'. Racine's contention is that, if the poetry is only good enough, even the most criminal

[1] Quoted by E. Vinaver, *Racine and Poetic Tragedy*, p. 103.

characters can be made sympathetic; and, if it is true, as the Abbé goes on to tell, that Racine wrote *Phèdre* to prove his point, we can judge his preaching by his practice. In other words, Racine trusted above all to his poetry to do what he thought right for tragedy. In the first and the last resort it is the poetry which counts and must be considered in its extraordinary and, for us, unaccustomed quality.

Racine's style has the same kind of simplicity as his dramatic structure and economy of action. It is formed by a resolute discrimination, a merciless rejection of anything which he considers below the proper majesty of his task. His vocabulary consists of no more than two thousands words, which is a tenth of the number in Shakespeare's, and he does not shrink from using the same phrase more than once if it meets a need. His is the antithesis of modern poetry which seeks at all cost to be individual and unusual and delights in unexpected images and unexploited observations. Though Racine admired Homer's gift for introducing the most humble details into poetry, he believed that this was impossible in French, which 'fuit extrêmement de s'abaisser aux particularités' and forbids the mention of 'des choses basses dans un discours sérieux'.[1] He drew a firm line between what is 'sérieux' and what is 'bas', and excluded much that we assume to be at home in poetry of any kind. He has very few metaphors, and some of these are commonplace and conventional. He abounds in abstract words, especially when he deals with personal and even private emotions. He makes little appeal to the visual sense and is shy of mentioning colours.[2] Even his flowers are never described more closely than as 'fleurs'. This exacting self-denial is dictated by his desire to keep his poetry serious; to make it conform to his notion that, if a drama is to have the universal character which is its right, it must be set at some distance from common life; to emphasize the difference of his characters, in the irresistible onslaught of their passions, from the common run of men; to maintain the majestic isolation in which they have their being. Racine's language conforms to his ideal of

---

[1] 'Calypso lui donne encore un vilebrequin et des clous, tant Homère est exact à décrire les moindres particularités: ce qui a bonne grâce dans le grec, au lieu que le latin est beaucoup plus réservé, et ne s'amuse pas à de si petites choses. La langue sans doute est plus stérile, et n'a pas des mots qui expriment si heureusement les choses que la langue grecque; car on dirait qu'il n'y a rien de bas dans le grec, et les plus viles choses y sont noblement exprimées. Il en va de même de notre langue que de la latine; car elle fuit extrêmement de s'abaisser aux particularités, parce que les oreilles sont délicates et ne peuvent souffrir qu'on nomme des choses basses dans un discours sérieux, comme une coignée, une scie, et un vilebrequin.' ('Remarques sur l'Odyssée, *Œuvres complètes*, éd. La Pléiade, ii, pp. 755-6.).

[2] J. G. Cahen, *Le vocabulaire de Racine*, pp. 93 ff.; Jean Pommier, *Aspects de Racine*, pp. 264-5.

simplicity in doing exactly what his dramatic purpose demands. The strength and the limitations of Racine's style lie in his unshakeable refusal to be lyrical. The spirit of song, which dances through Shakespeare and sheds a magic light on even the most obviously mechanical actions, would not only be distasteful to spectators who sharpened their thoughts on prose and expected poetry to share its virtues, but seem to Racine improper in tragedy. For him what matters is that the words should dominate the action, say exactly what it needs, and say no more, since even the smallest exaggeration or irrelevance must distract attention from the central, all-important task. In this he is far more ruthless than his Greek masters, whose words often take wing from the special situation to a larger and freer world which invites to vaster mysteries. Racine has an uncompromising notion of what dramatic speech ought to be, and lives rigorously up to it. Every line that he wrote cries to be spoken aloud and needs, if its full force is to be felt, to be spoken with care for every sound and intonation in it. So far from being monotonous, the flow of his couplets is in its own way as various as that of Virgil's hexameters; so skilfully does he shift his stresses and adjust his sounds. Even when a character speaks more than a hundred lines on end, like Mithridate in forecasting his plans to invade Italy, or Théramène in telling of the death of Hippolyte, the temper changes continually and many different sources of poetry are struck. The glory of this style lies partly in its texture, into which every theme is woven with a consummate feeling for its tone and temper, and partly in its continuity, which sustains the varied sequence of themes in unflagging and unfailing music.

There are moments when Shakespeare, towards the close of a tragic disaster, abandons imagery and makes his characters speak in the plainest of plain words, because any ornament would be untrue to their feelings and plain words alone fit the broken soul in its last agonies. So the dying Antony says to Cleopatra :

> Of many thousand kisses the poor last
> I lay upon thy lips.

So Racine, who begins a tragedy almost at the point at which Shakespeare begins a fourth act, not only shrinks from decoration but maintains his own kind of plainness through the whole length of a play. Though he is a master at varying his tone and making it suit all kinds of occasion, this is, in his view, always the right language for the passions, which are in themselves so personal and compelling that they do not need to be made more particular or to have their quality enriched by imagery. The words must fly straight to the target and hit the central point of emotion. Such an ideal would be unattainable if Racine did not build his plays on the contrast and conflict of many different passions, each of which demands its own kind of poetry. Nor would it be successful if he were not able to find their own appropriate poetry for the whole range of situations which make his plots. In his practised and immediate understanding of humanity nothing eludes him or defeats his capacity to present it in its full appeal. He has a dramatic, passionate poetry not only for all levels of love from the most selfish to the most self-sacrificing, but for almost every other emotion which troubles, inflames, or perverts the hearts of men. Clarified and toughened in his creative genius they come out in their primeval violence and compel our fascinated attention.

It is not enough to say that Racine's style is plain or simple. This it certainly is in its restricted vocabulary and its unfailing lucidity. But it is also supremely calculated in that its simplicity is shaped to a deliberate formality. This is necessary not only to give the right air of distance and majesty but to keep the passions in their place. Without it they would sweep all before them, and the whole discipline of the poetry would be ruined. But this formality takes a special form. It concentrates an extraordinary charge of emotion in a narrow space and makes this the more effective through its firm hold on it. Racine learned from the Greeks that, if the passions are to be displayed successfully, they must not be allowed to rant and rave. But he left his masters behind in imposing a far more rigorous formality, which indeed reflects something central to his being. Because he was himself at once extremely sensitive to the appeal of the passions and determined to master them by understanding them, he needed this stylistic discipline in his poetry to help him to fuse passions and understanding into an indivisible unity, in which each strengthens, completes, and absorbs the other. It is just because the passions with which he deals are so powerful that he curbs them with a highly precise, controlled, and formal language. Unlike Pushkin, who writes with a comparable clarity and simplicity, he does not venture far away from the passions; unlike Virgil, who is no less deeply concerned with them, he insists that everything must be clarified and understood beyond doubt or question. The fusion of the passions and the understanding means that Racine's style is often pointed and always concise and exact. His taut, powerfully charged lines rise from his unified outlook, from turning his whole compassionate attention to the engrossing spectacle of human behaviour.

This poetry is applied not to vague, general situations but to men and women, who are indeed compounded of familiar elements but are unmistakably individuals in their firmly articulated personalities. Racine treats of human nature in its conflicts and confusions, but seizes on the unity of impression which these produce and which has an intimate, personal appeal. His characters speak from their innermost, inalienable selves with an unfailing truth to the heart. They are as independent and self-sufficient as the characters of Homer or Shakespeare, and in none can we see an image of Racine himself or even a projection of his ideas and predilections. They live of their own right in their own passion-stricken world, and the strong light of poetry beats on them as they uncover the springs of their being. So in her reproof of Burrhus Agrippine reveals all that her pride of birth and station means to her :

> Certes, plus je médite, et moins je me figure
> Que vous m'osiez compter pour votre créature,
> Vous dont j'ai pu laisser viellir l'ambition
> Dans les honneurs obscurs de quelque légion,
> Et moi qui sur le trône ai suivi mes ancêtres,
> Moi, fille, femme, soeur et mère de vos maîtres.

So Ériphile describes how, after her first terror and horror of Achille, she sees him in quite a different light :

> Je le vis; son aspect n'avait rien de farouche;
> Je sentis le reproche expirer dans ma bouche.
> Je sentis contre moi mon cœur se déclarer;
> J'oubliai ma colère, et ne sus que pleurer.

So Phèdre, tormented by jealousy for the love of Hippolyte and Aricie, sees it in all its innocent happiness, when she throws the torment of her solitude and her guilt into her imagination of them :

> Les a-t-on vus souvent se parler, se chercher?
> Dans le fond des forêts allaient-ils se cacher?
> Hélas ! Ils se voyaient avec pleine licence.
> Le ciel de leurs soupirs approuvait l'innocence;
> Ils suivaient sans remords leur penchant amoureux;
> Tous les jours se levaient clairs et sereins pours eux.

Such passages record states of mind which are fundamentally not uncommon, but in Racine's passionate simplicity they are exalted to a peculiar power and given an extraordinary degree of life.

More remarkably, Racine provides a no less powerful poetry for characters who are swayed by passions so black and ugly that we might think them to be beyond the sway of so harmonious an art. But he rises without apparent effort to these criminal occasions and gives to wickedness its own revealing voice. When Iago discloses his hideous depths, he usually speaks in prose, but when Néron decides to break his promise to Agrippine and kill Britannicus, his words of calcu-lated, cold-blooded savagery have their own terrible force :

> Elle se hâte trop, Burrhus, de triompher.
> J'embrasse mon rival, mais c'est pour l'étouffer.

When Hermione rejects Andromaque's appeal for help in trying to escape with her son to some remote refuge, her vanity and her jealousy conspire to mask her hatred with a freezing disdain :

> Je conçois vos douleurs. Mais un devoir austère,
> Quand mon père a parlé, m'ordonne de me taire.
> C'est lui qui de Pyrrhus fait agir le courroux.
> S'il faut fléchir Pyrrhus, qui le peut mieux que vous?
> Vos yeux assez longtemps ont régné sur son âme.
> Faites-le prononcer; j'y souscrirai, Madame.

When Roxane refuses Atalide's offer to surrender Bajazet to her, the flood of her black fury is held in the bounds of an ironical, murderous ambiguity :

> Je ne mérite pas un si grand sacrifice :
> Je me connais, Madame, et je me fais justice.
> Loin de vous séparer, je prétends aujourd' hui
> Par des nœuds éternels vous unir avec lui.

Racine's poetry rises directly from his understanding of human beings in all their range and complexity and derives its strength from the insoluble paradoxes of their nature.

This art is so fitted to human passions and so closely interwoven with them that it lacks the sudden flights into the empyrean which we find in Shakespeare. But if we wish to judge poetry by its impres-sive single lines and to treat these as touchstones or talismans, many such can be found in Racine. No one knows better how to clinch an occasion with a line of astonishing force and concentration, and such lines may legitimately be isolated and enjoyed for their own sake. But his true strength lies in making them obey a commanding pattern and be indispensable to it. They are not thrown in haphazard by an inspired whim or merely as decorative additions; they contain the essence of an occasion which has already been introduced with a wealth of powerful, if less breath-taking, poetry. For instance the famous line

> Dans l'Orient désert quel devint mon ennui !

is all the more impressive when it comes in Antiochus' speech to

Bérénice, because he has already declared his love for her and now tells of his misery when he was left without her in Palestine. When Andomaque shrinks from the attentions of Pyrrhus, she begs him to go back to Hermione in words which reflect all her helpless desire to be left alone with her sorrows :

Retournez, retournez à la fille d'Hélène.

But this is only the crown of an appeal in which she has uncovered the pathos of her unprotected widowhood. So an even more famous line, which used to be quoted by advocates of 'la poésie pure',[1] because it had, as they claimed, little or no meaning, is actually the climax of Hippolyte's conviction that something fatal and accursed has broken into his happy existence :

Cet heureux temps n'est plus. Tout a changé de face
Depuis que sur ces bords les dieux ont envoyé
La fille de Minos et de Pasiphaé.

Though these lines caress the ear, they fascinate and hold us because they are charged with dismay and horror. Racine's poetry yields its full reward only when we respond alike to its intellectual strength and its emotional intensity.

Racine is singularly free of double or ulterior meanings, vague echoes, symbolical intentions, and indeed most means which seek to extend the domain of poetry beyond its immediately intelligible subject. He aims at making every thought and emotion clear, at showing their union in its provocative, indissoluble strength. He insists that this must be itself in all its richness, with all its own attraction, and he sheds on it the life-giving splendour of his style. So far from encouraging our thoughts to range in vast speculations about the nature of things, he pins them down to the special case, and demonstrates how absorbing it is. No matter how complex it may be, he presents it in a transparently simple form, which leaves no room for doubt and grips our whole conscious and emotional attention. This poetry is indeed not always maintained at the same point of intensity. Not only does it vary with the moods of the characters, but there are some moments when the need to explain a situation invites no more than merely machining lines, and other moments when the passions have not yet burst into full flame and must be treated with a quiet decorum. But this variety of tone is

---

[1] So Proust makes Bloch quote the line as 'un vers assez bien rythmé, et qui a pour lui, ce qui est selon moi le mérite suprême, de ne signifier absolument rien' (*Du côté de chez Swann*, éd. N.R.F., 1929, i.p. 129), and the Narrator speaks of 'la beauté dénuée de signification de la fille de Minos et de Pasiphaé' (ibid., p. 133), cf. also H. Bremond, *La poésie pure*, pp. 36, 93, 116.

essential to the whole effect. It prepares the way for the tremendous occasions when the poetry soars effortlessly to the most difficult tasks and with its radiant lucidity presents a crisis in its full imaginative appeal. For example, when Hippolyte defends his innocence to his father, he breaks into a line which is as limpid as the day which it invokes :

Le jour n'est pas plus pur que le fond de mon cœur.

In this, which Paul Valéry calls 'le plus beau de vers',[1] intellectual meaning and poetical enchantment are inextricably fused, and each strengthens and completes the other. If we wish to know what pure poetry is, we need not waste effort in trying to distil some magical or metaphysical essence; it is enough to respond to lines like this, which do all that poetry can and embody all the qualities which we ask from it.

Racine knew and interpreted in his own way the famous saying of Aristotle that the function of tragedy is to arouse pity and fear and in so doing to purge as of such emotions.[2] But it is not always very relevant and certainly not central to his art. The formula is too narrow for his achievement, in which almost every emotion is aroused and the purgation which follows is not a mere negative riddance but a transformation into something positive and enthralling. He does not attempt to show that the disasters which he dramatizes are resolved by some ultimate harmony, or that they can be explained and justified by religion or philosophy, but through his imaginative insight into his characters, who are so fatal to themselves, the emotions aroused by their destinies are mastered and transcended in what he calls 'majestic sadness'. This is his solution for the problems raised by tragedy, and for it he relies on the power of his poetry. Without its transfiguring influence his events would often be unbearably painful, but through it their horror is absorbed in an excited and exalted understanding. Its special, its overwhelming claim is that it is a poetry of humanity in its complexity and its contradictions, in its errors and its crimes, often ruined by its own violence, often corrupt and unredeemed, but for that very reason close to much that we know in ourselves and cannot, without betraying our human ties and loyalties, reject or deny.

---

[1] *Tel Quel*, ii. p. 78.

[2] In his interpretation of Aristotle's much disputed words περαινουσα την των τοιουτων παθηματων καθαρσιν (*Poet.* 1449^{b}27), Racine follows the Latin version of Nicolaus Heinsius, *per misericordiam et metum conficiens huiuscemodi perturbationum purgationem*, and translates 'qui, excitant la pitié et la terreur, purge et tempère ces sortes de passions'. (J. Racine, *Principes de la tragédie*, ed. E. Vinaver, pp. 11-12.)

IX

EDWARD FITZGERALD

[Lecture delivered at the Inauguration of the British Institute for Persian Studies, at Tehran, on 11 December 1961]

IN THE nineteenth century England, despite its reputation for ruthless conventionality, was a happy home for eccentrics, for men who with an almost unconscious confidence pursued their private whims and maintained a curious innocence from the world around them. To this select and agreeable company belonged Edward Fitz-Gerald. He was not, strictly speaking, English, but Anglo-Irish, coming from a family long settled in Ireland but regarding itself as an outpost of English manners and superiority, and confirmed in its belief by an ample income and several large houses. Though FitzGerald lived to be 74, his life was undramatic, and such dramas as befell him he took with a philosophical calm. Even when his father lost his money trying to find coal on his Manchester estate and was declared bankrupt, FitzGerald's existence was not troubled. His wants were few; he had no appetite for luxury or display. When some of his old friends, notably Thackeray and Tennyson, became prominent figures in London society, FitzGerald preferred the company of farmers in Suffolk and made a special friend of one Joseph Fletcher, a sailor, whom he called 'Posh' and thought 'a gentleman of Nature's grandest type', forgiving him his bouts of intoxication and his uncertain touch with money. To the more dramatic events of his time he paid little attention. He was not interested in the sensational strides of natural science; he thought most contemporary writers, including Tennyson after his first work, sadly imperfect; he was deeply distressed by what he regarded as the rapid decay and imminent dissolution of the British Empire. He developed agreeable oddities of dress and manner, wearing indoors a top hat and a silk dressing gown, and out of doors a plaid shawl wrapped loosely round his shoulders, and very short trousers, which stopped just below his knees. He kept himself alive by maintaining a calm routine, and when he tried to break it, always regretted the attempt. When he was nearly fifty, he married a woman older than himself, but she had social ambitions which were highly distasteful to him, and he soon separated from her. When years afterwards he met her by accident, he held out his hand to her, but withdrew it at once, saying, 'Come along, Posh,' and walked away. His life lacked any obvious purpose, and though at first he was conscious of this and a little troubled, it soon became a habit and even a philosophy. He wrote letters to his friends about the small matters of every day, and they remain among the most subtle and charming letters written in English. He pursued his literary hobbies with a quiet persistence, and in the end it was clear that this man, who seemed to be wasting his undoubted talents, had discovered where they lay and made at least one triumphant use of them.

FitzGerald loved words and had a natural gift for their use, but he lacked the mastering, driving impetus which makes a truly creative writer. Though he enjoyed the practice of writing, as his letters abundantly show, and though he was an acute and exacting critic of the work of other men, he was incapable of forming a large design for any literary undertaking of his own. His gift was for sensibility and the niceties of observation, for finding the right, unassuming words for what caught his fancy in nature or books or human relations. His refusal to join in the ardours and struggles of other men meant that he had very little to write about, and his emotional life, confined as it was to his friends, gave him no inspiration. When he was twenty-two years old, he wrote a little lyric, 'The Meadows in Spring', which is in its own quiet way original and graceful and true to himself. It catches a tranquil, relaxed mood, which was indeed to be the dominating mood of his life, and shows how early he had settled down to his characteristic quietism. It begins :

> 'Tis a dull sigh
>   To see the year dying,
> When winter winds
>   Set the yellow wood sighing :
>   Sighing, oh ! sighing.

> When such a time cometh
>   I do retire
> Into an old room
>   Beside a bright fire :
>   Oh, pile a bright fire !

And there I sit
  Reading old things,
Of knights and lorn damsels
  While the wind sings—
    Oh drearily sings!

I never look out
  Nor attend to the blast;
For all to be seen
  Is the leaves falling fast;
    Falling, falling!

This is not a great poem, but it has certain qualities. The use of the unrhymed line at the end of each verse catches very aptly the mood of peace and resignation and lack of effort. The half-conversational language shows, as FitzGerald was to show on a much greater scale later, his dislike of the artificial vocabulary which the Victorian poets imported from an imaginary medieval world. The theme of withdrawal into books is entirely true to FitzGerald's temperament, and it is not surprising that he writes in a mood of reminiscence as if, at the age of twenty-two, life held nothing in store for him.

FitzGerald wrote a few more occasional poems, none of them so good or so revealing as this. He saw that he was not really the man to write poetry at the only level at which it is worth writing. He had therefore to find some other, less direct means to express himself, and it was some time before he found it. He had the makings of an excellent critic, and his letters give many examples of his independence from current fashions, his sharp eye for faults and failures, his understanding and admiration of the great masters, his precise and sensitive feeling for words. But he wanted more than this. Criticism might be good enough for conversation and correspondence, but it was not a life's work, and despite all his modesty and self-depreciation FitzGerald dreamed of writing something that would be remembered and endure. The question was how to do it. His own demon was not strong enough to drive him into truly creative activity, and he was not content merely to discuss the works of other men. In his spare time he edited a book of maxims, which revealed the unconventional range of his reading and his eye for a terse or pointed sentence. But this kind of scholarship did not satisfy him. Hidden away in him was something which called to be put into words of beauty and power, and yet defeated his first efforts to express it rightly. FitzGerald was in the awkward position of feeling that he had something important to say and yet not being quite sure what it was.

FitzGerald's first sustained and serious attempt to write a book was *Euphranor,* published in 1851. It is modelled on a Platonic dialogue, in which four Cambridge undergraduates discuss with a doctor, who is twice their age, subjects that undergraduates in all times tend to discuss. In it FitzGerald has a serious purpose, to charge English schools first with failing to look after the physical development of youth; secondly, with paying no attention to the usefulness of education in fitting a man for a career. The first charge sounds odd today, when for a century our schools have been vociferously accused of preferring physical to mental training, and even in Fitz-Gerald's day many schools had established the cult of compulsory games as a moral antidote to the more violent relaxations of an earlier generation. The second charge is more far-sighted, and is still a subject of hot debate, especially on the relation of science to society, in which FitzGerald was not interested. Both come unexpectedly from FitzGerald, who was in no sense an athlete and had little curiosity about industry or business or administration. *Euphranor* is written with the same charm and grace as the letters and has many happy observations and alluring cadences. Yet it fails sadly when we compare it with its Platonic models. We miss the closely knit argument, the intellectual structure, the appeal to first principles, the merciless and unforgiving cogency with which a debate is conducted, the fusion of close and even difficult thought with an easy conversational style. FitzGerald has the style, but not the strength which is needed to give body to it, and his principles are too like prejudices to be impressive. He himself soon thought little of *Euphranor* and called it 'a pretty specimen of a chiselled cherry-stone'. He was right, and yet it reveals something in FitzGerald which was to come to the fore later and was already at work in him. In setting out the case for physical education he was speaking for the Greek world which he knew and loved from books, and his statement of the case is a quiet challenge to the Victorian society in which he lived. From early days he had rejected some of its favourite assumptions, and now he had seriously begun to look for some alternative to them. He presented his views with tact and restraint and decorum, but he had shown the first signs of revolt and indicated the direction in which he was to move.

Poetry was the art which FitzGerald most loved and admired and wished to practise. Recognizing that he could not be a great poet in his own right, he decided to devote himself to the translation of poetry, and with this for the rest of his life he was mainly occupied. The three languages which concerned him were Greek, Spanish and, above all, Persian. Greek he had studied at school and at

Cambridge and knew with the thoroughness inculcated by a well-established discipline; Spanish and Persian he learned with the help of his friend Edward Byles Cowell, who was a man of most unusual gifts and, despite the lack of a formal education, took up Persian, Sanskrit, Norse, Italian and Spanish, to end up as Professor of Sanskrit at Cambridge University. FitzGerald met him in 1846 and formed with him a friendship which lasted until his own death. Cowell was an excellent scholar, who combined a very wide range of reading with a thorough knowledge of the languages which he read and a real enthusiasm for their literatures, and though Fitz-Gerald was never to know Spanish or Persian so well as Cowell, he inspired FitzGerald with his own excitement, taught him how to study new languages, engaged in a long and scholarly correspondence on points of detail, and put him on to new topics when his ardour began to flag. It is a pity that in translating Greek, on which FitzGerald could so easily have got expert advice, he relied on his own judgement and sought for no Cowell to assist him. Cowell's direct contribution to Persian studies in England was not nearly so great as that of Sir William Jones or Browne or Nicholson, but indirectly, in his own sphere, he may have had more influence than any of them, since it is through him that one Persian poet became an established English Classic.

In translating from Spanish and Greek FitzGerald's methods were very much his own. He translated eight plays of Calderon, the *Agamemnon* of Aeschylus, and the *King Oedipus* and the *Oedipus at Colonus* of Sophocles. The results are always readable, even distinguished, but the methods are certainly eccentric. First, FitzGerald thought nothing of omitting passages which did not appeal to him. This might not matter if the omitted passages were unimportant either for their own sake or because they did not contribute to the structure of a complete work of art. However, if they bored FitzGerald, or for some reason he took against them, they were left out. Secondly, he took more than legitimate liberties with the text when he fused two separate and quite different plays of Sophocles into a single play. The two plays about Oedipus differ in manner, in intention, in tragic interest, in the actual quality of their poetry, and to make them one, FitzGerald had to leave out important characters, soften the asperities of the first play, obscure the age of Oedipus, who is a young man in one play and an old man in the other, spoil the detective interest of the first play and the religious interest of the second. Thirdly, FitzGerald disliked anything too elaborate and mannered, and this did not make him an ideal translator of Calderon, who wrote in the high manner of Spanish rhetoric, or even of Aeschylus, with his bold, unexpected phraseology and his complex, metaphorical lessons. If these got in the way, FitzGerald pushed them aside and simplified and lowered the more musical and more melodious passages of Aeschylus and the tone of the text. Fourthly, FitzGerald was not a lyrical poet, and the more melodious passages of Aeschylus and Sophocles were beyond his reach. He reduced the first to much less than their full scale; the second he did not attempt to translate but used instead the poor versions of an eighteenth-century rhymer called Robert Potter. His gift was much more for philosophic or reflective verse than for lyrical or even dramatic poetry, and though his lines have always a noble resonance and often a real sweep and splendour, they are not dramatic. We can read them with pleasure, but we cannot imagine that they could be spoken successfully on the stage. He prefers the fine sweep of noble sentiments to human situations, and general remarks about the human state to particular instances of it. All this means not merely that he was an unfaithful translator, but that he did not really find the right medium for his own views. Tying himself, as he did, to drama, he shirked the issues that in fact most troubled and most interested him. The result was not a faithful version, and FitzGerald did not intend it to be one; but in that case, it was equally not an independent work of art which conveyed the richness and the oddity of FitzGerald's own personality.

At the same time, FitzGerald needed the *persona* of some other poet in order to discover and express himself, and at least he saw that, whatever else a translation must do, it must live as poetry in its own right. 'Better a live sparrow than a stuffed eagle' was his own comment on his work, and there is much to be said for it. He did not necessarily have to accept the views of the authors whom he translated and was paradoxically more at home in the religious passages of Calderon than in the courtly and worldly. What really stirred him was the kind of poetry which deals with general ideas, but in such a way that they are transmuted and transfigured by an individual, imaginative treatment of them. FitzGerald felt at home with this and made it fit his own more troubled ideas. His error was to try to find it in Greek and Spanish. Greek tragedies were too austere, too remote for his feminine, melancholy nature; Calderon was too elaborate and too dignified. He had still to find what he really needed, and it came to him unexpectedly. To realize himself as he wished FitzGerald had to set himself at some distance from his own life and society. In a foreign language, in a distant past, in ways of thought that had not been touched by Christianity, in ideas and ideals not familiar to western Europe, in poetry richer and more heavily loaded than any other known to him, FitzGerald found his release and his means of self-expression, and his final, complete, satisfying and inspiring refuge was the poetry of Persia.

As with Spanish, the first impulse came from Cowell, in the winter of 1852. Cowell later said of it; 'I suggested Persian to him and guaranteed to teach the grammar in a day. The book was Jones' grammer, the illustrations in which are nearly all from Hafiz. Fitz-Gerald was interested in these and went on to read Hafiz closely.' Fitz-Gerald carried the grammar, which was that published by William Jones in 1771, about with him for a year, translating the passages in it and writing to Cowell in January 1853 : 'The Persian is really a great amusement to me.... As to Jones' Grammar, I have a sort of love for it.' For the next eighteen months, he studied poems by Sa'di, Ferdowsi, Hafiz, Jāmi, and Attār, and read many books about Persia and its people. Then in the summer of 1854, with Cowell's help, he read Jāmi's *Salāmān and Absāl,* and began to translate it, very much according to his own rules, omitting what did not interest him, elaborating what did, and giving much more care to some passages than to others. He told Cowell that he had 'compacted the story into a producible drama and reduced the rhetoric into perhaps too narrow a compass'. Yet though he thought his version the best thing that he had yet done, it did not meet all his inner needs. He did not like its more complex thoughts and said of it : 'I shall bundle up the celestial and earthly shah so neatly that neither can be displeased, and no reader know which is which. Trust an Irishman where any confusion is wanted.' But what he himself really wanted was not confusion but a clarity and firmness which the poem did not give him, at least in the form that he desired : 'I wanted to secure a palpable image of the diety *scrutinizing* the world he made and moves in *through the eyes* of his master-work, Man, and to edge and clench it with the sharp corner-stone of rhyme in that very word scrutinize.' In the end FitzGerald produced a version of a poem whose actual story he found boring, but there was much else in it to excite him, and it has more sustained power than his translations from Greek and Spanish. Moreover, it tells much about himself, especially when he deals with its speculative and metaphysical passages. In his first version he translated the opening lines not only with an unusual power but with an unexpected fidelity to the original.

> Oh Thou, whose memory quickens Lovers' souls,
> Whose fount of joy renews the Lover's tongue,
> Thy Shadow falls across the world, and they
> Bow down to it, and of the rich in beauty
> Thou art the riches that make Lovers sad.
> Not till thy secret beauty through the cheek
> Of Laila smite does she inflame Majnun,

And not till thou have sugar'd Shirin's lip,
The hearts of those two Lovers fill with blood.

The mystical conception of love has caught FitzGerald's imagination, and he breaks out into words that would have been beyond
his scope but for the Persian text in front of him. Over twenty years
later FitzGerald published a revised version of the poem, and his
new translation of these opening lines shows how much he has
thought about them and how much further he has moved from them :

> Oh Thou, whose Spirit through this universe
> In which Thou doest involve thyself diffused,
> Shall so perchance irradiate human clay
> That men, suddenly dazzled, lose themselves
> In ecstasy before a mortal shrine
> Whose Light is but a shade of the Divine;
> Not till thy Secret Beauty through the cheek
> Of Laila smite doth she inflame Majnùn;
> And not till Thou have kindled Shirin's Eyes
> The hearts of those two Rivals swell with blood.

Some of the first sweep and power and ecstasy has gone, and yet
FitzGerald is more at home in his new version, more at ease with
the idea of love as a divine power working through the universe.
Salāmān and Absāl opened new vistas to him, and, as he slowly grew
accustomed to them, he made them fit his inner longings more
closely.

For FitzGerald the trouble with *Salāmān and Absāl* is that he was
not equally interested in the whole poem throughout. He conscientiously translated much of it, but the narrative portions called for
talents which he did not possess, and he made a grave error of judgement when, for the sake of variety, he put some passages into the
jaunty metre of *Hiawatha,* for which his original provided no excuse.
The poem introduced him to a new kind of religious poetry, and it
was this that fascinated him and kept him to it, but in the meanwhile he had found something else of a different kind, which was
to satisfy much more of his nature and to excite the full exercise of
his genius. In July, 1856, FitzGerald told Tennyson : 'I have been the
last fortnight with the Cowells. We read some curious infidel and
Epicurean tetrastichs by a Persian of the eleventh century—as savage
against destiny, etc., as Manfred—but mostly of Epicurean pathos
of this kind—"drink for the moon will often come round to look
for us in this garden and find us not".' Behind this lay Cowell's discovery, in the Bodleian Library at Oxford, of a manuscript of Omar

Khayyám written in 1460 on thick yellow paper, in purple-black ink, profusely powdered with gold. It contains 158 quatrains which Cowell copied out and sent to FitzGerald. FitzGerald was fascinated by them, collected more information from the French Scholar, Garcin de Tassy, got hold of a Calcutta text of them, and in the summer of 1857 could read no other books. At first he played with the idea of translating it into rhymed Latin verse in the medieval manner, and a specimen of this was sent to Cowell. It was probably no more than a joke, though FitzGerald wrote to Cowell : 'You will think me a perfectly Aristophanic old man when I tell you how many lines of Omar I could not help running into such bad Latin'. By the autumn of the same year he had finished the first draft of his translation into rhymed English verse, and in 1859 he published anonymously, in an edition of 250 copies, bound in brown paper, his *Rubaiyat of Omar Khayyám,* at the price of one shilling a copy.

At first it attracted no notice whatsoever. For two years it lay on the shelves of Quaritch the publisher, who, giving up all hope of selling it, dumped the copies into his bargain box at the price of one penny each. Some unknown man of great perception saw it there, bought a copy, and showed it to Dante Gabriel Rossetti, who returned to the shop with his friend Swinburne, to find themselves charged two pence a copy. As Swinburne wrote : 'We were extravagant enough to invest in a few more copies at that scandalous price'. From Swinburne and Rossetti news of the book was passed to William Morris, Burne Jones and Ruskin, and by 1868 the book appeared as a rarity in Quaritch's catalogue at the price of three shillings and sixpence, and FitzGerald wrote to him to say that the price made him blush. While the Pre-Raphaelites took up the poem in England, the American scholar and critic, Charles Eliot Norton, saw Burne Jones' copy and made the poem known in the United States. In all this, nobody was more surprised than FitzGerald, who had not attached his name to the book and read with pleasure the statement in a newspaper that it was the work of 'a certain Reverend Edward FitzGerald, who lived somewhere in Norfolk and was fond of boating'. Off and on the poem was to occupy FitzGerald for the rest of his life. He published new editions of it, each greatly revised, in 1868, 1872 and 1879. It made his name in select circles, but he did not live to see the enormous popularity which it had in the last ten years of the last century and the first twenty years of this. Produced in every shape and size and print, ornamented often with the most startling or most inappropriate illustrations, given freely as a Christmas present by elderly relations to their nephews and nieces, parodied and copied and maltreated from comic papers to Rudyard Kipling, it shared a strange popularity with other vastly inferior works which were thought to make no claims on the intelligence of their recipients. It was set to music with luscious accompaniments suited to contralto voices and thought to reflect all the lure and luxury of the East. It even became a symbol for those who paid more than serious attention to food and drink, and the Omar Khayyám Club in London, with its ceremonious and carefully chosen dinners, passes far beyond the poet's own satisfaction with a loaf of bread and a jug of wine. FitzGerald would have been amazed, amused, perhaps even a little shocked. It was not in the expectation of such a future that he translated the quatrains of the astronomer-poet of Persia.

FitzGerald was himself somewhat surprised that Omar should appeal to him so much as he did. Omar was a man of strong appetites and a strong predilection for wine; FitzGerald was a vegetarian and seldom drank anything stronger than beer. Omar did not attempt to hide his taste for women; FitzGerald was shy of them and liked them only for their conversation. Omar played a large part in public affairs; FitzGerald was a recluse even in his own small section of rural society. Omar speculated boldly about the universe; FitzGerald, at least outwardly, conformed to the Church of England, though it must be admitted that his local clergyman remonstrated with him about his laxity. FitzGerald was attracted to Omar as to a poet quite outside his previous experience, and all the more seductive because he lived in a world so unlike FitzGerald's own and had so marked and so powerful a personality. He wrote to Cowell: 'I thought him from the first the most remarkable of the Persian poets, and you keep finding out in him evidences of logical fancy which I had not dreamed of'. That FitzGerald should prefer Omar to Hafiz or Ferdowsi indicates that this usually balanced and sagacious critic had been swept off his feet, and it was not only the quality of Omar's poetry which had done it. FitzGerald had a strong taste for what he here calls 'logical fancy', and by it he means something akin to metaphysical poetry, which treats ideas imaginatively and enriches and expounds them through symbols and images. He had liked this in Calderon, and he liked it in Omar, but behind it was something else which exerted a stronger attraction on him and about which he was not quite so happy.

FitzGerald owed his knowledge of Omar to Cowell, but he knew that Cowell, who was a devout member of the Church of England, could not take Omar entirely to his heart. He was quite frank about it and wrote to Cowell in December 1857: 'In truth, I take old Omar more as my property than yours; he and I are more akin, are we not? You see all his beauty, you don't feel with him in some respects as I do. I think you would almost feel obliged to leave out the part of Hamlet in representing him to your audience, for fear of mischief. Now I do not wish to show Hamlet at his maddest; but mad he must be shown, or he is no Hamlet at all. . . I think these free opinions are less dangerous in an old Mahometan or an old Roman (like Lucretius) than when they are returned to by those who have lived on happier food'. FitzGerald was right in thinking that Cowell felt some responsibility for introducing Omar to FitzGerald; for many years later, in 1898, after FitzGerald's death, when the Persian scholar, Edward Heron-Allen, proposed to dedicate to him a book on Omar and FitzGerald, Cowell wrote :

> 'I yield to no one in my admiration of Omar's poetry as litera-
> ture, but I cannot join in the Omar cult, and it would be wrong
> in me to pretend to profess it. So I am deeply interested in
> Lucretius . . . but here again I only admire Lucretius as "litera-
> ture". I feel this especially about Omar Khayyám, as I unwit-
> tingly incurred a grave responsibility when I introduced his
> poems to my old friend in 1856. I admire Omar as I admire
> Lucretius, but I cannot take him as a guide. In these grave
> matters I prefer to go to Nazareth, not to Naishapur.'

Cowell was quite right. What fascinated FitzGerald in Omar was not merely its strangeness, nor its purely literary quality, nor even its metaphysical ingenuity, but its point of view. This appealed to him more deeply than the Olympian grandeur of Sophocles or the mystical fervour of Calderon, or the philosophic sweep of *Salámán and Absál*. No doubt he had many serious reservations about Omar's philosophy and would certainly neither admit nor think that he accepted it in its entirety. No doubt he believed that he liked it simply for its purely poetical qualities, irrespective of its senti-ments, though this is not an easy position to maintain and usually conceals an element of self-deception somewhere. Yet Omar fascin-ated FitzGerald in more than one way, and the fascination was by no means merely aesthetic. FitzGerald was at heart a practising Epicurean, in his love of a quiet life with its tranquil consolations, and untroubled security, enjoying the passing moment and not look-ing beyond it, free alike from action and from the decisions which action demands. More than this, as a modern Epicurean, Fitz-Gerald could not but speculate about the nature of the universe and its government. His Christian upbringing and allegiance meant little to him, and in some moods he saw an encompassing darkness, to whose central mystery there was no clue, but which raised awkward questions and prompted various answers. The inconsistencies and the contradictions in his agnosticism found an echo in Omar, and when he turned the quatrains into English, the strength and the passion of his words show how fully FitzGerald was at home. On one side there is a profound scepticism, which asserts that it is useless to ask questions because no answers can be found to them.

> Why, all the Saints and Sages who discuss'd
> Of the Two Worlds so learnedly, are thrust
>   Like foolish Prophets forth; their Words to Scorn
> Are scatter'd, and their Mouths are stopt with Dust.

On the other side is a positive conviction that the universe has its own ghostly guidance, which is indeed alien to any teaching of religion :

> Then to the rolling heav'n itself I cried,
> Asking, 'What Lamp has Destiny to guide
>   Her little Children stumbling in the Dark?'
> And—'A blind Understanding!' Heav'n replied.

FitzGerald may have had reservations and qualifications, and certainly did not treat literally all that Omar said and he himself translated, but how seriously he treated him and liked him can be seen from his association of Omar with Lucretius : 'Men of subtle, strong and cultivated intellect, fine imagination, and hearts passionate for truth and justice, who justly revolted from their country's false religion and ... with no better revelation to guide them, had yet made a law to themselves'. The words 'with no better revelation to guide them' are a saving clause which FitzGerald puts in, no doubt sincerely, but equally there is no doubt about his admiration of Omar, as of Lucretius, for his bold and independent outlook, and though he does not say that he himself shares it, he would hardly display this degree of admiration if it did not in some respects appeal to him.

FitzGerald's treatment of Omar has its characteristic idiosyncrasies. He has been accused of adding and falsifying, of making too much or too little of what he found before him. He certainly treated Omar on his usual principles of translation, determined that 'at all cost a thing must live', but in his curious way he was more faithful than he is commonly thought to have been. In the final form his poem has 101 stanzas, and it has been calculated that of these :

> Forty-nine are faithful translations of single quatrains to be found in the Bodleian MS., copied for him by Cowell, or in the copy of the text which he got from Calcutta.

Forty-four are traceable to more than one quatrain and may be
called composite, but not in the last resort unfaithful.

Two are inspired by quatrains found by FitzGerald in the
French version of J. B. Nicholas, published in 1867.

Two are quatrains reflecting the whole spirit of the original
poem, but may be classed as FitzGerald's own inventions.

Four are traceable to other poems by other poets, notably Attār
and Hafiz.

At least FitzGerald treated Omar with more respect than he treated
Sophocles, and even his additions have been skilfully adapted to
the dominating tone and temper.

Examples of FitzGerald's methods will illustrate what he had in
mind and what success he achieved. First, he took from Hafiz the
quatrain :

> Before the phantom of False morning died,
> Methought a Voice within the Tavern cried,
>   'When all the temple is prepared within,
> Why nods the drowsy Worshipper outside?'

FitzGerald has completely changed the context and therefore the
intention of the lines, but they fit very well into his scheme, and he
puts them in at this point because they provide a useful link to get
his subject going at the start. Secondly, from Attār comes :

> Earth could not answer; not the seas that mourn
> In flowing purple, of their Lord forlorn;
>   Nor rolling Heav'n, with all his signs reveal'd
> And hidden by the sleeve of night and morn.

This gives a new strength and majesty to the sense of utter ignorance
which afflicts mankind and fits very well in FitzGerald's presentation of it. Thirdly, FitzGerald composes verses of his own which
reflect and summarize the general spirit of Omar, but are not based
on his actual words. Such is the quatrain :

> Iram indeed is gone with all its Rose,
> And Jamshyd's Seven-ring'd Cup where no one knows;
>   But still a Ruby kindles in the Vine,
> And many a Garden by the Water blows.

This little distillation of poetry in the master's manner is needed in
its place to provide a transition to the theme of wine, and Fitz-
Gerald's words are a remarkable example of *pastiche*. He has so
absorbed Omar that he speaks like him in his own voice.

Apart from these small and successful aberrations from the text,

FitzGerald treated it in other ways which may seem to be high-handed but are also justified by success. First, he chose from a larger number available 101 quatrains, and omitted those which did not appeal to him. He then arranged his selection to suit his own design. This was permissible because the original quatrains were single, separate poems which could be arranged in any order because each stood in its own right and was not part of any unifying design. But FitzGerald, who treated Omar seriously, decided to make a single poem of the various quatrains, because this would stress their underlying philosophy. There is a real development through the poem from the dawn, with which it starts, to the resigned melancholy of the end. This development has not the logic of an argument or an apology; it follows a natural sequence of emotional states, as the poem passes from the ignorance and insecurity of man to the consolations of the grape. FitzGerald's *Rubaiyat* is by his own choice and skill not a mere string of stanzas, of which almost any might take the place of any other, but, as he himself calls it, 'something of an Eclogue, with perhaps less than an equal proportion of the "drink and make merry", which (genuine or not) recurs over frequently in the original'. Secondly, FitzGerald reduced all the stanzas to the same shape and to the same scheme of rhyme. He kept the unit of four lines, made all of them the same length, and rhymed the first, second and fourth lines, leaving the third unrhymed. The result is remarkably effective, and we can see what FitzGerald means when he says that 'the penultimate line seems to lift and suspend the wave that falls over into the last'. The stanza so formed is irrevocably associated with the names of Omar and FitzGerald and has found a lasting place in English poetry, being used even for so unexpected a task as Mackail's translation of the *Odyssey*.

At the same time FitzGerald certainly played some minor tricks with the text, and these throw some light on his ulterior intentions. Take, for instance, a famous and much quoted stanza :

> Oh Thou, who Man of baser Earth didst make,
> And ev'n with Paradise devise the Snake :
>   For all the Sin wherewith the Face of Man
> Is blacken'd—Man's Forgiveness give—and take !

Asked much later about the last line Cowell wrote in 1903 :

> 'There is no original for the line about the snake; I have looked for it in vain in Nicholas. FitzGerald mistook the meaning of *giving* and *accepting* . . . and so invented his last line out of his own mistake. I wrote to him about it when I was in Calcutta, but he never cared to alter it.'

Fortunately we have FitzGerald's answer at the time to Cowell's criticism :

> 'I have certainly an idea that this *is* said somewhere in the Calcutta manuscript. But it is very likely I may have construed, or remembered, erroneously. But I do not *add* dirt to Omar's face.'

In fact FitzGerald got the idea not from Omar but from Attār, and so absorbed it that he forgot the source. But it is exactly the kind of effect that he seeks and loves, and we can understand that, having done it, he was not going to withdraw or alter it.

FitzGerald altered his poem greatly in the four editions of it which he published at intervals, and though we may feel that many of his corrections take away some of the first freshness, there is no doubt that FitzGerald, who was an excellent critic of his own work, made them with due deliberation because they represented more closely the poetical effect which he wished to produce. In each he tends to get further away from the original text and to speak more confidently in his own voice. Take for instance one quatrain on the theme of drinking while we may. In the first edition it runs :

> While the Rose blows along the River Brink
> With old Khayyám the Ruby Vintage drink :
> And when the Angel with the darker Draught
> Draws up to Thee—take that, and do not shrink.

In the second edition this has been remodelled :

> So when at last the Angel of the Drink
> Of Darkness finds you by the river-brink,
> And, proffering his cup, invites your Soul
> Forth to your lips to quaff it—do not shrink.

The rose by the river and the whole conception of drinking with old Khayyám have disappeared, and the stanza is devoted to the single, powerful image of the draught offered by the angel of death. It is more sombre, more pointed, more concentrated. Then in the fourth and final form the quatrain reads :

> So when that Angel of the darker Drink
> At last shall find you by the river-brink,
> And, offering his cup, invite your Soul
> Forth to your lips to quaff—you shall not shrink.

The Angel has become more remote and more mysterious, and the last line is now not a command but a prophecy. This is what will happen, and there is no gainsaying it. FitzGerald has hardened and condensed his style to get this effect, and there is no doubt that he rewrote it because it said what he really wished to say.

In making his alterations FitzGerald had a clear notion of what the style of his poem should be, and in this he presents a marked independence from any Victorian practice. The Victorians suffered from a taste for archaic, literary words. In their rejection of the neatness and point sought so ardently by the eighteenth century, they sought to convey an air of romance by certain affectations of speech—not merely medieval words long passed out of currency, but inversions, such as putting the adjective after the noun, or twisting the order of words to make them look more impressive. They did this because they thought that the poetry of their immediate predecessors was unduly prosaic, and they thought that this was a good way to counter and correct its influence. FitzGerald did not agree with them. He was no great admirer of Victorian poetry, and thought that most of it compared poorly with even such work as that of Crabbe. On the other hand though he saw much to admire in Pope and Cowper, he felt that they did not belong to his world and could not teach him anything, and in this he was certainly right so far as his love of exotic situations and striking fancies was concerned. The result was that he stood in a middle position between the dominating styles of the eighteenth and nineteenth century, and instead of being perplexed and defeated by this, he took triumphant advantage of it. He was a man of the nineteenth centuries in his romantic affection for the past, for strange places and strange names, for flaunting statements about the nature of reality, for rich, decorative effects, for the graces and subtleties of nature. But he had his roots in the eighteenth century—in his love of point and paradox, of sharp epigram and lyrical wit, of personal statements which tell the truth in a concise and striking way without any adventitious ornament. His peculiar, indeed his unique success was that he fused these two sides of his nature into a single style. At one time the nineteenth century seems to dominate in such a stanza as :

> One Moment in Annihilation's Waste,
> One Moment, of the Well of Life to taste—
>   The Stars are setting and the Caravan
> Starts for the Dawn of Nothing—Oh, make haste !

or

> I sometimes think that never blows so red
> The Rose as where some buried Caesar bled ;
>   That every Hyacinth the Garden wears
> Dropt in its Lap from some once lovely Head.

Here indeed FitzGerald speaks with the luxurious melancholy of
his time and finds an imagery which suggests vast distances in space
or long tracts of time, but he casts his words in a strict and economical mould. Nothing is otiose or flabby. At other times the
eighteenth century comes to the fore, and in the background we
hear the disciplined march of the heroic couplet :

> Myself when young did eagerly frequent
> Doctor and Saint, and heard great Argument
> > About it and about; but evermore
> Came out by the same Door as in I went.

or

> Indeed, indeed Repentance oft before
> I swore—but was I sober when I swore?
> > And then and then came Spring, and Rose-in-hand
> My threadbare Penitence apieces tore.

In such cases there is much that Pope would have liked, but Fitz-
Gerald is richer and warmer and less self-conscious. And though we
may distinguish the two strands in him, the important fact is that
he unites them in a style which is at once highly coloured and
strictly drilled, bold in its sweep and yet careful of every step that
it takes, straightforward as common speech and yet loaded with
imaginative association at every point, reckless and ironical, outspoken and controlled, passionate and witty. All this FitzGerald
learned from Omar, but he learned it so well and made it so intimate
a part of himself that he stands in his own right as a unique poetical
personality.

Through Omar FitzGerald found the deliverance that he needed
from certain misgivings and uncertainties. Of course he did not take
everything that Omar said at its face value and was very far from
preaching a gospel of drink. For him no doubt the vine and its
products were symbols of the happiness which he hoped to find, and
indeed often found, by avoiding the troubles and entanglements of
an active life. As such they enabled him to state with unusual power
the troubles which gnawed his spirit, as indeed they gnawed the
spirits of other men, but were not easily publicized in Victorian
England. The complacent religion of his time forced him into opposition because he saw that it did not meet his real spiritual needs,
and, though in his daily life he treated it with a polite tolerance, in
his inner self rebellious powers were at work, urging him to complain
about the scheme of things which aroused not merely his discontent
but his condemnation. He felt, as the Greeks felt, that human life
was a shadowy affair at the mercy of dark, incalculable forces, and

7

he found in Omar his instrument to speak of his disillusion and his distress. In this respect he was the forerunner and almost the guide of some Victorian rebels, who did not share the current optimism and reverted to those denunciations which Shakespeare gives to some of his characters when their worlds are shattered around them. Yet he differs greatly from them. He has much more tenderness and love of life than James Thomson in the prolonged gloom of *The City of Dreadful Night;* his outlook is much gentler and easier to understand than Housman's acrid and disdainful vision :

> It is in truth iniquity on high
>> To cheat our sentenced souls of aught they crave,
> And mar the merriment as you and I
>> Fare on our long fool's-errand to the grave;

he gives far more scope to human effort and choice than do Thomas Hardy's Spirits of the Years :

> O Immanence, That reasonest not
> In putting forth all things begot,
> Thou build'st thy house in space—for what?

> O loveless, hateless ! past the sense
> Of kindly eyed benevolence,
> To what tune danceth this immense?

FitzGerald felt the force of these questions, but shrank from answering them in his own voice or with any final assurance. His translation of Omar is the record of his quarrel with himself, of the conflict between his natural desire to take things as they come and not complain, and something which forced him to look away from the creeds and assurances of his youth and to find some sort of answer in Omar's Epicurean nihilism. At least this left the human affections intact and gave a brief, if precarious, dignity to his pleasures. If pressed about his views, FitzGerald would have said that he did not know what they were, and that much of Omar was not really acceptable to him. Yet in his inner self, away from the compromises and falsities of his time, he found something which caught his heart and his imagination. In him the Victorian melancholy was set on a philosophic basis, where it could be exorcized only by a recognition that what we have is after all worth having, even if its career is brief and uncertain. At times he might wish to get more than this, to break out into complaint and denunciation, but in the end he knew that it was useless, and it is this sense of his human limitations which gives a special tenderness to some of his darker foreboding and doubts :

Ah, Love ! could thou and I with Fate conspire
To grasp this sorry Scheme of Things entire,
  Would not we shatter it to bits, and then
Re-mould it nearer to the Heart's Desire !

Yet Omar taught him that such questions, and the desires that made
him ask them, were in the end futile, and that it was better to enjoy
things as they come. This was the lesson that FitzGerald, certainly
an apt and ready pupil, learned from his master and transformed
into his own high poetry. It was because he was able to identify
himself with Omar on this central issue that he wrote his masterpiece, and fulfilled a wish which he had expressed in 1851 before
he had heard of the *Rubaiyat* :

'I was thinking ... to myself how it was fame enough to have
written but one song—air, or words—which should in after days
solace the sailor at the wheel, or the soldier in foreign places !
to be taken up into the life of England.'

His prayer was answered on a scale which he could never have
imagined, and it was Persia that answered it for him.

X

POETRY AND THE FIRST
WORLD WAR

[The Taylorian Lecture, University of Oxford, 1961]

THE OUTBREAK of war in August 1914 struck Europe with appalled
amazement. Though for years politicians and publicists had prepared the way for it, and though ordinary people had commonly
discussed it as much more than a mere possibility, very few expected
it to come when it actually did. It had for so long been a mere idea
that, when it was suddenly transformed into brutal reality, it came
as a cataclysmic shock to millions of men and women who were
forced overnight to adjust to it not only their daily habits but their
familiar assumptions and outlooks, their challenged convictions,
and their haunting dreams. In this adjustment, which, as the war
continued, became increasingly exacting and difficult, poets played
a special part. In all belligerent countries they tried to express in
forceful words what the new situation meant for the human spirit,
what issues were really at stake, what was the significance of the
crisis and the conflict which ravaged the minds no less than the
homes of men. The great bulk of their work was of course ephemeral
and has long mouldered in deserved neglect, but enough has survived the probing tests of the years to have a place in our memories,
and it is with this part that we may concern ourselves. It provides
no facts which we cannot learn better from elsewhere; it does not
begin to compete on their own ground with history or the realistic
novel. But it does what nothing else can do. It not only gives a coherent form to moods which at the time were almost indiscernible
in the general welter of emotions, but incidentally provides a
criticism of them, not indeed consciously or overtly, but through the
character of its approach and the power or insight with which it
gives them shape. It enables us to see through the eyes of an unusual few what the war meant to them, and, just because they were
themselves caught in it, we can share their experience and learn from

it. What they created survives for its own worth and is not without relevance to ourselves today. They stand for many points of view, and some of these may be alien, if not repellent, to us, but in all their variety and divergence there is a discernible pattern, which is an inner record of this gruesome climacteric in human affairs and discloses how men tried to grasp it with their imaginative understanding and so to come to terms with it and master its menace in themselves.

A tragic paradox of the war is that it was actually welcomed by the great majority of those who found themselves caught in it. Of course nobody had the slightest prevision of what infernal shapes it would take, and for the moment crowds were bewitched by the lure of unprecedented excitement after years of drab routine. But something deeper and subtler was also at work. Before 1914 it was impossible not to be aware of a growing belief that war was certainly unavoidable and even in some sense desirable. This mood received eloquent support from some poets, who in their opposition to prevailing tendencies of the age became, in their several ways, prophets of doom. In Germany, where the military spirit was most ardently cultivated, a few poets foresaw its inevitable conclusion in bloodshed. The Expressionists, in particular, were haunted by the spectacle of present savagery and by spectres of coming catastrophe, and in these war held pride of place. So in 'Der Krieg' ('The War') George Heym, who died in 1913, turned his gruesome forebodings into a primeval, blood-curdling myth, in which the incarnate spirit of war sets out on its ghastly progress :

> Auf den Bergen hebt er schon zu tanzen an,
> Und er schreit : Ihr Krieger, alle auf und an !
> Und es schallet, wenn das schwarze Haupt er schwenkt,
> Drum von tausend Schädeln laute Kette hängt.
>
> Einem Turm gleich tritt er aus die letzte Glut,
> Wo der Tag flieht, sind die Ströme schon voll Blut.
> Zahllos sind die Leichen schon in Schilf gestreckt,
> Von des Todes starken Vögeln weiß bedeckt.

. . .

> On the hills already has his dance begun;
> And he cries out : 'All you fighters, up and on !'
> Shaking his black head he starts a clanging sound;
> Loudly from a chain a thousand skulls ring round.

Like a tower stamps he on the light's last glow;
Where the day flees, full of blood the rivers flow.
Countless are the corpses on the shelves now laid;
Mighty birds of death have them in white arrayed.

The violence of Heym's horror is mirrored in his hard, metallic imagery, and the abrupt crash of his heavily loaded lines. He does not trouble to explain why war is coming, but he knows that it is, and in his sense of outraged justice he does not find it unwelcome.

Close to this mood was another, based on the conviction that only through some vast sacrifice and redemption could society be purged of its complacency and its grossness. So Stefan George, who both in his aims and in his art was far removed from Heym, was equally outraged by the spiritual aridity which he marked everywhere in the Germany of William II. He, too, claimed the authority of a seer, but he was also a teacher, the pioneer of a purified culture which was to breathe a refreshing vigour into the jaded present. He had long fought for his new realm of the spirit, but by 1913 he felt that he had largely failed because his countrymen were corrupted by false and futile causes. Unlike Heym, he did not regard war as an inevitable end; rather he discerned a progressive impoverishment of the soul as it sank ever deeper into sloth and unconcern. In the material abundance around him he saw only dearth, and it was this that he wished to heal, but the cure which he proposed was as devastating as the disease :

> Zehntausend muß der heilige wahnsinn schlagen
> Zehntausend muß die heilige seuche raffen
> Zehntausende der heilige krieg.

. . .

> Ten thousand must the holy madness strike,
> Ten thousand must the holy sickness seize,
> Tens of thousands the holy war.

If Heym saw war as an inescapable consequence of the military ideal, George came even to desire it. It was of course to be a war of his own choosing, a holy war fought for his own ideals and inspired by his own spirit, but it was none the less war. His ardent ambition to redeem his age had become a crusade, which may indeed be impressive in its hope of an unreckonable, god-given change of heart, but still calls for uncounted sacrifices.

What Heym and George did in Germany had its counterpart in Russia, where a bitter sense of political frustration sharpened the

issues and inspired an even more desperate outlook. While Heym's
fevered imagination was limited to actual war, Alexander Blok foresaw a vaster, less definable destruction. Before 1914 he prophesied
a boundless wrath to come, and contrasted the blind carelessness of
men with the fearful chaos that awaited them. In 'Голос из хора'
('Voice from the Chorus') he speaks of the pitiful pettiness and self-
sufficiency of human relations, and then delivers his terrifying forecast of what the future holds in store :

> И век последний, ужасней всех,
>   Увидим и вы и я.
> Всё небо скроет гнусный грех,
> На всех устах застынет смех,
>   Тоска небытня . . .

> . . .

> The last age shall be worst of all,
>   And you and I shall see
> The sky wrapped in a guilty pall;
> Laughter on lips shall fail and fall,—
> Anguish of not-to-be . . .

For Blok this was the fated doom of mankind. He did not justify
it or desire it, but he believed that it would surely come. In his clairvoyant, tragic way he spoke for a generation broken by defeat and
driven to find its chief consolation in the privacy of the affections,
but he thought that this was an abdication of responsibility which
could end only in universal agony. His older contemporary, Valery
Bryusov, assumes a similar doom in his 'Грядущие Гунны' ('The
Coming Huns'), where he welcomes the prospect of a barbarian invasion which, by destroying churches and books, will put new life
into decaying bodies, while perhaps a few men 'in catacomb, desert,
and cave' will save from the past the little that deserves to be saved
from it. Bryusov has none of Blok's compassionate anguish, and his
poem is the ruthless utterance of a hardened aesthete who so hates
the tedium of his circumstances that he will pay even this price to
relieve it. Yet he comes to a conclusion not very different from
Blok's. Both poets foresee an enormous destruction and have no
doubt that it will come.

Such black forebodings were in fact countered in their own time
from an unexpected quarter by a poet of whose work western Europe
as yet knew nothing. Before 1910 Constantine Cavafy, a Greek poet
living in Alexandria, wrote his own version of the expected doom in
περιμένοντας τοὺς βαρβ άρους ('Waiting for the Barbarians').
Setting his modern theme in the decline of the Roman Empire, he
tells how a city waits excitedly for the arrival of Barbarians and
prepares to receive them with high honour. It is well aware of their

vanity, gullibility, and ignorance, but it accepts and even welcomes their advent. Then, with a splendid stroke of irony, news comes that there are no Barbarians any more, and the poem closes:

καὶ τῶρα τί θὰ γένουμε χωρὶς βαρβάρους;
δι ἄνθρωποι αὐτοὶ ἦσαν μιὰ κάποια λύσις
.   .   .

And now what will become of us without Barbarians?
These people were some kind of a solution.

Cavafy deftly turns their own weapons against those who wish for some violent change by showing that, however eagerly they may desire it, it is illusory, that, however sick civilization may be, it cannot put any hope in this kind of salvation. Cavafy's scepticism was fully justified, but it did nothing to undermine the morbid desire for catastrophe which possessed some of his contemporaries. Before 1914 the vision of coming bloodshed haunted the minds of poets, and, whether they merely foresaw it or actually desired it, they believed that it would come and prepared others to regard it as inevitable. No doubt they appealed to diverse and contradictory elements in their contemporaries, to various convictions that men had grown soft from too long a peace, that finer instincts were corrupted by the pursuit of wealth, that increasing mechanization stifled the arts, that modern organization allowed no place for adventure or glory or heroism, that a growing obsession with personal ties weakened the sense of public duty. But, whatever the actual appeal of these poets might be, there is no doubt about their influence. They gave vivid forms to ideas that were already lurking in many minds, and, when at last the war came, much had been done to make it acceptable.

The outbreak of war stung poets to work. Here indeed was a theme worthy of their attention, and they did their best for it. Love of country is far too deeply ingrained in human nature for most men not to feel grave anxiety and fear when their land is in danger, and their first reaction is that they must do all that they can to save it. In this first onrush of devotion they are not likely to specify very particularly what they love in their country or why they are ready to sacrifice themselves for it; it is enough that it is threatened. In their immediate response they are confident that, though they may know little about their cause, it has a paramount claim on them. They are suddenly aware that they belong to something much larger than themselves and have towards it obligations which they cannot shirk. So Karl Bröger in 'Bekenntnis' ('Confession') feels that he is urged on by something almost beyond the reach of words:

Immer schon haben wir eine Liebe zu dir gekannt,
bloß wir haben sie nie mit einem Namen genannt.
Als man uns rief, da sogen wir schweigend fort,
auf den Lippen nicht, aber im Herzen das Wort
Deutschland.

. . .

The love that we now feel for you we long have known;
Simply, we never called it by a name of its own.
When we were summoned, silently forth we stirred,
With nothing on our lips, but in our hearts the word
Deutschland.

This is typical of much simple patriotism, and, though it is not very subtle, it is quite honest. For the moment, the emotional pressure is so strong that it hardly allows analysis of what it means. In a like mood Thomas Hardy makes his soldiers sing :

What of the faith and fire within us
    Men who march away
    Ere the barn-cocks say
    Night is growing gray,
Leaving all that here can win us;
What of the faith and fire within us
    Men who march away ?

Despite his habitual doubts and misgivings, Hardy knows the temper in which men go to war, and though, as he shows later in the song, there is more in it than faith and fire, yet these are its foundation, and there is something grave and touching in their very simplicity.

Yet love of country is not merely an emotion. Every man who feels it finds something in his country which is peculiarly characteristic of it and which he loves just for that reason. When it comes to specifying or formulating what this is, the modern poet is at a great disadvantage in comparison with his forerunners in ancient Greece. Living as they did in small city-states, in which almost everything was familiar and part of their special heritage, the Greeks knew for what they fought. But the modern soldier, who is an infinitesimal part of some huge administrative agglomeration and no more than a single tactical unit in an army of millions, is left with little to love but an abstraction. This will take him a certain distance, but before long he may feel that he must justify and explain his position or get others to do it for him. So Rudyard Kipling certainly spoke for the great mass of Englishmen in 1914 when he asked :

> What stands if Freedom fall?
> Who dies if England live?

If in England the older generation saw the younger as fighting for an ideal of justice and order, in France the issue was even simpler. The ideal of 'la France', which is in mortal peril, stirred Paul Claudel to write with powerful, if disturbing, eloquence about the lengths to which the common soldier would go in doing his duty. Claudel is not afraid of realistic colour, even if later he tempers it with other associations. So when he begins a poem

> Dix fois qu'on attaque là-dedans, 'avec résultat purement local'.
> Il faut y aller une fois de plus? Tant que vous voudrez, mon Général.

he starts with the bare language of the official communiqué, and then he begins his supporting argument, that the French soldier will fight for France to the last sacrifice demanded of him. Whether the war is waged for English 'fair play' or for 'la France' or for 'holy Russia' or for 'deutsche Gerechtigkeit', it has become more than a struggle for survival, and the emotional outburst which carried away poets in the first days has been replaced by something more imposing.

Yet in this we feel that something is lacking, that the poets have not probed the matter to its depths and are to some degree the victims of moral and literary prepossessions. They try to address their minds to the unprecedented situation, but they do not see it as it really is. In particular there was a serious danger that they would look at the fearful holocaust of modern warfare through romantic spectacles and see it falsely. It was easy to compare modern soldiers with medieval knights, but the comparison was usually absurd and sometimes nauseating. A. E. Housman indeed made the mistake but avoided the worst consequences by his wilful fancy that the modern soldier faces fewer dangers than his predecessors and is, at least in his own opinion, inferior to them :

> So here are things to think on
> That ought to make me brave,
> As I strap on for fighting
> My sword that will not save.

Here there is a redeeming irony, but we cannot offer the same defence for a famous verse by Walter Flex :

Der Stahl, den Mutters Mund geküßt,
  Liegt still und blank zur Seite.
Stromüber gleißt, Waldüber grüßt,
  Feldüber lockt die Weite![1]

.   .   .

The blade my mother's lips have kissed
  Hangs at my side and glistens;
Gleams over streams, greets over woods,
  Calls over fields—the distance!

It is bad enough that a soldier should have his bayonet kissed by his mother, but it is almost worse that he should see himself lured onward by some nameless and endless quest. Yet mistakes of this kind were made everywhere just because poets did not yet see the reality of war beyond the mirage of misleading associations. To this error the apocalyptic poets made their own contribution. A truly alarming case is the 'Fünf Gesänge' ('Five Songs'), which Rainer Maria Rilke wrote on the outbreak of war. This detached, solitary, internationally minded figure, with his refusal to surrender himself to human ties, and his endless probing into himself, was irresistibly carried away by the declaration of war and for a few days flung aside all his earlier convictions, as in dithyrambic language he glorified the coming of war as an irruption of ancient gods, a return to primeval energy, an intrusion of reality into a realm of illusions. He who had so exploited his sensibility as the only condition of creative work now felt that he was absorbed into some larger unity, in which he could find a vastly extended and reinforced existence. He conceals none of the horrors of war, but takes a fierce delight in its breaking of all bonds and its creation of a new, inhuman self:

Andere sind wir, ins Gleiche Geänderte: jedem
sprang in die plötzlich
nicht mehr seinige Brust meteorisch ein Herz.
Heiß, ein eisernes Herz aus eisernem Weltall.

.   .   .

We are others, changed into resemblance; for each
there has leapt into the breast
suddenly no more his own, like a meteor, a heart.
Hot, an iron-clad heart from an iron-clad universe.

When passions are roused to this pitch, they are not all likely to work in the same direction. In the heavily charged atmosphere of

[1] I am indebted to Mr George Hill for my knowledge of this poem.

the time some poets regarded the war as a necessity which they had themselves foretold. This did not mean that they always opposed it. Indeed, Valery Bryusov almost welcomed it as a preliminary to revolutionary changes in the world and the release of a new spirit of freedom. For him it was at once a fulfilment of the fantasies of H. G. Wells and a modern counterpart of Roncesvalles, and without displeasure he foresaw it spreading to every land and every sea. To Blok, on the other hand, it was a heart-breaking tragedy. He believed that by its assent to war 'civilization signed its own death-warrant', and, though he had almost foretold it, it brought him nothing but anguish. His few poems of the time are the record of his struggle to keep his faith in humanity and in Russia, when almost everyone was carried away by a fury of destruction and death. He watches with pitying dismay the troops going to the front, and in their songs and hurrahs finds nothing but the menace of enormous slaughter on the blood-stained fields of Galicia. In his passionate devotion to his country he will have nothing to do with war, and he proudly proclaims that he has never betrayed the white flag. Though now he sees the crosses on the graves of his brothers and knows that friend and foe are alike sunk in a deadly dream, he still clings to his love for Russia and trusts that, like the star of Bethlehem, it guides him in the darkness. The world now at war was as empty as it had been in peace, and everywhere he felt a numbing sense of futility :

> Есть немота – то гул набата
> Заставил заградить уста.
> В сердцах, восторженных когда-то,
> Есть роковая пустота.

· · ·

> All dumb. Alarms have struck affrighted
> On lips that close together press.
> In hearts that were before delighted
> There is a fated emptiness.

Perhaps out of this evil some good might come, but Blok did not see its shape or put his trust very firmly in it. For him the war was a senseless agony for which he saw no consolation and no solution.

Despite his remoteness from Blok in almost every personal and literary respect something of the same kind was felt by Vladimir Mayakovsky, who in 1914 was in his twenty-first year. From boyhood he had been a revolutionary, and had already been three times in prison. As a poet he was a Futurist, who had before the war helped to compose *A Slap in the Face of the Public Taste*, which derides the literary past of Russia rather in the manner of Giacomo Marinetti's more notorious manifesto. Mayakovsky's genius drove him to seek startling effects through up-to-date, even brutal imagery, and he might have been expected to follow Marinetti in glorifying war for its furious sensations and its mechanized modernity. At first, on his own testimony, he 'took the war excitedly' and 'thought of it in its decorative and noisy aspects', but he soon felt 'hatred and disgust for it'. He had seen through Marinetti's vociferous nonsense, and he knew that his own revolutionary aims allowed no compromise with war. His long poem 'Война и мир' ('War and the Universe'), finished in 1916, shows how far he went in his condemnation of it. His realistic understanding of it was not in the least impaired by his Futurist manner; indeed, the novel character of his imagery, drawn from many unexploited quarters of experience, adds to his gruesome picture of insane brutality. He sees the war as a gladiatorial show, which needs another Nero to enjoy it; the whole world is a Coliseum, and the waves of every sea are the velvet curtain hung over it. Under his satirical jabs and his savage irony against those who think it good to 'burn and ravish to the music of machine-guns' he hides his unquestionable pity for the millions of all countries who 'die on a stone in a hole'. He differs from Blok in his ability to look beyond the frontiers of Russia to the whole world and beyond the appalling present to a more comforting future. He is sustained by his confidence in the coming of revolution, and this keeps him sane through the strain of war. But despite their manifest differences, when these two poets denounced the war, they saw in the Russian scene something which was concealed from most men by the self-sacrificing devotion which drove millions of Russians to death. In due course the Russian people came round to the opinion of its leading poets and accepted Lenin largely because he promised peace.

These attempts to grasp the war as a whole and to see it as a natural or cosmic process were made largely by men who were far from the front or at least took no active part in the fighting. They had the advantage of detachment and the freedom to look at things in a wide context without the distracting urgency of the battlefield. To write about the war from the inside was a different matter, and, when poetry began to come from those who had a first-hand knowledge of battle, it took a new character. It showed that war was not at all what literary convention assumed, and it emphasized aspects of it which were commonplaces to fighting men but disturbing novelties to those who stayed at home. It is from such moments that we get the most revealing and most authentic poetry of war, based on a perceptive acquaintance with its real character and an un-

premeditated response to its unforeseen demands. It illustrates beyond dispute how wrong established notions of war may turn out to
be when they are tested by hard facts.

First, those who knew of events only from hearsay could not
imagine the incredible variety of battle and of the moods which it
evokes. When a man is inextricably dependent on his circumstances,
every little thing in them makes a powerful impression on him. He
must at all costs acclimatize himself to this strange and unaccount-
able world of war, and his moods will cover the whole range of which
he is capable. There is no standard reaction to war; each man takes
what comes, as it comes, in his own way. For some, indeed, it was,
at least at the start, a novelty so extraordinary that it was impossible
not to enjoy some of its moments, and this attitude certainly had its
advantages for anyone who had to endure its strains. So Guillaume
Apollinaire, bursting into the lilt of a popular song, sings of his
delight in his new role on horseback :

> As-tu connu Guy au galop
> Du temps qu'il était militaire
> As-tu connu Guy au galop
> Du temps qu'il était artiflot
> A la guerre.

Of course war brought deliverance from the irking routine of urban
life, and for this reason it was natural to welcome its brighter occasions. But, more than this, by its very difference from everything
that they had hitherto known it could set poets' imaginations to
work as they sought to find a place for themselves in it, to feel somehow at home, to adapt their habits of mind to its fantastic demands
and sensations. If they were glad to be rid of old restraints, they
might still wish to replace them by a new background which could
give them comfort and confidence. Some of them found this in the
natural scene in which they now lived and moved, and, as they
extended their contact with it, they formed a close intimacy with
the earth, and, since they had lost most of their familiar supports,
they developed almost a religious attitude towards natural things
and felt themselves to belong to their company. This is the mood of
Julian Grenfell's 'Into Battle', in which he feels the spring in his blood
and speaks of it not with the external detachment of a mere on-
looker but as someone who cannot but respond to it with all his
being and recognize in it a source of enhanced vitality and sustain-
ing comradeship. What before he had known casually and distantly
now sets the rhythm of his actions, and his discovery of it has the
strength of an inspiring revelation :

> The fighting man shall from the sun
>   Take warmth, and life from the glowing earth;
> Speed with the light-foot winds to run,
>   And with the trees to newer birth;
> And find, when fighting shall be done,
>   Great rest, and fullness after dearth.

As he sees his surroundings in this new light, the poet settles more happily into them, and the whole business of battle becomes less alien and less formidable when it reveals its similarities with more familiar and apparently quite different things. So the Russian poet, Nikolai Gumilev, who enjoyed soldiering and excelled at it, tells with fascinated curiosity of a bombardment in a wood :

> Как собака на цепи тяжелой,
> Тявкает за лесом пулемет,
> И жужжат шрапнели, словно плечы,
> Собирая ярко-красный мед.
>
> А «ура» вдали, как будто пенье
> Трудный день окончивших жнецов.
> Скажешь: это – мирное селенье
> В самый благостный из вечеров.

.   .   .

> Like a watch-dog, whom a great chain ties,
> Comes a bullet barking in the wood;
> Shrapnel buzzes like a swarm of bees
> Gathering its honey bright and red.
>
> Sound 'Hurrahs !' far off, as if it were
> Fag-end of a reapers' work-day done;
> You could say : 'A quiet village here
> In the holy light of evening sun.'

The surprises and the paradoxes of war invite its participants to identify its uncouth scenes with others from a very different order, and by this means not merely to bring it into the range of intelligible experience, but to reveal the strange ways in which the imagination is touched by its unforeseen surprises. Unfortunately this mood, which was easy enough in the first months of the war, became vastly more difficult to sustain as the armies settled into the squalid monotony of trench-warfare with its desolated landscapes and its numbing frustrations, but at first the poetical imagination helped to make the war less unnatural by marking its unexpected moments of intimate charm.

Conversely, there were other poets who from the very outset hated and denounced the war, and yet got out of it something which was both less and more than hatred. However fiercely they might condemn it, it exerted a sinister hold over them. A striking case of this is the Russian Futurist, Viktor Khlebnikov, who fought as a private soldier on the eastern front from early in the war until the dissolution of the Russian armies. A leading figure in the *avant-garde* of poetry, he experimented with words and images in the hope of making his poetry tougher and harsher, and war provided him with many opportunities for effects which suited his peculiar tastes. It appealed to him by its elemental disorder, its reduction of life to its lowest terms, its chaotic brutality which made him believe that the earth had returned to the sway of savage, primeval gods. His packed, forceful lines and his bold improvisations in vocabulary reflected his isolation from other men and his imperviousness to the common claims of humanity. His revolutionary ardour was perfectly sincere and set him in principle against the war, but in practice he displayed his feelings largely in his love of rasping shocks and grim surprises. His imagination was set to work by such themes as a dead man lying in a pond, soldiers caught in battle as in a mousetrap, the merciless torment of rain and snow and wind, the flame and smoke of bombardments, the burning of villages and the wreck of forests. In these he feels at home, because he sees in them a reversion to a distant, disordered past for which his anarchic temperament craves. He creates his own mythology for the battlefield and likes to see in its routine survivals from pagan rites. So in 'Тризна' ('Death-feast'), he presents in the cremation of dead soldiers an ancient death-feast, in which modern military drill is part of the ceremony. As soldiers stand in silence and watch the pyre set alight, the smoke which rises from it recalls the flow of great rivers, the Don and the Irtish, and symbolizes the overpowering domination of nature when artificial restraints are removed. In Khlebnikov's love of horrors there is a streak of perversity, but it is none the less in character in a man who looked forward to the collapse of his world. For him also war transforms what he sees, and gives to it a fierce enchantment.

From his knowledge of war as it really is the poet may start again towards a wider vision of it and try to see it in a fuller perspective without reverting to the old abstractions and falsities. It is impossible to present its illimitable chaos, but what counts is the poet's selection from it of what really strikes or stirs him. This is what Georg Trakl, who died on the eastern front in December 1914, does in 'Im Osten' ('On the Eastern Front'). He applies to the whole shapeless panorama of battle his gift for images which form a centre for a host of associations and must be taken at their full value as each appears :

> Den wilden Orgeln des Wintersturms
> Gleicht des Volkes finstrer Zorn,
> Die purpurne Woge der Schlacht,
> Entlaubter Sterne.
>
> Mit zerbrochnen Brauen, silbernen Armen
> Winkt sterbenden Soldaten die Nacht.
> Im Schatten der herbstlichen Esche
> Seufzen die Geister der Erschlagenen.
>
> Dornige Wildnis umgürtet die Stadt.
> Von blutenden Stufen jagt der Mond
> Die erschrockenen Frauen.
> Wilde Wölfe brachen durchs Tor.

. . .

> Like the wild organ-notes of a winter storm
> Is the dark wrath of the people,
> The purple wave of the battle,
> Stars that have lost their leaves.
>
> With ravaged brows, silver arms,
> Night beckons to dying soldiers.
> In the shadow of the autumn ash
> The ghosts of the slain are sighing.
>
> A wilderness of thorns girdles the town.
> From blood-stained steps the moon hunts
> Terrified women.
> Wild wolves burst through the door.

Here the individual elements are taken from fact and give a true picture of war, but they gain a special significance because they also point to something beyond themselves, of which they are both examples and symbols. Trakl shows that the soldier-poet is fully capable of seeing beyond his immediate situation with an insight denied to those who have no experience of actual battle.

Though Trakl looks upon war from the anguished solitude of a prophet, he draws no conclusions and makes no forecasts. Yet it was not impossible for a fighting man to let his vision pierce beyond the actual carnage and to divine with an apocalyptic clairvoyance its meaning in the scheme of things. This was what Isaac Rosenberg did. In the British army he had little in common with his fellow poets. They were officers; he was a private soldier. They cherished a trust in a privileged and happy England which had only to survive the war and return to its old ways; he, brought up in poverty and frustration and conscious of his alien origin, shared none of their romantic dreams. For him the war was indeed a cosmic event, which he believed to be needed to purge the injustices of society and to bring back sanity to men. As such he welcomed it when it came, and as such he continued to believe in it when others had lost their nerve on finding that their vaulting hopes were false. He was convinced that the war was an inevitable part of an historical process, in which England, driven by a desire for self-destruction, by an 'incestuous worm' eating into its vitals, was passing to the doom of Babylon and Rome. He had something in common with the Russian revolution-aries, but he differed from Mayakovsky in believing that the war was necessary to attain what he desired, and from Khlebnikov in taking no pleasure, however grim or perverse, in it. He did not deceive himself about its actual cost, and hardly any poet has written with so unshrinking a candour about the actual appearance of battle. As a human being Rosenberg was racked by the agony and the waste which he saw, but he steeled himself to endure it, because he be-lieved that only through such an ordeal could the injustices and falsities of his world be discredited and destroyed. In his view Eng-land was paying a price for her cruelties, and, though the price was indeed heavy, it must none the less be paid. For this cause Rosen-berg was ready to sacrifice himself, and he fulfilled his pledge when he was killed in April 1918. He spoke very much from his own point of view, but what he said is an enlightening corrective both to those who saw nothing in the carnage and to those who saw nothing beyond it.

A second matter on which there is a wide divergence between the non-combatant and the combatant views of war is in their treatment of death. Those who are not in constant contact with it cannot but be deeply affected by it, and not only express their grief freely but see in death much more than its immediate presence. Death in battle has long had its own glory, and it is understandable that Rupert Brooke, who died before he had seen any fighting except at Antwerp, should proclaim :

Blow out you bugles, over the rich Dead.

But this was not how the average soldier treated it. So far as the prospect of his own death was concerned, he usually observed a private fatalism, which made speculation superfluous, and in the deaths of others, however deeply he might feel a personal loss, he knew that it was useless to lament or do anything but hide his feelings in a situation where death came all the time and hardly called for special remark. This of course did not deceive anyone, and was not intended to do so; it was the dignity of silence in the face of something on which there was nothing to say. The soldier has to adjust his mind to death. He does so by treating it as nothing unusual, and in his topsy-turvy world he is not wrong. This note of superficial detachment is what Guillaume Apollinaire catches in 'Exercice' :

> Vers un village de l'arrière
> S'en allaient quatre bombardiers
> Ils étaient couverts de poussière
> Depuis la tête jusqu'aux pieds
>
> Ils regardaient la vaste plaine
> En parlant entre eux du passé
> Et ne se regardaient qu'à peine
> Quand un obus avait toussé
>
> Tous quatre de la classe seize
> Parlant d'antan non d'avenir
> Ainsi se prolongeait l'ascèse
> Qui les exerçait à mourir.

With solicitous understatement Apollinaire tells of the deaths of four men behind the lines as if it were nothing unusual, and so indeed it was. But behind this quiet exterior there is a real compassion at the impartial cruelty of death which suddenly breaks into the soldiers' routine and destroys them, when in their talk about the past they pay no attention to the future, which suddenly falls upon them. Apollinaire's art speaks for a whole order of human beings of whom he is the representative, and presents these casual deaths in the spirit in which any soldier would, in his inarticulate way, feel about them.

The paradox of death in war is that despite its presence life must go on without interruption and that even the most gruesome relics must not be allowed to break into the living soldier's hold upon himself, which is at all times precarious but none the less the centre of his sanity and his ability to act. The contrast between what he feels or does and the surroundings in which he does it is one of war's most violent discords, and in it we can see how the human spirit adapts itself to the most horrifying circumstances simply because it

must exert itself and endure. Something of this kind is in the mind of
the Italian poet Giuseppe Ungaretti in 'Veglia' ('Watch') :

Un' intera nottata
buttato vicino
a un compagno
massacrato
con la sua bocca
digrignata
volta al plenilunio
con la congestione
delle sue mani
penetrata
nel mio silenzio
ho scritto
lettere piene d'amore

Non sono mai stato
tanto
attaccato alla vita

.   .   .

A whole night long
crouched as a neighbour
to a companion
massacred
with his mouth
turned into a snarl
towards the full moon
with the congestion of his hands
piercing
into my silence
I have written
letters full of love

I have never been
so greatly
attached to life.

In the struggle to maintain his individuality Ungaretti has to resist
any invasion of it by distress at the dead body. He is fully aware of it,
and his words are not in the least lacking in humanity. He marks the
horror of death in the snarl on the dead man's face and is painfully

conscious of the way in which the dead hands push towards him,
but he struggles against the horror, exerts a complete command over
himself—and writes love-letters. It is his escape from the hideous
unreality of war into the reality of his affections, and it gains greatly
in seriousness from the chilling circumstances in which it all takes
place.

A third matter on which the fighting soldier has his own ideas
is the enemy. At home enemies may be denounced as inhuman
barbarians, ready to destroy the hearths and shrines of lands more
civilized than their own. Therefore patriots, safely esconced in the
rear, fulminate against them, but the average soldier soon sees that
in this there is little truth. Living in his own isolated world of the
trenches, he feels that the enemy are closer to him than many of his
own countrymen, and especially than the invisible commanders who
from a remote security order multitudes to a senseless death. On no
point is there a sharper contrast between home and front, and in
England we may mark the extremes, on one side by Kipling's.

> It was not part of their blood.
>   It came to them very late
> With long arrears to make good,
>   When the English began to hate,

and on the other side by Siegfried Sassoons'

> O German mother dreaming by the fire,
> While you are knitting socks to send your son
> His face is trodden deeper in the mud.

In Germany no less pungent a contrast can be found between one
end of the scale with Littauer's 'Hymn of Hate' and another with
ordinary soldiers, who felt, almost despite themselves, the curious
brotherhood into which battle draws its antagonists. So in 'Brüder'
('Brothers'), Heinrich Lersch comes close to what many men felt as he
tells of a dead man hanging on the barbed wire in front of his trench.
He feels that this man is his brother, and at night he thinks that he
hears him crying. He crawls out to bring him in and bury him, and
then he sees that he is a stranger. He draws his conclusion :

> Es irrten meine Augen. Mein Herz, du irrst dich nicht :
> Es hat ein jeder Toter des Bruders Angesicht.

. . .

> 'Twas my eyes were mistaken. You, heart, were not misled;
> There's the look of a brother on every man that's dead.

In France we find similar contrasts. At one extreme we may put
Claudel's 'Derrière eux', which in righteous anger denounces the
Germans for shedding innocent blood and foretells their defeat and
punishment by the implacable justice which they have aroused
against them. It has its own proud fury when Claudel elaborates
how in the end the Germans will be undone by the very forces which
they have themselves set in action :

> Retranche-toi, peuple assiégé ! tends tes impassables réseaux de
>   fil de fer !
> Fossoyeyurs de vos propres bataillons, sans relâche faites votre
>   fosse dans la terre !

but it moves in too exalted and too personal an atmosphere to speak
for the common soldier. What he felt is more truly represented by
René Arcos in 'Les Morts', which with poignant understanding
develops the theme that in war the true defeated are the dead of
both sides and that their defeat is that of all humanity :

> Serrés les uns contre les autres
> Les morts sans haine et sans drapeau,
> Cheveux plaqués de sang caillé,
> Les morts sont tous d'un seul côté.

The strange, compulsive fellowship of war breaks across familiar
distinctions and differences and shapes new relations for those who
live in it. What binds one man to another is not some abstract cause
or theoretical obligation but identity of effort and suffering, and this
brings even enemies together. The merciless, mechanical rules of
warfare insist that opponents must continue to kill one another, but
they do not do so in hatred, and they know that they have something indisputably in common with those whom they try to kill.

The unique universe of the battlefield, imprisoned by its inexorable discipline, its neglect of everything except the immediate needs
of war, and its lack of every familiar consolation, shapes men's habits
to fit its all-embracing demands. As soldiers shed their false notions
of it and learn to see it as it really is, it cannot but dominate their
being. Yet just for this reason most men struggle against its tyrannical claims and create some private refuge for their own thoughts
and fancies and dreams. In this way they assert their right to be
themselves and, so far as lies in their control, they master their
circumstances by refusing to surrender to them. What is true of most
soldiers is, in a special degree, true of poets, who know all too well
the struggle between their secret selves and the enforced exactions

of war, and, because this is clearer to them than to others, they speak for others with a greater authority. All belong to one company and share the same conflicts without and within. That is why the man who struggles to maintain his inner life against the inroads of military necessity gains strength from the presence of others around him. They may not be so vividly conscious of the need as he is, but they too wish to be themselves, and he knows that on this issue they are with him and he with them. Like them, he leads a double life, exterior and interior, active and withdrawn, public and private. This is what Ungaretti, who felt the paramount claims of keeping his inner integrity, understood when he wrote 'Italia' ('Italy') :

Sono un poeta
un grido unanime
sono un grumo di sogni

Sono un frutto
d'innumerevoli contrasti d'innesti
maturata in una serra

Mal il tuo popolo e portato
della stessa terra
che mi porta
Italia

E in questo uniforme
di tuo soldato
mi reposo
come fosse la culla
di mio padre

.   .   .

I am a poet
a unanimous cry
I am a clot of dreams

I am a fruit
of innumerable contrasts of grafting
ripened on a wall

But your people is borne
by the same earth
that bears me
Italy

> And in this uniform
> of a soldier of yours
> I take my rest
> as if it were the cradle
> of my father.

If a poet is to make all that he can of war, this is a well-chosen position, since it enables him to maintain his own personality and to reflect what is in the hearts of his fellows. By this means he will escape from the rhetoric and the falsity into which circumstances might otherwise delude him, and he will speak with truth about war as it is for those who take part in it.

To maintain such a balance is not at all easy. It calls for an unusual combination of detachment and commitment which few can attain, and those who aim at it must keep their senses and their sensibility awake and refuse to be enticed from the truth as they see it. Ungaretti's small volume *Allegria* (*Joy*), written with a highly critical and selective control, reduces to their essence, almost to their minimum, his experiences on the Italian front. Of actual battle he writes almost nothing, and the main effect of war on him was to sharpen his love of nature and to encourage him to examine his own feelings with a new delicacy and precision. He was fortunate in enjoying the prospect of an Alpine landscape, which could never be shelled into a bog of slimy mud, but it is its very simplicities that touch him, its stars, its stormy skies, its slopes of velvety green, its flowers in abandoned gardens, its river Isonzo to remind him of other rivers which he has loved. The savage contrast of war makes him look affectionately at the scene around him and through the delight which it gives him he keeps his confidence in himself and turns what he sees into images for his own imaginative introspection. Though many of his poems look like an escape from an oppressive reality into dreams and desires, they are rather his efforts to keep his inner self alive by getting the best that he can from his circumstances. His inner and outer lives have almost become one, as each penetrates the other and gives it a new meaning. Thus in a piece so short and concentrated that it recalls a traditional Japanese poem, he sums up his feelings about soldiers :

> Si sta come
> d'autunno
> sugli alberi
> le foglie

.   .   .

> They stand as
> in autumn
> on the poplars
> the leaves

It is the merest sigh in the wind, and yet is it born from many months of war and from the loving admiration which Ungaretti feels for the men among whom he has lived.

Like Ungaretti, Guillaume Apollinaire found exactly the right equipoise which enabled him to write about the war as he really knew it. But while Ungaretti found security by enriching and examining his inner thoughts, Apollinaire's ebullient, expansive nature took in with delighted curiosity all the unparalleled novelty of the front. He had always sought new sensations, and now he had them in abundance, so that there was little in the enormous disarray of battle which escaped his attention or failed to strike a spark from him. He responded equally to sights and sounds, to human situations, and the obstinate persistence of nature. He marks with perfect felicity the sound of guns at night :

> Les canons tonnent dans la nuit
> On dirait des vagues tempêtes
> Des cœurs où pointe un grand ennui
> Ennui qui toujours se répète

the fireworks used as signals :

Ce sont des dames qui dansent avec leurs regards pour yeux et cœurs

an exploding shell :

> Comme un astre éperdu qui cherche ses saisons

or a machine-gun :

> La mitrailleuse joue un air à triples-croches.

He builds exalted fancies out of the wasted scene, and sees the whole battlefield as a 'palais du tonnerre' rich in undiscovered treasures and glittering with its own magnificence. Nor is he unaware of the human beings around him. He compares soldiers, in their bubbling and bursting vitality, with bottles of champagne. He feels the speechless pathos of an African from Dakar, who is entirely lost in this uncouth world of war, thousands of miles from his own village and people and gods. He knows the strain and excitement of a night before an attack :

Nuit violente et violette et sombre et pleine d'or par moments
Nuit des hommes seulement
Nuit du 25 septembre
Demain l'assaut
Nuit violente ô nuit dont l'épouvantable cri profond
    devenait plus intense de minute en minute
Nuit qui criait comme une femme qui accouche
Nuit des hommes seulement.

Apollinaire saw the war from all angles, knew its worst as well as its best moments, but kept throughout his independent, observant, imaginative awareness of it. Of all the poets of the war he was most at home in it and got the most out of it. His unfailing candour and his irrepressible humanity enabled him to master its horrors and to find much that fascinated him in the most unexpected quarters. He took events as they came, including a wound in the head, from which in the end he died, and by seeing things without any false associations he was able to exert his transforming imagination and turn the battlefield into a new world which, despite its appalling peculiarities, could be related to much that in very different circumstances men know and love.

To few men is it given to maintain a balance like that of Ungaretti or Apollinaire, and it soon became almost impossible to do so. Early enough there seemed to be no prospect that the war would ever end, and meanwhile millions of men were being slaughtered in conditions from which all glamour and glory had departed. The armies were locked in a diabolical grip from which there was no escape, and poets, both inside and outside the actual struggle, began to see that it was even worse than their worst fears had anticipated. It seemed useless to look for peace, and earlier moods of enthusiasm and exaltation turned into Stoical resignation and fatalistic acquiescence. In Russia, where the enormity of the slaughter and the pitiful return which it brought fostered darker moods, Blok, sunk in a paralysis of melancholy, could in March 1916 only ask how long it would all last :

Идут века, шумит война,
Встает мятеж, горят деревни,
А ты всё та ж, моя страна,
В красе заплаканной и древней.–
Доколе матери тужить?
Доколе коршуну кружить?

> Centuries pass. Loud blares the war,
> Rebellion rising, hamlets burning,—
> But you, my country, as before,
> Your age-old beauty red with mourning!
> For how long must the mother weep?
> For how long must the vulture sweep?

He had indeed foretold undecipherable disasters, but in this un-remitting agony he felt that Russia was fated to be tortured for no purpose and to no end. In Germany George soon realized that the actual war bore no resemblance to the crusade for which he had once yearned, and saw in it an empty show, lacking even the old glitter and pomp. He was deeply distressed by the deaths of young friends upon whom he had set his high hopes, and he felt that the best he could do was to comfort the few who were still precariously alive. For himself he expected nothing that was worth having. He believed that the war merely intensified the faults which he had long deplored in his country and that the enormous sacrifices were made in no worthy cause :

> Das nötige werk der pflicht bleibt stumpf und glanzlos
> Und opfer steigt nicht in verruchter seit.
>
> .   .   .
>
> What duty needs to do stays blank and lightless,
> No sacrifices rise in evil times.

George wrote for himself and a few friends, feeling that his main convictions were still right and that the whole ghastly business of war was irrelevant to them.

What these men felt at home found its counterpart at the front. Almost from the very beginning of the war, certainly from the futile massacres of 1915, there were soldiers who were not fooled by propa-ganda or beguiled by the lure and the intoxication of battle. They had accepted its horrors and its sacrifices in a clear knowledge of what they really were and perhaps in a faint hope that in the end some good might come out of them. The pathetic lot of the unconsidered rank and file could not but touch deeply those who had any care for humanity, and the anonymous equality of war made all soldiers look like victims driven to some merciless slaughter-house. This is what Carl Zuckmayer catches in his 'Morituri', as he watches troops marching in the night :

> Truppen marschieren bei Nacht.
> Alle Gesichter sind gleich :
> Fleckig und bleich,
> Helmüberdacht.

> Soldiers by night on the march.
> Every face is the same :
> Blanched under grime,
> Helmeted each.[1]

But it was in these unreckoned and unrecognized instruments of battle that poets saw the huge pathos of war. Such men were expected to endure almost more than any men before them had endured, and it was an astonishing achievement that they were able to do so. Yet such endurance was on a perilous edge. Try it too hard, and it might collapse. It was of this that Jean Marc Bernard was already conscious, when before his death in June 1915 he wrote in the form of a prayer :

> Vous nous voyez couverts de boue,
> Déchirés, hâves et rendus . . .
> Mais nos cœurs, les avez-vous vus?
> Et faut-il, mon Dieu, qu'on l'avoue?
>
> Nous sommes si privés d'espoir,
> La paix est toujours si lointaine,
> Que parfois nous savons à peine
> Où se trouve notre devoir.

The strain which was already making itself felt at this date came near to breaking-point later, and the poets could not but take notice of it and respond in their own ways to it.

In 1916 the reckless and unrewarding battles of Verdun and the Somme left few illusions even among poets of the older generation who were far from the front. In 'Gethsemane' Kipling faced one of the more gruesome inventions of the war without attempting to glorify or palliate it. In the British army itself the change of mood was voiced by Siegfried Sassoon and Wilfred Owen. They were torn by an agonizing conflict in themselves. They felt a deep responsibility to their fellow soldiers, whose sufferings and sacrifices they were ready to share to death, and they felt that, in spite of everything, they must stay with them and that any attempt to shirk their duties was an unthinkable dereliction of honour. On the other hand their natures were ravaged by the uncontrollable havoc of war, the mutilation of bodies and minds, the ignorance and the indifference of the higher command. From this quarrel in themselves their poetry gained a special strength. While Sassoon turned to sharp satire which struck at incompetent leaders and hysterical patriots, Owen could

[1] Translated by Christopher Middleton.

not hide his conviction that the war was a monstrous catastrophe, mitigated only by the warmth of human affections which welled up from its destructiveness. Owen's famous words that 'the Poetry is in the pity' fit both poets, and it is this compassionate conviction that has won them an honoured place in our memories. In their Stoical endurance no less than in their human tenderness they spoke with authority and understanding for victims, alive or dead, in a war which had got out of human control and was grinding the world to pieces.

In Germany, too, something of the same kind was happening, not quite in the same way or in the same spirit or with the same art, but undeniably troubling and indicative of the change which the unceasing carnage worked in the hearts of men. Just as the Expressionists had foretold the brutal destructiveness of modern war, so now, conscious that they had been right, they turned their harsh, uncompromising manner to vent their resentful fury at the increasing brutality. In speaking at the top of their voices, they left little to subtleties and undertones, and it is not easy to detect in their outbursts the compassion which moves their English contemporaries. Yet their bitterness arises from a respect for human life, and though it is primarily a weapon of attack, it has much to defend that is worth defending. Their fault is not that they lack humanity but that in making every word strain at the same level of indignant denunciation they tend to numb our senses and to weaken the force of their own impact. Such is the case with Johannes Becher's 'Päan gegen die Zeit' ('Paean against the Age') which denounces war with such an accumulation of gruesome images that at a first reading we are almost stunned. Yet, as we accustom ourselves to its strident tones, we see that behind his merciless parade of horror Becher has both pity and passion :

> Du Zeit der schwanken Throne !
> Tyrannen öde Brut.
> Kasern-Gewürme schlingen.
> Haut-Trommeln ringsum springen
> Gleich Niagara los . . .
> Fleisch-Rücken fetzen Knuten.
> Verdorrt treu Brüder flattern
> In Gift-Wind-Feuern bloß.
>
> •   •   •
>
> Age of the tottering throne !
> Tyrants' desolate brood.
> Barrack-worms twist on the ground.
> Skin-drums raised all around

> Like Niagara blare . . .
> Flesh-backs ripped by the knout.
> Brothers, shrunk, flap about,
> Stark, in poison-wind-fire.

Becher presents his case with an eruptive violence because he hates the age in which he lives, but he is no way resigned to it. He attacks it in the hope of discrediting it and getting something better. While Wilfred Owen was content to say that all that a poet can do is to warn, Becher uses poetry as an instrument of political action. His purpose is to redeem the present suffering by winning from it a unity of mankind in 'Allverbrüderung', and since he is moved by such aims he can afford to present his case with a ferocity worthy of the opponents whom he assails.

Becher's revolutionary mood had its counterpart in Russia at the same time, but, whereas in Russia it was soon absorbed in the universal ferment of revolution, in Germany it turned sour as it wasted itself against obstacles which were too strong for it. Towards the end of the war Berthold Brecht wrote his 'Legende vom toten Soldaten' ('Legend of the dead soldier'), which is in its own way a masterpiece of indignant horror, a savage, disillusioned myth of what death in battle really means. In the form of a traditional ballad, with the simplest and most ordinary words, Brecht tells his tale. The Kaiser, in a pretence of grief over a soldier's death, decides that some action must be taken. A medical commission digs up the soldier at night. A doctor pours spirits into him, has him cleaned by a parson, and puts a woman on either side to support him. They paint his shroud in the national colours of black, white, and red, and, to an accompaniment of military music, shouts, and cheers, the ghoulish procession passes through villages :

> Und mitten drin der tote Soldat
> Wie ein besoffner Aff.
>
> .   .   .
>
> And the dead soldier in the midst
> Went like a drunken ape.

The excitement is so frenzied that in the end nobody notices the dead soldier :

> So viele tanzten und johlten um ihn,
> Daß ihn keiner sah.
> Mann konnte ihn einzig von oben noch sehn,
> Und da sind nur Sterne da.

Die Sterne sind nicht immer da,
Es kommt ein Morgenrot,
Doch der Soldat, so wie er's gelernt,
Zieht in den Heldentod.

. . .

Round him so many danced and yelled
That no one saw him there.
You could see him from nowhere but on top,
Where only stars could stare.

But the stars are not always there.
A morning rises red;
The soldier, who has learned it all,
Is, like a hero, dead.

Brecht's gruesome and yet heart-felt myth exposes, among other pretences, the popular notion of glory. The parade of a corpse as a living hero marks the absolute discord between what is said at home and what is known at the front, between sentimental make-believe and the ruthless finality of death. The parade 'mit Tschindrara und Wiedersehn', with its crowds and cries and music, is a ghastly travesty of military pomp, but for those who know what this costs in flesh and blood it is a just image of it. The macabre fancy that a dead man cannot be left at peace in the grave turns the myth into nightmare, but it remains close to what many men felt when they contrasted the actual character of their duties with the unreal abstractions by which they were dignified in public mouths. For Brecht the war has ceased to be anything but a heartless, meaningless exercise in showmanship, whose only aim is to feed the vanity of a ruling caste. The spirit which once sent men to war, and the rewards and the consolations which it offered, have ceased to have any significance for him, and his disillusionment becomes an anarchic irony which destroys a whole edifice of manufactured sentiment.

It is a long journey from the first outbursts of exaltation in 1914 to Brecht's rejection of everything which once gave glamour to war. Nor even in 1918 was Brecht representative of a large number of people, since most were too numbed by horrors and too occupied with daily necessities to revolt in his ruthless fashion. Yet the remarkable changes in the prevailing temper of poets during the war are a just commentary on it, and the best among these poets spoke truly for millions of other men who could not speak for themselves. As we now see it in retrospect, the poetry of the war was not the voice of a minority or an opposition, but gave clarity and emphasis to feelings which might still be inchoate but were certainly at work in countless soldiers. The claim of the poets on posterity is that in their own special medium they made a brave attempt to grasp the war as they saw it. In its enormous monstrosity it could be understood only in fragments from individual angles through personal experience, and this is what the poets succeeded in doing, with truth and power. Modern war provides no material comparable with that of the *Iliad* or even of *Henry V,* and the poets have to take it as they find it. Their record of what they found has its own tragic distinction. They spoke for mankind in one of the cruellest ordeals to which it has ever been subjected, and their work bears testimony to what happens when malignant circumstances obliterate the familiar landmarks of civilization and rob man of his last assurance that anything in his existence is secure.

XI

THE PROPHETIC ELEMENT

[Presidential Address to the English Association, 1959]

WHEN THE Muses appeared to Hesiod on Mount Helicon, they put in his hand a branch of olive-wood and breathed into him a divine voice that he might celebrate the things that shall be and that were aforetime. That a humble Boeotian farmer should make such claims for himself may surprise and shock those who regard the Greeks as the first rationalists and their poetry as a dawn breaking through the long Babylonian night. But Hesiod was not alone even among the Greeks in asserting the poet's dominion over so vast and so formidable a field. Claims like his can be found in many ages and many places, and though not all poets were in the beginning prophets, there is abundant evidence for an ancient and intimate connexion between poetry and prophecy. Before the Romans were touched by Greek influences, they had no word for 'poet', and their rude indigenous verses were the work of *vates,* who were nothing more or less than seers. Some of the most splendid poetry of the Hebrews is contained in prophecies which reveal their character at the start with some such formula as 'It shall come to pass' and proceed to foretell disaster and doom. Their claims may be less comprehensive than Hesiod's, but they are of the same kind, and if we wish to find a parallel to him we have it to hand in a Kara-Kirghiz of the Tienshan mountains, who said to the traveller Castrén: 'I am a shaman, who knows the future, the past and everything which is taking place in the present, both above and below the earth.' We need not take such claims too literally, and perhaps the shaman himself was conscious that his pretensions were a little exorbitant, even if he owed them to the dignity of his profession. After all, what a Tatar shaman means by 'everything' is not likely to coincide with our own idea of it. But it is at least clear that at a certain stage of its development poetry is largely concerned with the revelation of a special kind of knowledge and is the task of prophets who get their information from the Muses or a god or a familiar spirit or the strange voyages of their own disembodied souls. It has the special authority of revelation, and from this comes much of its power and its influence.

Conceptions of this kind may seem to bear very little resemblance to our usual conceptions of poetry, and indeed the civilized world has for many centuries had little use for the belief that poetry is essentially prophecy. Outside the legitimate prognostications of theology there is no sign of it in the Middle Ages, and in the Renaissance it is limited to occasional outbursts of patriotic or crusading fervour against aliens and heathen. But in the last 150 years the notion has revived and taken root and flourished, not indeed on its old terms with all its old claims but with so striking an originality that it has set its mark on our literature and forces us to consider whether after all the poet may not in some circumstances be also a prophet and combine the two roles in a single art. This spirit first appears in the Romantic age, which in its resistance to anything that savoured of natural philosophy felt that it must find its own alternative to such discouraging and desiccating theories. In England its first great exponent is William Blake, who in his gospel of the imagination sought to unseat such enemies of it as Newton and Locke, and makes claims for himself which take us back to a world of authentic prophets :

> Hear the voice of the Bard !
> Who Present, Past, and Future sees;
> Whose ears have heard
> The Holy Word
> That walk'd among the ancient trees.

Shelley does not go so far as this, but he had an exalted conception of the poet's mission and flung his far-ranging vision into a future where the wounds of mankind would be healed and its wrongs righted. Even Keats, who is often considered to be unduly occupied with the gifts of the senses, revolted violently against the scientific outlook and shared much of Blake's belief in the imagination. This was the first wave of the prophetic movement, and it arose naturally from the Romantic rejection of empirical knowledge and from its desire to make the poet regain some of his lost authority and speak about what really matters in human life.

This first wave seemed to have spent its strength with the deaths of Shelley and Blake, but towards the end of the nineteenth century a second wave, not unlike the first, broke upon the tidy shores of

Victorian poetry. This time the movement was indeed European, not in the sense that poets copied one another or drew their doctrines from a single master, but from a common urge of the spirit which was troubling more than one country. The long succession of mechanical inventions had broken the familiar assumptions upon which men had acted and either put nothing in their place or promoted the growth of a bleak intellectualism which starved the spirit of what it really hungered for. Though the poets who proclaimed the new gospel varied enormously from each other in personality and outlook and circumstances, all of them believed that poetry not only searches the present with the piercing penetration of vision but moves from this to forecast the future. They did not by any means confine themselves to this, nor were their forecasts very similar, except in their common forebodings, all too amply justified in the event, of vast bloodshed and the breakdown of many accepted securities and assumptions. Their prophecies are the more impressive because even before 1914 they diagnosed with a relentless accuracy the surfeit from which civilization had sickened, and which desperately cried out for relief in destruction. Nor has this wave yet receded. Though prophetic poets are, from the very nature of their gifts, rare, the prolonged crisis of our time has impelled some to speak in the full range of their powers, and though their purpose runs counter to the delicate, precise probings of the younger generation, there is no doubt that it speaks for young and old alike and makes a courageous attempt to grapple with our recurring anxieties and to see the facts as they are and as they will be. These poets derive their authority from their inspired insight, which they cannot resist or deny and must put into words. They feel that the ordinary methods of scientific or logical analysis are quite inadequate for the vast and terrifying issues before them and that their own kind of vision is a better way to the truth than the statistics and generalities with which publicists forecast the progressive starvation of man, or his drive to self-destruction, or his reduction to a flat and drab conformity of mind and habits. The company of prophetic poets is not large, but it is unusually distinguished, and it has proved by its practice that poetry is capable of more difficult and more adventurous tasks than are commonly expected of it.

A prophet does not and cannot confine himself to the future. He can foresee it only if he understands the present as it really is. To pass beyond the immediate moment to its meaning and its consequences calls for a special kind of vision, which sees and understands at its proper worth, in its inescapable significance, what is to most people invisible and even irrelevant. Such vision has little to do with the familiar world for its own ephemeral claims, or indeed with human actions whose main interest lies in the transitory throbs and thrills which they evoke. On the other hand, it is not an irrational activity. The poet who writes of what he sees through it works on quite as firm a foundation as any poet who relies mainly on his senses. Vision is often more vivid and more obviously trustworthy than what comes through the senses, and the poet rightly denies that it is an illusion. It is at the heart of his being and his work, and he would be a traitor to reject it. When its compelling urgency compels him to shape its gifts into words, it imparts to them some of its own forceful and fearful character. That is why truly prophetic poems are so unusually impressive. Because they are born from vision, which is itself an overwhelming experience, they concentrate the poet's powers on a single point and keep them at work under driving pressure. Because vision does not come when it is sought, and may come only at rare intervals, the poet tends to give to its presentation all the resources at his command and through it to realize his most generous scope and most personal utterance. It is closely related to a special insight, which is itself not vision but is inspired by it and works intimately with it in giving precision and immediacy to what it reveals. A natural field for vision is the human, historical scene, the fortunes of mankind as the poet sees them and the consequences which they are likely to bring. Prophetic vision differs from mystical in that it is concerned with the familiar world, and from sociological prognostications in that it moves not through the laborious processes of analysis and calculation but through sudden moments of illumination, when what lies beyond argument is seen in a fierce and disturbing flash of light.

In England the archetype of prophetic poets is William Blake. Before him it hardly existed, and after him even its most original exponents have either learned their first lessons from him or instinctively worked in much the same way that he did. In him are developed to an exemplary degree the main characteristics of a poet who is also a prophet. The foundation of his system is his rejection of anything which relies for the full truth upon natural philosophy, because this deals only with trivial and irrelevant appearance and is blind to anything that really matters :

> The Atoms of Democritus
> And Newton's particles of light
> Are sands upon the Red Sea shore,
> Where Israel's tents do shine so bright.

As the only possible alternative to this he offers the world of the imagination, and insists that it alone deserves the name of reality.

By it he means the world of vision, and in vision his whole life and
outlook and work were securely rooted. This vision is born from an
acute, sensitive, troubled awareness of the human state, especially in
its errors and frustrations and defeats. His vision of the future was
inspired by his passionate concern for the present and grew naturally
out of it. While he denounced the follies and the brutalities of his
time, he held out prospects of something better if men would only
obey their natural instincts and behave with the simplicity and
innocence of children. Like most prophets, he uttered both warnings
and encouragement, both counsel and threats. If he shared in the
Utopian ideals of the French Revolution and its English adherents,
he knew very well how hard they were to attain and how great a
change of habits and of heart they demanded. The hopes which he
offers may indeed be of a return to a lost paradise, to a Never-never-
land, the Beulah of his prophecies and the New Jerusalem of his
faith, but for him they are perfectly real, and he has no doubt that
if the right decisions are taken, such a return can be effected. In him
the poet and the prophet do not always work together, and as he
grew older he seems to have felt some strain in keeping them united,
and the prophet comes more to the fore than the poet, but when they
work together, as most notably in *Songs of Experience*, the result is
indeed both poetry and prophecy in their most concentrated and
most masterful form, and each gains immeasurably from being
united with the other in a single, indissoluble whole.

Blake illustrates an important point in the nature of prophetic
poetry, which might otherwise lead to misunderstanding. Though
Aristotle announced that poetry deals with the universal, most of us
would agree with Croce that every work of art is an entirely individual creation and must be inspired by an entirely individual outlook. That is why men like Yeats were so hostile to anything that
smacked of abstraction and asserted that, since nothing can happen
more than once, every poem must be the poet's personal experience
and nothing else. Yet we might think that prophetic poetry which
moves from the given scene into vast vistas beyond it must almost
be compelled to deal, sooner or later, with abstractions and at times
to speak not for the poet's self but for what he has in common with
other men. It does indeed deal with abstractions, but as if they were
individual issues. Its subjects are of enormous import and may even
lie outside the time-scheme in which our consciousness works, but it
treats them as single, special cases seen through the poet's own vision
and illuminated by his special insight. What might be a mere abstraction, lifeless and commonplace, becomes a particular issue, grasped
from both within and without in its full nature, but not dehumanized
or reduced to statistics. Blake, for instance, was gravely and

constantly troubled at the enforced denial of natural instincts by
what he believed to be a false morality which ruined the sweetness
and fullness of life. The problem which concerned him touches many
millions of people and can indeed be expressed in abstract terms,
and yet he sees in it a single, individual issue, as actual and as pres-
sing as any other in the world, and calling for his most earnest attention. What he made of it can be seen in a short poem which is of such
power that it conveys a whole vast situation in the most immediate
and most intimate way, and after reading it we feel that really
nothing more is needed to show exactly what he means :

> Ah, Sun-flower ! weary of time
> Who countest the steps of the Sun,
> Seeking after that sweet golden clime
> Where the traveller's journey is done :
>
> Where the Youth pined away with desire,
> And the pale Virgin shrouded in snow
> Arise from their graves and aspire
> Where my Sun-flower wishes to go.

The huge, impalpable issue, which might so easily have passed into
bleak abstractions, is grasped as something present and personal, and
shaped with so compassionate an understanding of what it means to
human beings that, though Blake forecasts the future as no more
than a hope or a prayer, his poem is authentically prophetic through
the unfaltering intensity of its vision.

Just as oracles often give warnings or advice rather than actual
forecasts, so prophetic poets are wise and right not to commit themselves too specifically on what will happen. If they did, their poetry
would lose much of its strength; for they would be guilty of assuming
the mantle of the journalist or the scientist and moving only on the
surface of things when they ought to be exploring the depths. What
counts is the spirit in which the prophetic utterance is made. The
matters which concern it must be displayed in their essential nature
and their relevance to the human condition as the poet sees it. He
can hardly do this unless he is carried away by something akin to
prophetic frenzy, by a sense of urgency so dominating that he must
surrender to it and do all that he can for it. His forecast needs not
by any means be always of evil, but it must always be given with
all the candour of which he is capable and make no concessions to
false hopes or exaggerated fears. Even forecasts of felicity gain
greatly from being born from conflicts and tensions and anxieties.
This is why, when at the end of The Dynasts Thomas Hardy, almost

in defiance of his own nature and his lifelong convictions, strikes a
note of hope, we welcome it and think that perhaps after all it may
be justified. This is what we must at least consider after all the tur-
moil and tumult of his epic-drama, and we accept it because it is
quite honestly offered as no more than a hope :

> But—a stirring thrills the air
> Like to sounds of joyance there
> That the rages
> Of the ages
> Should be cancelled and deliverance offered from the darts
> that were,
> Consciousness the will informing till it fashion all things fair.

By Hardy's standards this is asking for a lot, and he would not deny
that it may well be asking for too much, but because it rises from
the impact of harsh realities on his all too easily wounded humanity,
we accept it with gratitude and respond to the mood which it evokes.
Though the vision which inspires it may be discredited by bitter
disillusion, it is still a vision and throws a comforting beam of light
into the unfathomable future.

That something more than mere hopes and wishes is needed to
give substance to forecasts of good is clear from another poet who
practised the art with far more confidence than Hardy. Shelley believed that, if only superstition and tyranny could be overthrown,
all would be well with mankind. In itself his gospel, learned too
readily and too glibly from Godwin, lacks a living flame and reveals
its aridity in the rhetorical wastes of *Queen Mab*. But Shelley, without abandoning his high hopes, soon saw that he must ask what they
really meant and relate them to the actual world as he was beginning
to know it. So in *Hellas* after scenes of brutality and bloodshed the
final Chorus sings of the golden future which awaits the Greeks and
all mankind. We may feel that it is a little too golden to be convincing, and respond but coldly to the resourceful ingenuity by
which ancient themes are transferred to suit a reborn world. Indeed
these themes do not carry quite all the weight that they should, and
we are not quite sure how to take them. For instance, in one stanza
Shelley picks up a theme from Virgil's so-called 'Messianic'
Eclogue :

> A loftier Argo cleaves the main,
> Fraught with a later prize;
> Another Orpheus sings again,

> And loves and weeps and dies.
> A new Ulysses leaves once more
> Calypso for his native shore.

This is good enough so far as it goes, but it does not go very far. It sounds blithe and confident, but each of the three Greek myths on which it touches has its dark shadows, and we do not know how many, if any, of these we may read into Shelley's lines, and the result is that we are uncertain what to make of them and suspect that not enough hard thought has gone into their creation. We may profitably contrast with them Yeats's lines where he uses similar themes for a different purpose, to display the violence which a religious revolution brings into the world :

> Another Troy must rise and set,
> Another lineage feed the crow,
> Another Argo's painted prow
> Drive to a flashier bauble yet.
> The Roman Empire stood appalled;
> It dropped the reins of peace and war
> When that fierce Virgin and her Star
> Out of the fabulous darkness called.

This is far more forcible than Shelley's stanza because Yeats has thought out what the old myths really mean in their new setting, and leaves no doubt of what his forecast implies. Yet though we may rightly feel some misgiving at this stage of Shelley's song, at the end of it he shows on what convictions it is built, and breaks into a heart-felt appeal against the cruelty which he thought so unnecessary and so futile :

> Oh, cease !—must hate and death return ?
>   Cease ! must men kill and die ?
> Cease ! drain not to its dregs the urn
>   Of bitter prophecy.
> The world is weary of the past,
> Oh, might it die or rest at last ?

The abrupt change of tone and the return to harsh reality as the play has just dramatized it give the jolt that is needed to put the preceding stanzas into a new perspective. What has looked like too slick an optimism turns out to be a hope or a question, prompted by compassion for suffering and an ardent desire to alleviate it. Just because behind the glittering vision there is a warm humanity at work, we treat the prophecy more seriously and are ready to listen with closer attention to Shelley's hopes of future glory and enhanced endeavour. If he had not finished his poem in this way by revealing what really lies in his mind, it would have been more a dream than a forecast, more a drug than a vision.

If compassion can inspire hope, as in Shelley and Blake, it can also inspire darker moods and more formidable premonitions. Though the Second World War and the prolonged anxieties and agonies after it have stunned some poets into silence and driven others to turn away from the unintelligible storm outside to the intricate labyrinths of their own inner lives, yet the state of the world still calls for an authentically prophetic utterance, because these enormous catastrophes and menaces, these revelations of the fallen state of man, can only be interpreted by a seer who grasps them in all their horror and is courageous enough to speak out about them when others are silent. To the general unwillingness to face them in their dark potentialities there is a noble and notable exception. Dame Edith Sitwell has from *Gold Coast Customs,* written before the war but tragically aware of what lay ahead, until today responded with a passionate apprehension to the evils and the anguish of our time, and her poems about them are truly prophetic. They are inspired by the vision of a world perilously poised on a flaming abyss of its own making, and they foretell what will certainly happen if man pursues his present purposes of destruction and multiplies his means for it. Though she does not shrink from portraying the enormous horror of what she sees, she is moved throughout by compassion. If she displays what looks like hatred, it is inspired by love and directed against the soul of evil in the world. Though at times she cannot but burst into savage irony and bitter condemnation, yet the inexorable spirit that drives her is pity for the human state in its savage perversity and its blindness to its self-sought doom. It is this which enables her to write about the atomic bomb of 1945 in lines which contain no preaching and no propaganda, and yet are both tragically moving and unanswerably true to her own feelings and to those of many others, for whom in her Sibylline authority she speaks :

And if the ray from that heat came soundless, shook the sky
As if in search for food, and squeezed the stems
Of all that grows on the earth till they were dry
—And drank the marrow of the bone :
The eyes that saw, the lips that kissed, are gone
Or black as thunder lie and grin at the murdered sun.

The living blind, and seeing dead together lie
As if in love. . . . There was no more hating then,
And no more love. Gone is the heart of man.

In the appalling annihilation of living things by the bomb she sees a cosmic murder, an immeasurable crime committed by man against his own kind and the whole of nature. Her vision pierces beyond the ghastly furnace of Hiroshima to the whole present world, whose callous indifference to life it has revealed, and to the future which will exact retribution for it in the death of what alone makes life worth living.

Just as Blake turned from the pastoral idylls of *Songs of Innocence* to the agonized heart-cries and denunciations of *Songs of Experience,* so in our own time poets, who have begun in what seemed to be a secure seclusion of immaculate art, have been driven almost in despite of themselves to abandon it for the troubling and unloved responsibilities of prophecy. As a young man Yeats was content to live among dreams and ready to believe that they were his whole concern, but events were too strong for him, and with a characteristic self-knowledge he accepted the challenge and thereby made himself into the greatest poet of his age. The process was slow and came from small beginnings, such as local Irish quarrels about the Abbey Theatre or Hugh Lane's pictures. Even the First World War at first hardly touched him, and when Henry James asked him to contribute to a war-book edited by Edith Wharton, he wrote six lines which showed how obstinately he clung to his detachment :

I think it better that in times like these
A poet's mouth be silent; for in truth
We have no gift to set a statesman right;
He has had enough of meddling who can please
A young girl in the indolence of her youth,
Or an old man upon a winter's night.

In the covering letter which he sent with this Yeats wrote : 'I shall keep the neighbourhood of the seven sleepers of Ephesus, hoping to catch their comfortable snores till bloody frivolity is over.' Yet this is just what he could not do. Within less than a year his seclusion was shattered by the Dublin rebellion of Easter 1916, and thenceforward he knew that he could not shut himself up any longer in the 'great gazebo' from which he had hoped to watch the human scene with an artist's detachment. The Irish War of Independence and the civil war which followed it taught him that he could not neglect the fate of his own country, but so far from treating it as a perfunctory duty he gave himself to it with the full, ripe force of his genius. He who hated abstractions and thought that all poetry must be entirely

personal saw that the issues which now confronted him were indeed
his special concern, and as such he wrote about them.

Yeats's concern with the state of humanity lasted with him to the
end of his days, and it is significant that the last poem which he
wrote is not 'Under Ben Bulben', which he intended to be his literary
testament, but 'The Black Tower', which he completed a week before
his death as a symbolical myth of the fight for civilization which
troubled him in the depth of his convictions. Yeats's interest in
human affairs began with Ireland, but he made Ireland a microcosm
of that whole Western world which was passing through pangs of
death and birth and for whose survival he was anxious and afraid.
All that he had sought and loved was, he felt, in peril, and he must
make a stand for it and proclaim what the situation really was.
Poetry and prophecy are welded into a single whole just because
Yeats's vision is always his own, always free from abstractions and
commonplaces and stock ideas, always concentrated on the essence
of the situation as it affected him most deeply. His moods vary
greatly, and reflect the many sides of his proud, ironical, passionate
self. Though he saw everything from a uniquely personal point of
view, he was able to place what he saw in his own scheme of history
and to give it an additional strength from the associations which
this evokes. His own theories are never obtruded too crudely, and
their presence in the background even adds authority to the individual occasion. Thus in 'The Second Coming' Yeats takes for
granted a theory of cycles which govern the sequence of events,
and though he does not mention it, its presence in the background
gives a hint of inescapable doom and makes his theme more menac-
ing. He looks on the violence and the anarchy of the present and
then proceeds to his revelation :

> Surely some revelation is at hand :
> Surely the Second Coming is at hand.
> The Second Coming ! Hardly are those words out
> Than a vast image out of *Spiritus Mundi*
> Troubles my sight : somewhere in sands of the desert
> A shape with lion body and the head of a man,
> A gaze blank and pitiless as the sun,
> Is moving its slow thighs, while all about it
> Reel shadows of the indignant desert birds.
> The darkness drops again : but now I know
> That twenty centuries of stony sleep
> Were vexed to nightmare by a rocking cradle,
> And what rough beast, its hour come round at last,
> Slouches towards Bethlehem to be born?

This is in every sense a prophetic poem. The poetry finds a new dimension from the fearful, convincing nature of the prophecy and gains enormously from a subject so vast in its scope and yet grasped firmly in its ominous horror. We can see how much hard thought and practised insight have gone to its making, and we accept it as doing what only poetry can do when it throws all its powers into creating for others what the poet has seen in vision.

Prophetic poetry is at once in the midst of the events which concern it and at some distance from them. Its strength comes from its ability to combine a sharp understanding of a particular situation with an almost detached ability to see this in its many implications and consequences. The more violent or absorbing the present situation is, the more difficult it is for the poet to achieve this double approach to it and to bring both aspects together in a single experience. We might think that in the corruption and carnage of modern warfare it might be almost impossible to find such a unity, and yet it has been done more than once. A striking example is in a short poem by Isaac Rosenberg, who was himself killed in the First World War. He saw its horror with undeceived eyes and felt the immediate moment as only a man can who is in the middle of it, but he was able to see beyond this and to foretell what the war must mean in the scheme of things :

> A worm fed on the heart of Corinth,
> Babylon and Rome :
> Not Paris raped tall Helen,
> But this incestuous worm,
> Who lured her vivid beauty
> To his amorphous sleep.
> England ! famous as Helen
> Is thy betrothal sung
> To him the shadowless,
> More amorous than Solomon.

The 'incestuous worm' may owe something to Blake, and both Helen and Solomon are familiar from Yeats's use of them, but Rosenberg speaks in his own idiom about what he really knows. What he sees and foresees is the doom which England has embraced as a lover, and he knows that this will be her ruin as it was the ruin of Corinth, Babylon, and Rome. The terrible strength of his poem is that he is right. What he says so oracularly and yet so irresistibly is that this cult of death is something which we have bred ourselves and embraced in all the passion of unnatural love.

Prophetic poetry is concerned with humanity, with its desires for

more abundant life and its menace of man-made hells. In almost
every case where it succeeds the poet's vision is inspired by an over-
riding concern for mankind in its weakness or its wickedness. It is
this which provokes alike promises of ultimate felicity and warnings
of annihilating doom. Each of these two kinds of prophecy arises
from the same mood, from the same anxious and affectionate
solicitude which may express itself in many forms but remains constant to its central character. It may be complex and stir more than
one emotion in a single state of mind, and the conflict which it breeds
in the self may start other less majestic but not less truthful or less
significant responses than fear or hope or anger. Just because it is
held in control by the usual defences which we fashion for ourselves
against problems that outwit or defeat us, it may develop unexpected variations and half hide its essential seriousness in what
looks like gaiety or mockery or paradox. The fight which Blake
fought against natural philosophy has taken a new shape in our
time when physics, in its disinterested pursuit of knowledge, seems
indifferent whether it promotes the destruction of mankind or its
prosperity and happiness. Of this poets take notice, and though
their answer may not be so absolute or so uncompromising as Blake's,
yet it can be hardly less effective when it uses the right weapons.
So Robert Frost handles some of the more blood-curdling prospects
with his own unique combination of irony and humour and disturbing understatement. He spares his victims nothing by his skilful
device of asking what their activities really mean :

> Sarcastic Science she would like to know
> In her complacent ministry of fear
> How we propose to get away from here
> When she has made things so we have to go
> Or be wiped out. Will she be asked to show
> Us how by rocket we may hope to steer
> To some star off there say a half light-year
> Through temperature of absolute Zeró?
> Why wait for science to supply the how
> When any amateur can tell it now?
> The way to go away should be the same
> As fifty million years ago we came—
> If anyone remembers how that was.
> I have a theory, but it hardly does.

Frost is a prophet, but his weapon is mockery. He makes fun of the
scientists who plot these alarming enterprises, but behind the
mockery lies his sharp insight into their character and intentions

and his refusal to shirk what it all means. If at the end he almost
plays a trick on us, it is because he knows that we shall not be deceived, and the trick serves to emphasize the insensate nature of
the future as some men would wish it to be.

Poetry can also have its false prophets—false not so much in the
sense that their forecasts are not fulfilled as that they have not given
full consideration to them; for such an art demands the highest
degree of seriousness, self-knowledge, and truth to vision. This indeed was a fault of those poets in the nineteenth century who liked
to foretell the future but did not concentrate all their attention on
it. Tennyson, who understood so well man's nagging uncertainties
before his natural destiny, turned at times to prophecy, and, perhaps
from some lack of confidence in himself, spoke not from considered
convictions but from current ideas which he had not properly absorbed and made his own. When in *Locksley Hall* he dips into the
future, what he foresees is factually correct up to a point, but there
is something almost frivolous in his account of the coming Arma-
geddon in the sky :

> Heard the heavens fill with shouting, and there rain'd a ghastly
> dew
> From the nations' airy navies grappling in the central blue.

We, of course, have the advantage of after-sight and can with justice
complain that what rained on Coventry or the Ruhr is very inadequately described as 'a ghastly dew'. But not only has Tennyson's
imagination failed to rise to the occasion; there is also something
wrong in his whole approach. He sees the war in the air, but he does
not feel it, and he is more like a small boy playing with toy aero-
planes than a serious prophet of what is to come. Nor does he make
things better when he blandly supposes that the new means of destruction will lead, by some undecipherable process, to universal
peace and the rule of law. He has no good reason for thinking it,
and in his heart he may not even wish for it. He is merely repeating
a stock notion for its dramatic contrast with what precedes, and he
is certainly not moved by any deep concern for the fate of mankind.

The same inadequacy, which amounts almost to insincerity, may
be seen in some of Swinburne's political poetry. He was genuine
enough in his forecasts of emancipation from kings and priests,
though even in these he is hampered by his reverence for his master
Shelley and does not often think for himself, but at times, in his desire to say the kind of thing that is expected from a public figure, he
contradicts his own professed convictions, as when, for instance,
wishing to awake the Italians from their lethargy, he assumes a
highly authoritative manner and says :

Hearest thou,
Italia? Tho' deaf sloth hath sealed thine ears,
The world has heard thy children, and God hears.

For an old-fashioned atheist, who devoted many hundreds of lines
to denouncing God for not existing, this will not do. It is very close
to imposture, and it is not uncharacteristic of its time. The portentous, Titanic figure of Victor Hugo set an example, which many
were only too eager to follow, of fulminating with Olympian fury on
the issues of the day. In this there was nothing essentially new, but
the part was played with too resonant a fervour to be convincing,
and poets deceived themselves into thinking that just because their
subjects were indeed important, they had a special insight into them.
Though the omens might portend glorious or tragic possibilities, the
poets confined themselves to the surface, to the false appearance, to
the smash and grab of contemporary controversy, to the rhetoric
and the wrangling which belong to politics and not to poetry. Their
failure was that they did not look seriously enough at the given case,
that their concern was parochial and short-sighted, that they deluded themselves into beliefs which they did not really hold. They
assumed all the airs of prophecy and sought to speak with the voice
of thunder from Sinai, but they failed because they tried to say more
than they really meant, and for this very reason said less.

The prophetic approach to experience finds an appropriate technique in symbols. The word has many meanings, but in this context
a symbol is an object standing for something else which has so undefined and indeed so indefinable a character and contains such a
wealth of implications that it cannot be expressed in ordinary abstract words without its essential nature being obscured or misrepre-
sented or lost. Symbols make real even the most elusive themes which
flit on the edge of the consciousness or lurk in hidden memories or
flicker in associations beyond the range of descriptive thought. The
technique is not new and was exploited abundantly both in classical
antiquity and in the Middle Ages through the accepted myths of
religion, but whereas in them the symbols were traditional and easily
understood, in modern prophetic poetry new symbols have to be
found, since only by this means can the poet give full expression to
the highly individual issues which concern him. That is why Blake
turned to quite new purposes such ancient symbols as the rose or
found exactly what he needed in the sunflower and almost invented
a new mythology, with its portentous figures like Urizen, Orc, Los,
and Enitharmon, to replace not only biblical figures, who were too
respectable for his revolutionary purposes, but Greek gods and
goddesses, whom he despised as inventions of 'the silly Greek and

Latin slaves of the Sword'. That is why Shelley, absorbed in his not too different vision of the destiny of mankind, transformed his soaring fancies into shapes derived from classical mythology and found in Prometheus a type of suffering humanity and in the otherwise obscure Demogorgon a power lurking in the depths of being who should overthrow Jupiter, the enemy of mankind. That is why Yeats, after starting with Celtic mythology and finding that it did not really answer his needs, formed his own symbols and enriched them with new associations as he pondered over them and saw their ever expanding implications, till what begins as something solid and physical becomes metaphysical and even, in Yeats's sense of the word, mystical, as the tower stands in turn for established strength, the detachment of the soul, and the lost cause that still has its heroic defenders. That is why Dame Edith Sitwell uses, always with some new individual force, such symbols as the sun or ice or gold or corn or fire, and through them illuminates from different angles the realities which lie at the centre of her vision. It is idle to complain that not all these symbols are immediately intelligible or display their full range at a first reading; part of their strength is that they do not. It is their very mysteriousness, their way of eluding translation into common words, that gives them their strength and draws us back to them to see what they mean. They are almost the only method by which the prophetic poet can present his vision as he really sees and feels it, and because they have matured in his mind and formed a nucleus for his imaginative speculations, they are not decorative appurtenances but the very stuff of his poetry.

The use of symbols in prophetic poetry is relevant to the question of its truth; for it is through these that it gains the degree of emotional and imaginative precision which is indispensable to it. This is, of course, a different matter from the fulfilment or failure of its prognostications. They are in fact often fulfilled, but since they forecast not so much actual events as general movements and present even these largely through warnings or encouragements, their real task is to awake us to the urgent significance of what is happening round us and to what results it may lead. Their truth lies in their revelation of what contemporary events really mean for mankind and what fundamental issues are involved in them. We judge them from our own standpoint by the effect of candour and sincerity which they produce on us. We demand this from all poets, but from prophetic poets in a special degree. As we have seen, no prophet fails so disastrously as a false prophet; for his falsity discredits all his claims and makes all his messages ring hollow. If he is to make his proper impact, he must put the whole of himself into his work and appeal to our whole selves. Then we accept what he

says because we cannot shirk the spirit in which he says it, and give
to it our close and attentive care. With him it is a case of all
or nothing. If he is worth hearing at all, he must be heard to the end,
and conversely, if he loses our confidence at any point, he is unlikely to regain it. Now this is not necessarily true of all poetry, and
especially of such poetry as seeks simply to provide enjoyment. If
we do not happen to respond to it, it may not be the poet's fault,
and we cannot reasonably condemn him. But with prophecy the
whole position on which it is built demands that the poet be treated
seriously, and we apply to him standards which we should not apply
so rigorously to someone who makes less exalted or less exacting
claims. That is why we take on trust the elaborate theories of
existence which are embedded in the poetry of Blake and Yeats.
When we see them set out nakedly in a prose paraphrase with all
their glory gone, we may well think that they are unimpressive or
even positively wrong, but in the poetry where they belong and
realize their full being, we welcome them as courageous attempts
to diagnose our troubles with all the care of which they are capable.
If they are transfused into poetry we are less interested in their
factual fulfilment than in the appeal which their insight and
assumptions make to us who are participants in the whole human
scene.

Even in our time, when the need for prophetic poets is so amply
justified, they are rare. Their special response to events is not what
every poet feels, and despite their remarkable achievement they are
not very characteristic of the present age. They are sometimes derided for their majestic air, but without it they would be far less
formidable and make a far feebler impact. They are also attacked
because the issues which concern them are so much vaster than any
personal predicament that they may seem to be remote from common experience. But we are all involved in the same troubles and
have no right to shirk them. Prophetic poets may even be accused
of looking too avidly for a crisis and avoiding the congenial comfort
of ignorance and indifference. This is no doubt true, but it is right
to look for a crisis when there are signs that it exists, and to hide from
it is folly and cowardice. Against these unjustified objections we may
set the proved achievement of prophetic poetry. In an age when the
arts seem too often to have imprisoned themselves in their own
technicalities and poetry finds it hard to leave the ground just because it is so occupied with its method and its manner, it is both a
relief and a delight to find a class of poets who are indeed carried
off their feet by their subject and find through its wide scope that
freedom of utterance which is in danger of being forgotten in the

intricacies of personal self-examination. It is good that poets are still able to face large issues without abating their powers or falling into the false substitutes of rhetoric and argument, and that the technique of symbols, which was evolved largely for quite different purposes, should be applied with such success to events which touch us in far more than our rational minds. Prophetic poetry proves that there is nothing in the nature of a public subject which prevents it from being brought into poetry and that what matters is the vision which the poet has of it and his insight into its essential character and its relevance to the human state.

In exploiting the prophetic element poetry might seem to be reverting too easily to primitive methods and reviving an outlook which is alien to the intellectual discipline of our age. So indeed it is, and it is all the better for it. The rationalist spirit of our time has deluded us into believing that truth can be found only through proof and argument. This is certainly one way of finding it, but it is not the only way, and there are certain matters which lie beyond its reach. In our ordinary lives we all know how much we owe to sudden insight, to flashes of vision, to unexplained moments of confidence or foreboding. These are part of our human state, and we could not live without them. Nor is it difficult to justify our trust in them. They are in fact not irrational in the sense that they are against reason; they merely complement and help it. Nor are they instinctive, if by that we mean mere reactions to this or that stimulus. They arise from experience and practice, and behind them lies much that we have forgotten just because we have made it part of ourselves. They are as natural and as rational as the movements of our bodies, and they are no less necessary. The application of such training to contemporary events and the interpretation of their meaning is not a task for every poet. But there are a few who are unusually equipped for it, partly because they are deeply concerned with what is happening, but more because their understanding of it begins where logic and science end. What fires their vision is their sense of vastly important powers at work, and it is these which they try to grasp in their real significance and to delineate in words. The prophetic poet faces the world with an insight beyond that of ordinary men, and, just because he is a poet, his forecasts strike home as no others do. He may indeed be reverting to the primeval tasks of his calling, but that does not mean that they are not still needed. Indeed they are, if we are to understand what happens in the world not merely with our heads but with our hearts and consciences, and are thereby entitled to claim that we have not shrunk from reality or complacently believed that things are otherwise than they are.

INDEX